Livecasting in Twenty-First-Century British Theatre

Related Titles

Broadcast your Shakespeare: Continuity and Change Across Media
Edited by Stephen O'Neill
ISBN 978-1-3501-1882-9

Screening the Royal Shakespeare Company: A Critical History
John Wyver
ISBN 978-1-3501-7407-8

Shakespeare and the 'Live' Theatre Broadcast Experience
Edited by Pascale Aebischer, Susanne Greenhalgh and
Laurie E. Osborne
ISBN 978-1-3501-2581-0

Theater of Lockdown: Digital and Distanced Performance in a Time of Pandemic
Barbara Fuchs
ISBN 978-1-3502-3185-6

Toward a Future Theatre: Conversations during a Pandemic
Caridad Svich
ISBN 978-1-3502-4105-3

Livecasting in Twenty-First-Century British Theatre

NT Live and the Aesthetics of Spectacle, Materiality and Engagement

Heidi Lucja Liedke

methuen | drama
LONDON • NEW YORK • OXFORD • NEW DELHI • SYDNEY

METHUEN DRAMA
Bloomsbury Publishing Plc
50 Bedford Square, London, WC1B 3DP, UK
1385 Broadway, New York, NY 10018, USA
29 Earlsfort Terrace, Dublin 2, Ireland

BLOOMSBURY, METHUEN DRAMA and the Methuen Drama logo are trademarks of Bloomsbury Publishing Plc

First published in Great Britain 2023
This paperback edition published 2025

Copyright © Heidi Lucja Liedke, 2023

Heidi Lucja Liedke has asserted her right under the Copyright, Designs and Patents Act, 1988, to be identified as author of this work.

For legal purposes the Acknowledgements on p. x constitute an extension of this copyright page.

Cover design: Ben Anslow
Cover images: People on outside balcony of National Theatre during interval at Sunset. South Bank, London, England (© Paul Carstairs / Alamy Stock Photo); Camera viewfinder interface. Camera recording screen on black background. Vector illustration (© Veronika Zimina / iStock)

All rights reserved. No part of this publication may be reproduced or transmitted in any form or by any means, electronic or mechanical, including photocopying, recording, or any information storage or retrieval system, without prior permission in writing from the publishers.

Bloomsbury Publishing Plc does not have any control over, or responsibility for, any third-party websites referred to or in this book. All internet addresses given in this book were correct at the time of going to press. The author and publisher regret any inconvenience caused if addresses have changed or sites have ceased to exist, but can accept no responsibility for any such changes.

A catalogue record for this book is available from the British Library.

A catalog record for this book is available from the Library of Congress.

Names: Liedke, Heidi, author.
Title: Livecasting in twenty-first-century British theatre : NT live and the aesthetics of spectacle, materiality and engagement / Heidi Lucja Liedke.
Description: London ; New York : Meuthen Drama 2023. | Includes bibliographical references and index.
Identifiers: LCCN 2022060161 | ISBN 9781350340961 (hardback) | ISBN 9781350341005 (paperback) | ISBN 9781350340978 (epub) | ISBN 9781350340985 (ebook)
Subjects: LCSH: National Theatre Live (Great Britain) | Theater–Great Britain–History–21st century. | Theater–Production and direction–Technological innovations. | Technology and the arts.
Classification: LCC PN2596.L7 N355 2023 | DDC 792.09421/2–dc23/eng/20230209
LC record available at https://lccn.loc.gov/2022060161

ISBN: HB: 978-1-3503-4096-1
PB: 978-1-3503-4100-5
ePDF: 978-1-3503-4098-5
eBook: 978-1-3503-4097-8

Typeset by Deanta Global Publishing Services, Chennai, India

To find out more about our authors and books visit www.bloomsbury.com and sign up for our newsletters.

*In loving memory of my father.
And to my mother: Nie damy się.*

Contents

List of Figures ix
Acknowledgements x

Introduction: Locating livecasting – Twenty-first-century British
    theatre on the threshold 1
    Locating livecasting 6
    Constructing the live 8
    Distractions, slippages and turns: Spectacle – archive 13
    Research overview 16
    Aims and structure of the book 17

Part I Spectacle and materiality

1 Old new media: The optionality of the theatre space and
    different forms of embodiment in early live theatre and music
    broadcasting 25
    Early broadcasting technologies as substitutes 27
    Acousmatic livecasting in the nineteenth century:
        Visual landscapes 32
    Not a substitute for the real thing – The NT's dip into
        broadcasting in the 1940s and 1950s 38
    The launch of NT Live 40
    Then and now: The fifth auditorium 44

2 Watching others having fun – livecasting as spectacle 46
    The best of British theatre 47
    Spectacle and theatre on screens – images and deception 49
    Sports events, spectacle and NT Live 51
    Framing livecasting: Mediated spectacle and communitas 54
    Livecasting as affective spectacle: *A Midsummer Night's Dream*
        (Bridge Theatre/NT Live) 60

3	Capturing the atmosphere: The material-theatrical	75
	A word on wires, screens and electricians from a Brechtian perspective	77
	Theatrical and cinematic modes – filmed theatre	81
	Spatially extended atmospheres: The materiality of the theatrical space shifts	93
	Making the theatrical experience porous: Stuttering screens	98

Part II Engagement

4	Livecasting, liveness and the feeling I	105
	Spectator-centric theatre and modes of engagement with livecasts	107
	Livecasts, liveness and 'we'	111
	Bakhtinian and Benjaminian traces – fabrics of engagement	115
	I feel, therefore I am (a spectator)	117
5	Quasi-experts in the context of livecasting	125
	Immediacy and afterlife	131
	Quasi-experts at work: Liveness and after-liveness enabled by social media	136
	We are in it together: Critiquing the experience online	141
	Against a stagnation of theatre	142
6	Covidian theatre: The move to small screens and into homes	145
	Masks and socially distanced theatre	149
	Viral affect on screens	152
	Covidian theatre	154
	Retrospective synchronicity and NT At Home	160
7	Concluding discussion and future directions : What remains of livecasting?	173
	Responsible responsiveness and liveness	174
	What remains of livecasting?	178

Notes	185
References	199
Index	221

Figures

1	Cover of the issue of *Invention* (Vol. XIX, No. 872)	31
2	Screen capture of Twitter account of @abbielucas	55
3	Screen captures of @NTLive Twitter account	59
4	'I like your dungarees!' – Screen capture of a scene from *A Midsummer Night's Dream* directed by Nicholas Hytner	62
5	'Portrait!' – Screen capture of a scene from *A Midsummer Night's Dream* directed by Nicholas Hytner	65
6	Screen capture of a scene from *A Midsummer Night's Dream* directed by Nicholas Hytner	66
7	Screen capture of the Twitter accounts of @GozzaGood and @hvamitchell	67
8	Screen capture of the Twitter account of @albrees13	68
9	Puck jumps into the audience – Screen capture of a scene from *A Midsummer Night's Dream* directed by Nicholas Hytner	69
10	The affective arrangement of live theatre events versus livecasts	72
11	Screen capture of @NTLive Twitter account showing the filming equipment being set up in the Old Vic Theatre	85
12	'You Go Out Much?' – Screen capture of a scene from *All My Sons* directed by Jeremy Herrin	87
13	Screen capture of the final scene from *Julie* directed by Carrie Cracknell	89
14	Two pictures relating to the NT Livecast of *Small Island* directed by Rufus Norris	92
15	A sketch of the stage of *Antony and Cleopatra* directed by Simon Godwin in the National Theatre's Olivier Theatre	95
16	Screen capture of @NTLive Twitter account and exchange with @ClaireRonald on the evening of the livecast of *All About Eve*	100
17	Screen capture of the National Theatre's Facebook Page	146
18	Typology of Covidian theatre	156
19	Screen capture of the National Theatre's Facebook Page announcing the launch of NT At Home	162
20	Screen capture of *Frankenstein* GIF posted on the National Theatre's Facebook Page	163

Acknowledgements

Theatre remains and it attests to its energy that it does so via very different means. This book is the product of many encounters with theatre, performance and scholars whom it was a privilege to engage with. At the University of Koblenz-Landau, Stella Butter has been a wonderfully critical, attentive and friendly mentor. Her eye for detail and her talent for asking the difficult questions has shaped these chapters and left a distinctly structuralist imprint on many of them. I am also grateful to the University of Koblenz-Landau for supporting this publication with a small fund. Barbara Korte from the University of Freiburg sparked my interest in the topic, just like she had with the Victorians several years before that, and her constant encouragement has been a great motivation. The third mentor of this study was John London, my host during my two-year postdoctoral fellowship at the School of Languages, Linguistics and Film at Queen Mary, University of London (QMUL), generously sponsored by the Alexander von Humboldt Foundation. Our conversations were enlightening and educational in every way and I was lucky to profit from them.

From 2018 until 2020 I was part of the research environment not only at QMUL but also at the University of London as a whole. The colloquia and workshops, especially QUORUM and the events linked to the journal *Platform* at the Royal Central School of Speech and Drama, were inspiring and lively and made me feel welcome. As part of this, I had the chance to meet and talk with several researchers, whom I would like to thank for their comments and insights at different stages of the project: Jen Harvie, Nicholas Ridout, Alan Read, Clio Unger, Lisa Moravec, Duška Radosavljević and Megan Vaughan. I would especially like to thank Conor Moloney and Richard Huddleson, both for discussing my research with me and even more for their friendship and for spending many evenings attending performances both in big and tucked-away theatres in London.

I would like to thank my interview partners for the project, Ross MacGibbon, John Wyver and Matthew Amos, for their time and generosity in sharing their work with me.

Right at the beginning of my postdoc, I became a member of the Society for the Study of Contemporary Drama in English (CDE). In this context, I met several enthusiastic theatre scholars whom I would like to thank for insightful comments and suggestions at several stages of the project, and after-hours drinks: Marlena Tronicke, Anja Hartl, Monika Pietrzak-Franger,

Julia Boll, Anette Pankratz and Eckart Voigts, who also kindly agreed to write one of the reviews of the *Habilitation*.

The contacts with three scholars whose work I have been admiring for a while only manifested themselves virtually during the pandemic, and I am grateful for the exchanges with Pascale Aebischer, the late Martin Barker and Bernadette Cochrane.

Thanks also go to my students and colleagues at Landau, especially Thomas Gurke, for the pleasant working environment (and soup).

Great thanks go to the excellent staff at the British Library, the National Theatre Archive and the Senate House Library.

At Bloomsbury, the project was most expertly and swiftly guided through all stages of production by Mark Dudgeon and especially Ella Wilson. The anonymous reviewers who read either selected chapters or the final draft encouraged me in my work and provided lucid suggestions, for which I thank them.

I shall also like to thank all the performers, actors, actresses, directors, multi-camera directors, stage and production designers, and stagehands whose work it was my great pleasure, intellectual joy and sheer privilege to witness and interpret over the past few years all over London and during 2020–1 in the virtual space. I believe now more than ever that theatre expresses something at the very core of human existence; it is a threshold of revelation, as Harper Pitt has put it so wisely in Tony Kushner's *Angels in America*. Finally, I shall like to thank all the quasi-experts whose tweets form a vibrant fabric of this book.

On a personal note, I would like to thank my friends for their company, conversations and for letting me look at the bright side. To the late Jeanne-Marie Ebenezer: you have been the best of friends.

My greatest thanks, of course, go to Sarah for being there for me, for her loving support and for so much. I'm so grateful the 'acting thing' brought us together.

The past years have been overshadowed by unexpected losses. I cannot thank my mother, Joanna Liedke, enough for giving me some of her strength and for supporting me emotionally. It fills me with sadness that my father, Karl Liedke, is not with us anymore. I owe so much to him and especially his love for knowledge and critical thinking, and for integrity and academic rigour. He was a guiding light for me, and always will be. Ta książka jest dla Ciebie, Tatusiu. A Ty, Mamusiu, jesteś najsilniejszą osobą na świecie.

Introduction

Locating livecasting – Twenty-first-century British theatre on the threshold

When I attended the National Theatre (NT) Live screening of *Present Laughter* on 28 November 2019 at Rich Mix Cinema London, there was a lot of waiting involved. Before the show, I waited with the other ticket holders in the shared foyer and art gallery space on one of the floors of the Rix Mix, next to a room where a band was rehearsing with very audible percussions. While the email sent to ticket holders had stated that the livecast would start at 7.00 pm, the signs at the venue listed 7.15 pm as the starting time, which caused some anger and impatience at the Rich Mix, as the following exchange that I witnessed illustrates:

> Woman (to usher): Can you tell me the reason for the delay?
> Usher: It's just the way it is.
> Woman (to somebody else): ... 'Cause they sent me this email, not to be late, but it was supposed to start at 7!

Notably, what could have been turned into part of the experience – a playful and tongue-in-cheek remark on how the start was delayed because the actors were not ready yet – was merely dismissed by the usher, who, perhaps not used to impatient 'theatre' goers, looked at this as a mere technological issue and nuisance. There was a feeling of defamiliarization on the part of the ticketholders: we were attending a theatre play, but also not a theatre play in a cinema space and the delay was likely due to a disruption in the satellite transmission, something usually not connected with (analogue) theatre. In fact, this defamiliarization was kept up after we entered the cinema auditorium: the 'filmed live screening' (i.e. not a live broadcast – for scheduling reasons, the show had been filmed in the summer of 2019, see Buckeridge 2019) was framed by a slide with a PG-13 warning (because of some mild sex references and alcohol abuse in the play), thus a typically cinematic paratextual element. Before the actual screening began, there was a brief introductory film, filmed in an empty auditorium (it was not discernible whether that was an auditorium in the Old Vic Theatre – where *Present*

Laughter had run from 17 June to 10 August 2019 – or the NT), where the presenter, Dustin Lance Black, provided some background information. He was speaking in distinct American English and in a very enthusiastic manner which elicited giggling and laughter from my fellow cinema attendees. When the film from the Old Vic started, the first moments showed the atmosphere in the theatre that had left such an impression on me after I attended the theatrical event as well: in-situ audience members were getting to their seats, some still standing around and chatting with drinks in their hands. When the lights went down, there was a brief shot of the first couple of rows of audience members watching the stage, while The Shirelles' 'Will you still love me tomorrow?' was playing. Some people in the cinema started singing along. When Gerry and Joe kissed at the end of Act 1, a woman behind me shouted 'Yasssss!' and a few people applauded both after Act 1 and at the end of the screening.

I mention these actions and reactions observed among cinema attendees in order to draw attention to the multiple acts of negotiation which shape the experience of watching a (live) recorded theatre play in a cinema. From the outset, this situation is characterized by the complex interplay of different spaces. As Sophie Nield (2012) writes when thinking about the moment when a performance is (about to be) over in the theatre, the 'curtain call is an odd moment in many ways. Actors, who have often spent the last few hours pretending that the audience simply weren't there, now come forward, smiling and laughing, *to acknowledge their presence*' (emphasis added). The place in front of the curtain belongs to both the stage and the auditorium; it is an in-between. What Nield points to is a clash of different realities and differently real spaces belonging to different groups – the reality of the performance, the reality of the people behind the acted roles, and the reality of those watching them. In the cinema, the audience is not acknowledged directly, at least not by the performers, who cannot even see them. But there is another form of direct acknowledgement that is crucial here, namely strong prompters for entering social media spaces. The livecasting experience thus begins with moments of disorientation as the theatrical event is put in a cinematic setting, generating an unfamiliar hybrid space.

Being in an unfamiliar environment does not mean that one is lost – one can become familiar with the new environment or situation because one has a set of tools one can use to build a roof of familiarity above one's head. As Sara Ahmed notes,

> [e]ven in a strange or unfamiliar environment we might find our way, given our familiarity with social form, with how the social is arranged. This is not to say we don't get lost [. . .] But 'getting lost' still takes us

somewhere; and being lost is a way of inhabiting space by registering what is not familiar [...]. (2006, 7)

The livecasting setting is the unfamiliar-and-yet-familiar environment, creating moments of disorientation that, however, also take the spectators somewhere, namely to an experience of theatre that blends in with that of attending the cinema. The spectators are not unsettled by the unfamiliar, and if they are, then only momentarily; they become familiar with the dark rooms into which they have stepped. These are processes of negotiation that the spectators undertake willingly.[1]

* * *

This book was written at a specific point in time, one which constitutes a seismic shift in thinking about the live versus the digital, as one of the main minds behind NT Live, David Sabel, has put it in a talk a few weeks into the Covid-19 pandemic (Sabel 2020). Taking the year 2020 and the global presence of the pandemic as a caesura, my book in the main part focuses on the ways in which the NT has delivered its livecasts up until the point immediately before the pandemic, that is the years 2018–19. In the penultimate chapter of the book, I consider how this type of theatre found a new shape shortly after the pandemic had forced theatrical institutions all over the world to shut down. While up until 2019, livecasts for many viewers would have been extensions or add-ons to the live, perhaps substitutes (a rhetoric surrounding broadcast live events since the late nineteenth century, as Chapter 1 shows), the pandemic has shaken the ways we think about 'live' and 'digital' fundamentally. Now, the digital can be taken in more fully as creative, complex and curated content on its own merit. This book is driven by this insight which also, retrospectively, can make us change the ways in which we understand livecasts. It is indeed characteristic of the present moment that is difficult to distinguish the immediate past (pre-pandemic) from the present, as the two bleed into each other. The pandemic – as we are still coping with it – has had an impact on our daily lives and our perception (as scholars working in that particular field) of cultural phenomena and activities in particular. My account does not intend to yield entirely to the pandemic but indeed wants to analyse forms of enjoying theatre which have been developed in the second decade of the twenty-first century before Covid-19 changed everybody's perspectives on communal gatherings. It is impossible to ignore the pandemic, which is why my discussion links pre-pandemic livecasting with pandemic viral theatre. But *Livecasting in Twenty-First-Century British Theatre* strives to hone the extremely recent past of streamed theatre that will continue existing once the pandemic has eased its grip on people's lives.

* * *

NT Live creates specific ways of viewing, and together with the (remembered) etiquettes of theatre and those of cinema, these work as strategies in Michel de Certeau's sense (1988, 34–8) – or rooms, that are sometimes well-lit and sometimes dark. These strategies are met with tactics put in action by the audiences, negotiations to make the unfamiliar familiar, such as singing along and laughing at 'strange' pre-show features, or voicing one's response online and thus becoming visible participants in the livecasting event. As both NT Live and Royal Shakespeare Company (RSC) Live co-opt such audience responses on Twitter, 'collating and retweeting positive comments as part of their publicity campaigns' (Nicholas 2018, 79), the boundaries between strategies and tactics become blurry. The frame of the performance, which, according to Richard Schechner has as its anchors such practices as 'ticket-taking, passing through the gates, performing rituals, finding a place from which to watch', all of which is part of the 'ceremony' (2003, 189–90) of theatre-going, is dispersed in the livecasting context.

NT Live has been polarizing both audiences and theatre scholars since its launch. There are those who think it is a valuable way to access theatre, and those who reject it as some kind of scam, often an attitude partly motivated by a critical stance towards the NT as an institution that does not always manage to navigate the waters between meeting the expectations of an assumed audience and representing all that the British theatre world has to offer. The initiative evolves around satellite technology and elaborate filming equipment, thus also problematizing the status of the broadcast event as something other than theatre.

When NT Live celebrated 'Ten Years on Screen' in 2019, several famous actors, actresses and directors wished the initiative a 'happy birthday' in a trailer, saying how many amazing things it had achieved in the short time of its existence and how much of a difference it had already made. The specifics were missing – this is why, very simply put, *Livecasting in Twenty-First-Century British Theatre. NT Live and the Aesthetics of Spectacle, Materiality and Engagement* wants to get a clearer idea of the exact nature of this 'difference'. Superlatives and words of praise do not add anything to the conversation, but locating NT Live in developments in recent theatre history and the mediatization of theatre helps understand the cultural relevance of this hybrid theatre experience and what it has set into motion with regard to the future of theatrical performance.

When the dramatic text is transported from its position between two covers into its fleshed-out three-dimensional version on stage and then flattened again onto a cinema screen to be 'closer to home' for its audiences we are confronted with a new understanding of what theatrical performance is or should be. This development takes place within a context that is saturated with the penetration of social media into daily life, a context in which a picture of oneself taken by oneself is a selfie and thus a valuable commodity – that which used to be private can become public with the tap of a finger. When we are surrounded by and seek out screens and surfaces, this also has an impact on how we approach and consume art, and what we expect from it.

This is the age of the spectacularization of performance, the age in which spectacle is inextricably linked to new technologies, for example, the use of virtual realities (VR), intermedial projections or apps necessary to follow the narrative of a performance.[2] In the past three decades, 'performance practice integrating media has developed into a distinct genre that goes by a variety of names such as multi-media performance, intermedial performance, cyborg theatre, digital performance, virtual theatre, and new media dramaturgy, among others' (Bay-Cheng/Parker-Starbuck/Saltz 2015, 1), with each term reflecting a differently focused reliance on (external) media not traditionally integral to the dramatic process. This variety calls for a multiplicity of tools and methods to conceptualize the trends, rather than one 'totalizing narrative' (Bay-Cheng/Parker-Starbuck/Saltz 2015, 1).

Major theatre institutions such as the RSC cooperate with Intel to bring *The Tempest* back to life (in a Frankensteinian fashion, when the spirit Ariel is transformed into a VR projection with the help of a motion capture suit that the performer wears; see Evans 2017) and in the early summer of 2021, the RSC produced its first VR live online performance called *Dream*, which followed a performer playing Puck through a forest searching for the other spirits for about 25 minutes and resembled a computer game rather than a theatre play (Dream 2021). Despite the excitement of innovation, the potential to make theatre 'cool' again in the eyes of younger audiences and the practical benefits of creating media and digital departments and thus new jobs, these developments go hand-in-hand with the imminent danger that technology and spectacle are foregrounded rather than integrated. There is a risk, therefore, that this kind of theatre-as-spectacle resembles what Bertolt Brecht criticized as culinary theatre (see [1930] 1964, 33–41), a kind of theatre that is there to be consumed (and digested rather quickly). To conjure up Marshall McLuhan's maxim 'the medium is the message' (McLuhan 1964) in a nightmarish scenario, the technologies themselves are the spectacle.

This book takes up live theatre broadcasting as a phenomenon that has been around since 2009 with growing popularity and that is embedded on a threshold within twenty-first-century British theatre and performance. The impetus to speak of a threshold is motivated by the following observations: live theatre broadcasting is still a new, emerging performance trend; it combines several modalities, is thus inherently hybrid; and it demands a networking activity on part of the recipients, encouraging them to connect the NT Live experience with 'regular' theatre and tweeting about what they are seeing. It is this in-between status, the generic indeterminacy that is increased through the human encounter and that, I argue, creates breaks in the material (of the livecast): it is both a form of archiving material and also a kind of performance on its own right. This book develops the notion that livecasts represent the materiality of theatrical performance beyond 'mere' representation on the levels of spectacle and engagement. Taking the cue from performance studies' theorization, the livecasting phenomenon invites us to reflect on the materiality of (textual) form and the hybridity that 'the livecast' represents, namely a generic hybrid between performance, dramatic text and film.

Locating livecasting

The developments to incorporate diverse technologies into theatrical performances have unfolded over roughly the last three decades. As Steve Dixon and Barry Smith (2007) point out, it was the 1990s in particular that saw a boom in the use of 'digital performance', what they define as including 'all performance works where computer technologies play a *key* role rather than a subsidiary one in content, techniques, aesthetics, or delivery forms' (3). The examples they mention are indeed manifold and range from instances where screens with digitally manipulated images would be included on stage (in the work of Robert Lepage, The Builders Association, and George Coates Performance Works), to cases where video-conferencing software would make it possible for performers in different places to interact live on stage (see The Gertrude Stein Repertory Theatre and Kunstwerk-Blend). Further examples are the work of Merce Cunningham, who used images of virtual dancers on stage and, perhaps most radically, the work of performance artist Stelarc who 'wired his body up to the Internet and was thrown around like a rag doll by audience members in other countries who manipulated him using touch-screen computers' (Dixon 2; see also Broadhurst 2012, 229) in several performances. Modes of communication offered by stage and screen as 'performance media' (Lowe 2020, 2) – the use of screens on stage, as for instance in the work of theatre directors Ivo van Hove and Katie Mitchell, is only one illustration of that – have come together in cultural environments that are increasingly intermedial (see also Georgi 2014 for an insightful investigation of intermediality in British theatre and performance). The concept of 'convergence culture' (Jenkins 2006) can be understood as an umbrella term to grasp these parallel developments and point to the synergies and interrelationships across media forms more generally. Henry Jenkins defines convergence culture as 'the flow of content across multiple media platforms, the cooperation between multiple media industries, and the migratory behaviour of media audiences' and stresses that convergence 'occurs within the brains of individual consumers and through their social interactions with others' (2006, 2–3). Crucially, convergence is an ongoing process (2006, 16) that describes the 'collision' between old and new media and also the ways in which they are received by consumers and employed by producers and within the media industry.

Therefore, this is also the age in which spectacle can become that which *belongs* to the spectator via technology; everybody has access to it, at least theoretically. As a counter-reaction to that, positions are articulated calling for a more authentic experience in the sense that the experience with the artwork is not mediated and demands a, sometimes intimate, negotiation with it. This urge towards a more stripped-down encounter with art in general and performance, in particular, creates a tension. It is most visible in the manifold examples of immersive theatre that have appeared in the twenty-first century (see, for instance, Frieze 2016; Harvie 2013). In her insightful study, Jen Harvie, apart from sketching a vivid scenery of the peculiarities of the London theatre scene (a discourse my book seeks to continue), emphasizes the *potential* immersive theatre brings to the table: the potential for initiating social debate, social change, for actually bringing it about and – something that should not be underestimated – re-experiencing familiarities and familiar places. For instance, in a two-week performance intervention called *Fortnight* (2011–15), the company Proto-type Theater invited its 200 participants to 'be here, now' (Proto-type Theatre n.d.) by exploring the respective host city and to take part in events by following communications they received via mobile phones, electronic or postal mail. As two participants from their event in Lancaster put it, they liked being encouraged 'to ponder on things which [they] would normally never think about', be reminded of their 'childish vein' and be shown 'how to really look at life' (Proto-type Theatre n.d.). The immediacy of the experience here manifests itself in the sense that the participants are thrown back onto themselves, the technology or the surroundings do not provide a distraction but focus the attention on oneself. While all (or most) art can provoke such re-experiencing, the explicit use of technology pronouncedly blurs the boundaries between private and public space(s) when the same device that is used for daily activities is turned into a vehicle for artistic encounter. In *Fortnight*, the mediatized interaction happens in real time and connects the participants among each other and with the producer Peter Petralia (Petralia 2012, 7, 8, 10). While Harvie remains sceptical with regard to whether the envisioned changes can *actually* happen in this day and age (because the effects of neoliberalism cast their shadows on both those providing funding and those receiving it), one can observe an increasingly complex and fraught intertwining of technologies and experiences. On the one hand, the use of technologies can distract, distort and distance spectators from the performance; on the other hand, it can bring the two closer to each other, perhaps even enhance the experience and only throw into greater relief the pronounced reliance on spectators by major theatre institutions – oscillations that lie at the core of my study of live theatre broadcasting.

Constructing the live

In one of the talks offered as part of the 'Macbeth Talks' with the two leads of this production of *Macbeth*, Anne-Marie Duff and Rory Kinnear, which I attended on 30 April 2018 at the NT, the first remark the chair Tazeen Ahmad made to the audience was to share the event they were attending on 'whatever social media they were on'. Especially major theatre institutions such as the NT or the RSC depend on them more and more. All the livecasts come with their own hashtag, and as the discussions in the following chapters will repeatedly show, spectators are encouraged to be part of the event via the paradocumentational brim, and great care is taken to facilitate a comfortable experience of the livecasts in cinemas.

As Abbott and Read have put it, the concept of paradocumentation asserts 'a notion of unity between performances and their documents, borne in part from the technology of NT Live' (2017, 165); they define both official (leaflets, online articles promoting the performance, rehearsal shots) and unofficial (for instance, 'documents created by audience members'') documents as part of this paradocumentation, arguing that this term echoes 'a holistic approach to experiencing, interpreting, and creating records of a live-streamed play, advancing and extending the life of a single performance' (166). What these documents also do is break up the chronology between play and livestream: the same photos (usually rehearsal shots) are shown before a performance, the livestream, and later the Encore screening (i.e. the repeated screening of an NT Live stream). Thus, 'the logical sequencing of rehearsal to production to documentation is further altered: the rehearsal shots appear to occur *after* the performance has in reality aired *live*' (167). A solution to do away with this temporal confusion is to conceive of paradocumentation in spatial terms, which is why I use the image of the 'brim' as a stabilizing and constitutive part of the livecasting event.

What questions around chronology and how to capture and/or extend the performance's liveness also point to is that 'artists, producers and audiences [are] exploring new ways in which aliveness as an experiential force can be sustained, and perhaps even deepened, as theatre and performance find their way in an increasingly digital world' (Sullivan 2018, 73). The Tate Modern, too, has presented live performances since 2003 and additionally launched 'BMW Tate Live' as a way 'to progress the programme by creating a platform for innovation and a stage for emotion, learning to appreciate the transformational impact of new ideas and ensuring accessibility for audiences' (Tate n.d.b). What sounds like an example of vague verbosity includes three strands of activity from talks and events live at Tate Modern (which in itself would not be particularly innovative) to 'Performance Room', a series of performances 'commissioned and conceived exclusively for the online space and [. . .] broadcast live across the web' (Tate n.d.a). The performances are streamed live via Tate's website and YouTube Channel, where audiences can connect via the chat (Tate n.d.a).

What is emerging here is a new form of performance with new rules; the performance itself is not the sole focus anymore, what happens around it in the form of audience engagement has a central position as well. In other words: while audiences have always reacted in one way or another (in conversations, in private thoughts and sometimes even in written reviews) to art or performances they saw, in the present context an additional frame is established within which engagement is especially encouraged and within which it happens.

Jenkins has introduced a new perception of consumers (readers, viewers, users, etc.) as active participants in cultural production and reception, building on Alvin Toffler's concept of the 'prosumer', an active consumer who is 'increasingly being drawn into the production process' (1980, 290), blurring the boundaries between consumer and producer. Being a media consumer, as Jenkins, Ford and Green detail, entails several roles, such as translators, multipliers, appraisers, retro curators and pop cosmopolitans, all of which make up participatory culture (2013, 297).[3] As I show in Chapters 4 and 5, the roles of feeling spectators and quasi-experts need to be added to this list in the context of livecasting. This picks up on Eckart Voigts' call for new reception studies already in 2013 that 'will need to overcome the self-enclosure of merely thinking about audiences as consumers and start to fully grasp the fact that audiences are themselves producers, publishers and distributors of texts' (2013, 154) – for instance, as bloggers or contributors to the post-performance memory on social media.[4]

What the examples of the Tate Modern and the Macbeth Talks already demonstrate is the centrality of the spectators and how, first, types of theatre become popular that do not work without amateur 'actors', such as immersive theatre, and how, second, theatres (and other cultural institutions) increasingly court their audience's favours. The Old Vic does so, for instance, by introducing the position of Young Digital Creator (YDC) in 2018, who, among other things, on some performance nights takes over the institution's Twitter account and tweets videos from the interval or after the show. In this vein, the first YDC, Heather Pasfield, filmed twenty-four seconds of her crying after seeing *A Monster Calls* on 12 July 2018, which was viewed 3,941 times, as of 2 September 2018 (the video has been deleted from Twitter in the meantime). These developments indicate that this is, first, the age of 'every(wo)man experts' and second, the age of user-generated content, where everybody's opinion not only matters but has value in the sense of (cultural) capital. This becomes evident on pages such as Tripadvisor, Airbnb and others, but also plays a role in the way in which theatre institutions market themselves and target their audiences.

It is this uniquely post-postmodern[5] tension between older and more traditional forms of theatre and the timely use of technologies at the juncture of which this book locates the phenomenon of live theatre broadcasting, henceforth referred to as livecasting.[6] John Wyver prefers the term 'live broadcast' despite its television connotations; 'live relay [. . .] suggests that there is not a creative process being undertaken' and 'filming [. . .] suggests that it is recorded and reworked in some way' (interview in Stone 2016, 632). I am taking up Martin Barker's use of 'livecasting' (2013) because it is a new term for a new phenomenon and a poignant portmanteau term that also attests to the dynamic processes at play when a theatre show is recorded under the guidance of a multi-camera director.

The Metropolitan Opera in New York was the first to produce live streams of their performances in 2006 and the NT in London has followed suit since 2009. It is possible to see a selection of the NT's season at cinema venues around the world, resulting in what can only be thought of as 'a paradigm shift in theatergoing practices' (Sullivan 2017, 627). In 2019, the auditoriums on the Southbank were on average 91 per cent full across twenty-three productions (NT Annual Review 2018/2019). NT Live screened in 2,000 venues around the world and there were 6,632 screenings across the UK, reaching a total audience of 800,000 people worldwide (2018/2019). The first NT Live production in 2009, Nicholas Hytner's *Phèdre*, was watched by more than 50,000 people all around the world, roughly equivalent to the total in-house audience for the production's entire three-month run (Bakhshi and Throsby 2009, 2). The livecast of Turner's *Hamlet* starring Benedict Cumberbatch in 2015 was seen by over 225,000 people in twenty-five countries in October 2015 (Hawkes 2015) and was shown in 87 per cent of cinemas in the UK (cf. Gardner 2015; Hutchinson 2015).

It seems that livecasting has an effect on 'not just the surrounding theater ecology but potentially the cinematic landscape, too' (Sullivan 2017, 628). About 2,000 cinemas worldwide have broadcast NT Live screenings by now (see their homepage), and both major and smaller theatre companies work with broadcasting, either on big screens or online (for instance, the RSC since 2013, the Kenneth Branagh Theatre Company (KBTC) since 2015, Cheek by Jowl since 2015, and Table Top Shakespeare since 2015; Forced Entertainment has already live streamed their durational works to the internet in 2008, Etchells 2015). Several opera houses, such as the Royal Opera House (on BP Big Screens across the UK and internationally on YouTube) and the English National Opera (ENO).

Apart from 'inspiring' other theatre companies to follow suit, and more cinemas to take on showing livecasts because 'their best source of income is special events' (Hytner in Trueman 2014), NT Live also has an impact on the NT's self-image and working practices in three very different regards. First, the NT seems to reflect on the term 'national' more – as the then artistic director Hytner put it in 2013, it is 'better understood as reflecting the nation – its past, its present, what it has been, what it wants to be, what it shouldn't be. A whole spectrum of theatre should be produced every year that worries away at the "National" bit' (Smith 2013). While it started out as a national project and permission to use the prefix 'Royal' (which, however, is hardly used) was only given in 1988, the self-reflection can be said to become more conscious now, especially in the years after Brexit.[7] Second, and more practically speaking, NT Live has changed the equipment of the theatre. It also profited from the NT Future Redevelopment programme, which was initiated in 2010 and over the course of seven years raised 80 million pounds (from the Arts Council England, the Heritage Lottery Fund and individuals, companies, trusts and foundations – see NT Future n.d.). As part of it, there are now new in-house facilities for digital media and creative content development and expanded facilities, which enable NT Live to bring '[their] groundbreaking live broadcasts to cinemas across the UK and around the world, widening [their] international audience by a further 500,000 and supporting the increasing use of digital technology in NT productions' (NT Future n.d.) – one must note the use of superlatives in this phrasing from the NT's website.

The third point takes us back to the developments that I outlined at the beginning of this Introduction and indeed the pressure to comply with the trend to use technologies in theatre. As Stone observes, the NT 'has, in effect, transformed its theatres into film studios' (Stone 2016, 628). Tickets for those performances that are being broadcast live are available, but only with the additional disclaimer that they will be filmed because (a) audiences will see about seven cameras, usually two on rails, four static ones and one on a crane, and other filming equipment, and (b) audience members themselves will be seen. Greenhalgh, thus, is right in pointing out that the 'implications of embedded filming capacity will make for permanent change at the NT. Filming a particular production (or not) will affect all aspects of planning and design' (2014, 255). In addition, all this minute planning and coordinating is diametrically opposed to the idea of 'the ephemerality of live performance' (Stone 2016, 628). Those minds behind NT Live, such as Hytner, do not seem to find these issues as irreconcilable – as he put it when talking about his 1998 production of *Twelfth Night* that was broadcast live on PBS:

> You knew it wasn't *the real thing*, but as you couldn't be there at the big match, *you were glad* the cameras were there to capture it for you. *It didn't matter* that the actors were a bit sweaty and a bit shouty, because, like footballers, they were sweating and shouting live, in the moment. (Hytner 2018, 271, emphases added)

The livecast is described in terms of a sports metaphor and Hytner's statement hints at a worry and prejudice quite a few people have towards livecasts: namely that they look 'cheap', like those filmed plays sometimes shown on culture TV channels (the German channel 3sat, for instance, still occasionally transmits plays this way, with one static camera positioned at the back of the hall; the same goes for the German-French channel *arte*). Perhaps unwittingly, the editorial 'you' that is described here by Hytner is a sort of neoliberal couch potato, not *caring* that what they are seeing is not 'the real thing', simply 'glad' they can still see it – an attitude that would not constitute a successful PR slogan. 'It's not the real thing – but that doesn't matter?' The actual slogan used for NT Live is: 'Always the best seat in the house', without specifying what 'house' is actually meant. The liveness of the broadcast, therefore, is exclusively constructed through references to the simultaneity of the broadcast with the actual performance and not so much the location of either. In not 'needing' it, the spatial aspect is transcended while the temporal dimension – and especially the simultaneity of experiencing with others – acquires a new prioritized status.

Distractions, slippages and turns: Spectacle – archive

Livecasting opens up frictions, disruptions and slippages: between performance and text, actualization and potentiality, documentation and liveness/ephemerality, and presence and disappearance. 'Theatre' comes from the Greek *theatron*, which means a 'place for looking', that is, both a specific place *and* a form of sense perception and a focus on visuality. The Greek *theates* means 'spectator' and *theasthai* means 'to behold'. Yet both of these are under contestation in theatre livecasts: the place of the cinema venue, of course, still matters for the livecast attendees, but strictly speaking the place of the theatre only matters remotely – (co-)*temporality* rather than co-spatiality comes to the foreground. While 'traditional' theatre is defined as an activity (Balme 2008), Balme also refers to Eric Bentley's formula of theatre as 'A impersonates B while C looks on (1965, 150)', thus already hinting at the constantly negotiated question surrounding the passivity or activity of the spectator. For livecasts, Bentley's formula has to be adjusted to 'A watches as B impersonates C while D looks on' – whether A sees D, however, differs from livecast to livecast and will be taken into account in my discussions of the performances.

These frictions, between closeness and distance, immediacy and media(ti)zation, also coincide with shifts within the field of theatre studies. While in the beginning, the discipline of theatre studies was centred on historical research and the study of dramatic texts, it now concentrates also on live performance (perhaps more so in the British and American tradition than in that of *Theaterwissenschaft* in Germany – for comprehensive overviews see Balme 2008 and Fischer-Lichte 2004). For the purposes of the argument here it suffices to refer to one seminal text, Jerzy Grotowski's *Towards a Poor Theatre* (1968), which calls for an 'aesthetic purity' of theatre:

> The theatre must recognize its own limitations. If it cannot be richer than the cinema, then let it be poor. If it cannot be as lavish as television, let it be ascetic. If it cannot be a technical attraction, let it renounce all outward technique. [. . .] There is only one element of which film and television cannot rob the theatre: the closeness of the living organism. (Grotowski [1968] 2002, 41)

Grotowski's call, thus, is for an organicity and immediacy of acting and the moment in which it unfolds; what he describes as 'the closeness of the living organism' is later captured as 'leibliche Ko-Präsenz' of actors' and spectators' bodies by Erika Fischer-Lichte (2014, 47). And it is also a call for a valorization of that element, which only theatre has to offer: the experience of a Here and Now.

In recent London theatre productions one can occasionally see a going back to what Grotowski might have pictured as purity (e.g. *Sea Wall; My Name is Lucy Barton*[8]) but all in all, the impression that one receives is superseded by the need to establish and create comfort and happiness (echoing something akin to what Sara Ahmed' postulates as the 'duty to be happy' [2010]). This is not to say that contemporary (London) theatre productions are concerned with happiness; the range of topics covered by the plays that have been put on stage recently is varied (and ranges from narratives of personal loss, such as *A Monster Calls* [Old Vic, 2018] to modernizations of canonical texts, such as *Wild Duck* [Almeida, 2018], *The Tragedy of King Richard II* [Almeida, 2019], to musical adaptations that indeed ooze joy, such as *Twelfth Night* [Young Vic, 2018] and *White Teeth* [Kiln Theatre, 2018], to name just a very few). Yet great efforts are made to ascertain that the viewing experience is a happy, comfortable one, along several axes: the audience is prepared beforehand via email newsletters and on social media about what to expect via trailers, rehearsal photographs, a digest of (preview) reviews; at least one actor/actress is usually well-known and hyped up as such, which again means that one knows that it will be worthwhile; the duration of the show and of the interval are announced in the programme, in the aforementioned email announcements and in the case of livecasts through the presenter, so that one knows exactly how to time one's evening. There is hardly any room left for surprises or uncertainties that might cause impatience or anxiety. Paradoxically perhaps (or quite logically), the spectacle turn in theatre, as I want to call it, that is, the date around which the first livecasts were produced roughly coincides with the happiness turn as identified by Sara Ahmed – she locates it as occurring from the year 2005 onwards when more and more publications on the science and economics of happiness started to appear (see 2010, 3; see also a special issue of *New Formations* on happiness, edited by Ahmed). The spectacle turn points both at the spectacularity (as in eventness) and grandness of what is to be performed. Happiness, or to be happy, is an individual responsibility; there is hardly a feeling that is more difficult to define in general terms. This is why theatre – if it wants to connect with people – needs to be designed in a more personal and responsible way. This more personal shape is linked closely to a comfortable and (yet) spectacular form of consuming art.

There is a final turn that I want to mention at this point and that I will revisit at the end of my book: the archival turn. It specifies two main categories of my analysis that complement each other, liveness and the archive/documentation (see Bucknall and Sedgman 2017; Giannachi et al.

2012). For a little than over a decade now (since 2009), there has existed a need in both performance studies and performance practice to raise awareness on the impact that digital curation and archiving have on the past, present and future of the field, which coincides with the time when both the Metropolitan Opera in New York and the NT started producing live broadcasts. While the NT does not make livecasts available to the public on DVDs afterwards like the RSC, there are still copies preserved that can be accessed in the NT Archive. Toni Sant (2017) calls for the need to re-validate the term 'documentation', which has hitherto been mainly used as a generic and contentious term, and think about it 'as the simple *process* of creating and organizing documents towards providing documentation that is available for long-term access' (2017, 1, emphasis added). In contrast to the performance itself, the term documentation, understood generically, tends to be relegated to the sidelines as being of a secondary value both by performers and performance scholars and arts administrators (2–3). Yet Sant then endows documents with a certain kind of power by saying that they 'provide ways to access *memories* of performance events or momentary experiences of them' and that they are 'open to interpretation, re-interpretation and other forms of re-use . . . *regardless of the original context*' (3). To emphasize that they function like gateways to memories is suggestive of a much narrower conception of Aleida and Jan Assmann's 'kulturelles Gedächtnis' (2006, 2013), or cultural memory. This also suggests that there is something like a (subjective) uniqueness that surrounds each performance event and is captured in memories of it, reminiscent of Walter Benjamin's *aura*. To say that these documents are open to (re-)interpretation and re-use, however, implies a much more permeable and flexible understanding of a performance event that it is far from disappearing in the moment of its presentation.

With regard to livecasts, the question of liveness a complex one.[9] They are in fact primarily marketed as (immediate) experiences. Yet each live transmission *is* a recording and is made on only one night, and not for instance, on several nights, and then edited into one 'perfect' version. In line with Sant's specification above of documentation as a (powerful, creative) process rather than 'mere' fossilization, those archived livecasts, I argue, can never be static or finished because they are surrounded by a paradocumentational brim consisting of pre- and post-production assessments both by professionals and especially by what (partly unwittingly, in a process of being hailed as unpaid labourers) becomes an amateur review community on social media. In contrast to other cultural texts, livecasts are not only made up of the filmed content of the theatre performance but also the (informal) texts surrounding them and the feedback loop they create in the virtual space. In fact, the way they are 'treated' by audiences positions them in the realm of popular culture:

this is not to say they *are* popular culture as broadcast theatre can hardly be considered a mainstream pastime activity. NT Live is produced by and thus carries the (economic, ideological) interests of the biggest player in the field of British theatrical production. But including and even fostering such lines of force that open the field to participatory culture, the initiative makes available the resources necessary for people to make their own meanings (see Fiske's definition of 'popular culture' [2001, 2]).

Of course, documents of performances are not the same as performances; but livecasts preserve memories of performances and as such contribute to creating an emotional history of a specific moment in culture for their viewers. While Sant elaborates that the main reason why performance documentation is underplayed is because it is rarely recorded 'with the same level of precision, commitment and discipline as the creation of the other essential parts of the performance itself', almost as 'an afterthought' and 'something far removed from the experience of being in the same place and time as the original event' (Sant 2017, 4), and all of this is redefined when it comes to livecasts. Commitment and precision are as outspoken as in the case of the production itself and the recording of the performance is a *fore*thought.

Research overview

This book provides an analysis of livecasting coming from the field of performance of cultural studies, focusing on NT Live and the years 2018–20 and connecting it to the discourses around spectacle, materiality and engagement. It is embedded in the context of recent research on the topic in the form of very nuanced articles and book chapters, such as Cochrane and Bonner (2014), Wardle (2014), Stone (2016), Sullivan (2017), Way (2017), Cochrane (2018), Wyver (2019) and Lowe (2020). The only short monograph to date on the phenomenon comes from the field of media studies and sociology, namely Barker's *Live to Your Local Cinema* (2013). His book offers a useful overview of what has been done in the realm of liveness and mediation in cinema and theatre, and his assessment of the audience experience is insightful, yet it covers only the year 2009 and functions as a starting point for further investigations. He emphasizes the importance of audience research in the field and outlines key questions for the event cinema industry as a whole. As a complement to that, Wyver (2014b) maps the early history of theatre broadcasting in the UK and offers invaluable insights into the technical craft behind twenty-first-century broadcasting technologies.

Other publications that zoom in on selected aspects of livecasting are articles by Daniel Schulze (2015), Susanne Greenhalgh (2014), Bernadette Cochrane (2018) and Lauren Hitchman (2018). Greenhalgh (2014) offers an overview of the role of livecasts for the distribution of Shakespeare's work, establishing a contrast between the strategies of NT Live and the RSC (which releases DVDs of some livecasts). She refers to livecasting as a 'hybrid form' which introduces new challenges to the reviewer and discusses what kind of effect film has on theatricality. Hitchman (2018) takes up this question of hybridity and, using Walter Benjamin as a theoretical framework, thinks of liveness in this context as a condition of perception and not transmission.

In addition, there are scattered articles on the topic (by Purcell 2014; Sullivan 2017) and two collections edited by Stephen O'Neill (2017) and Pascale Aebischer, Susanne Greenhalgh and Laurie Osborne (2018), the latter of which provides a very helpful reference point for my book. What is striking is that most of these discussions come from the field of Shakespeare studies, however; while my project wants to take into account Shakespeare's plays as well, its aim is to conceptualize livecasting as such *and* analyse selected livecasts not only of Shakespeare's plays.

Aims and structure of the book

Livecasting in Twenty-First-Century British Theatre adopts a culturally materialist perspective to keep in mind the hybrid quality and potential of new media as coupled with performative arts and film. Livecasting specifically has an impact on the landscape of theatre but also that of film because it could influence future film adaptations of stage productions. Yet it does not reflect the complexity of livecasts to refer to them merely as that which they are not (*actual* performances, *actual* films) or that which they have an influence on. Cochrane and Bonner (2014) are right to emphasize that livecasts need to be considered as a distinct art form,[10] but I would like to pick up a claim introduced by Cochrane more recently in 2018, namely that they are adaptive instantiations in their own right (2018, 340 and 342). While I agree that it is necessary to speak of the distinctiveness of a livecast as an art form, this may narrow down the discussion too much to the aesthetic and to form. The term 'adaptive instantiation' allows for more flexibility and a broader discussion, which is why I develop it further in this book with the concept of 'crossover'. The capacity of this new art form to both mediate and spectacularize the performance that it is based on, to foreground its materiality and to create multiple layers of engagement that are then added to the art form on its paradocumentational brim is what makes it truly distinct.

Linked to this understanding of liveness and the experience of it as being subject to change and under historical contestation, an underlying assumption that helps consider livecasts and their status as crossovers is the following claim by Mikhail Bakhtin. Bakhtin regarded the genre of the novel as the perfect form yet his theses are applicable to drama, too:

> The living utterance [*performance; livecast of performance*], having taken meaning and shape at a particular historical moment in a socially specific environment [*post-2009 livecast technologies*], cannot fail to brush up against thousands of living dialogic threads, woven by socio-ideological consciousness and around the given object of an utterance [*reviews surrounding it; PR campaigns; social media feedback*]; it cannot fail to become an active participant in social dialogue. After all, the utterance arises out of this dialogue as a continuation of it and as a rejoinder to it – it does not approach the object from the sidelines. (Bakhtin 1981, 276–7 additions in brackets mine)

Building on the earlier considerations, the following hypotheses will guide this book. They form the grid of my argumentation, which is then filled in by the respective chapters. The conceptual triad of spectacle, materiality and engagement points to the three central characteristics of twenty-first-century theatricality in a medial context, which are contingency, risk and spontaneity:

Hypothesis 1: Livecasts foster a multi-modal engagement with the translated source and are a constitutive part of the *spectacle turn*. A Bakhtinian reading of livecasts suggests that they bring forth a movement towards a humanization of cultural perception (cf. Cutchins 2017, 85) and remind us that texts are not dead things but begin and end with the human voice (Bakhtin 1981, 252–3). In this context, especially the role of other spectators as carriers of affect contributes to the affective experience of livecast spectators.

Hypothesis 2: More unstably than other media, livecasts stand on the threshold of different media and temporalities. Their status can be termed interdetermination, which plays on the notion that they are interdetermined with regard to their genre, venue and reception, and interrelated with the paradocumentational brim surrounding them. Therefore, the usual primary/secondary hierarchy with regard to livecasts (the theatre performance is presented as primary, while the livecast is secondary) needs to be broken up; so does the binary opposition of 'live' and 'recorded'. As Purcell (2014), Cochrane (2018, 342) and Parsons (2014, 101) point out, broadcasts are multi-faceted products in their own right, they are crossovers, which also extends to describe the eventness of livecasts, emerging out of adaptive processes (see also Lowe 2020). When the usual binaries surrounding theatrical performance become blurry, that which performance is made of – its *materiality* – is foregrounded. Thus, in livecasting the agency and materiality of the performance elements are moved centre-stage or rather centre-screen. The livecast is positioned on the spectrum between film and theatre and, while incorporating especially cinematic aesthetics, is the hub for a new kind of theatricality, the material-theatrical, which manifests itself through objects and the interplay of different spaces.

Hypothesis 3: In analogy to the notion that the experience of an adaptation seems to be a recognition of two things at once, livecasts extend this moment into a prolonged experience thus creating a vital archive and prolonged liveness that is motivated by reception processes. They open the doors to amateur reviewers more than 'regular' theatrical events and – more importantly – allow different forms of *engagement*. For this reason, they are part of the discourse around participatory culture and in the case of livecasts these responses on the paradocumentational brim belong to the arrangement of the livecast. Apart from the opportunities it opens up, one must also ask critically whether the potential of this multi-modal complexity is not complemented with experiential simplicity. The varied forms of reception, however, have hitherto been neglected in the critical discourse and therefore also deserve their place in the assessment of contemporary theatrical and livecast reception.

* * *

This book is interdisciplinary at its core, which both bears great potential and is a responsibility for me as a scholar. It aims to examine the phenomenon from the perspective of performance studies, cultural studies, and with insights from performance philosophy,[11] literary and cultural theory, and theatre history at a point when the British theatre (industry) has to position itself with regard to changing medial conditions and changing audiences. As far as methodology is concerned, the approach is also interdisciplinary and combines close readings of both the productions and their reception with auto-ethnography and netnography and embeds these discussions in their sociocultural contexts. My positionality (at the time this book was written) is that of a 'early career researcher' with an educational background in literary theory, English literature and culture and drama studies, who has lived in Germany, the United States and the United Kingdom. My perspective is Eurocentric and I focus on the Western cultural context, yet my own background is that of a migrant (my family is from Poland) and a queer person, so these biographical facts inform my perspective and fuel my interest in margins of all kinds.

The book is structured as follows: because of the complexity of livecasts, the concepts spectacle, materiality and engagement form the anchors for the analysis. Part I presents the historical and sociocultural backdrop for my analysis. In Chapter 1, I introduce the electrophone as an early form of live theatre and music broadcasting as an acousmatic experience in order to think about how theatrical space has been made optional already in earlier forms of mediated theatre. Chapter 2 embeds livecasting within the spectacle turn and, using *A Midsummer Night's Dream* (2019a, NT Live/Bridge Theatre) as a case study, argues that the affective arrangement differs when one looks at livecasts versus live theatre performances because the thresholds of intensity characterizing both settings are crossed/played with differently. As a consequence, the effect of the spectacular set-up of the livecast creates a new manifestation of mediatized communitas. Chapter 3 adds the concept of 'materiality' to the discussion of livecasts. My approach is informed by calls within theatre scholarship to study and acknowledge the role of objects, props and (backstage) craft more generally 'to understand the complete theatre event' (Monks 2014, 176). The chapter argues that in the livecasting setting the material conditions of production are especially emphasized. The livecast is positioned on the spectrum between film and theatre (performance) and, while incorporating especially cinematic aesthetics, is the hub for a new kind of theatricality, the material-theatrical.

In Part II, I use the term 'engagement' as a central concept to denote scalable levels of involvement. The decision to work with this concept is informed by recent developments in performance and audience studies that see the term being used in order to capture the relations of audiences to contemporary media and culture. In their Call for Papers to a special issue on the concept of the journal *Participations*, editors Martin Barker and Sue Turnbull identify several markers of the term's rise, among these its use in branding and marketing, digital media industries and studies about audiences published between 2013 and 2021[12] that have featured this term in their titles and sought to address the idea in action with particular connections to transmedia. My motivation does not only rely on these – although representative – quantitative markers, but is of a qualitative kind as well as my aim is to make fruitful use of the implications of the term to describe the processes in play when audiences get into contact with livecasts.

Two main strands are central to my use of the term 'engagement': (a) engagement is understood as a pull and active allure to describe a series of calls to kinds of involvement enacted both by a live theatrical event but also differently in its livecast counterpart, and (b), engagement is used to describe an enacted sense of being part of a communitas of watcher-participants, enabled by the ways in which the livecast is filmed (the focus of Chapter 2 in connection with the spectacle), or a hailing of spectators as 'feeling I's as orchestrated by the digital/medial environment of the livecast. Thus, Chapter 4 asks what impact livecasting technologies have on the experience of their spectators and what contribution they make to thinking about ways of engagement. It argues that, on the one hand, livecasting opens up new possibilities of audience participation and fosters a multi-modal (Kress 2010) engagement with the 'translated' sources. On the other hand, this new paradigm of spectatorship, seems to foster the manifestation of the 'feeling I', one's own and personal position with regard to the cultural product witnessed rather than critical (i.e. more rational, reflected) responses.

Chapter 5 introduces the 'quasi-expert' in order to consider the potential of livecasts for a shift in participation discourses and a more democratic form of critical discourses by quasi-experts. It discusses how this figure and the new processes of engagement with a theatrical event are shaped by live broadcasting as a new form of mediation and mediation of liveness especially.

Chapter 6 was written at a moment in time of theatrical exception against the background of the Covid-19 pandemic. While it is thus a timely complement to the analysis conducted in the previous chapters, it continues and links up to the discussions of the tensions between non-mediated and mediated theatre, and more crucially, the tensions emerging out of the interaction between spectators and mediated performance. I use the term 'Covidian theatre' to refer to plays which, in the wake of social distancing and lockdowns, explicitly address audiences *at home* and/or use various means to activate the pandemic frame. I am interested in the different levels of engagement a new platform such as NT At Home fosters. In sum, the chapters concerned with the concept of engagement investigate what kinds of engagement livecasts bring about, how they challenge theatrical affects (in contrast to cinema viewing, for instance) and in what ways they create new forms of involvement.

Chapter 7 is a concluding discussion to this book and revisits the notion of interdetermination with regard to livecasts discussed in the Introduction and then places the livecasting discourse in the context of ongoing debates around liveness and the archive to emphasize, once again, how livecasts necessitate a thinking that resists a binary logic, such as the archive versus the live or fleeting.

Rather than presenting separate case studies, the considerations and theoretical discussions in my book are accompanied and illustrated by analyses of livecasts produced between 2017 and 2020 by the NT and, to a lesser extent, the RSC as the two biggest companies in this field, consisting of close readings of the livecasts and taking into account the reception of them on social media. These productions are: *Macbeth* (NT Live 2018), *Julie* (NT Live 2018), *Romeo and Juliet* (RSC 2018), *Antony and Cleopatra* (NT Live 2018), *The Madness of King George III* (NT Live 2018), *All About Eve* (Noel Coward Theatre/NT Live 2019), *All My Sons* (Old Vic/NT Live 2019), *Small Island* (NT Live 2019), *Present Laughter* (Old Vic/NT Live 2019) and *A Midsummer Night's Dream* (Bridge Theatre/NT Live 2019). This is complemented with interviews that I conducted with multi-camera directors Ross MacGibbon (Chapter 2) and Matthew Amos (Chapters 3 and 7), and the RSC producer John Wyver (Chapters 4 and 5).

Ultimately, this book asserts a paradoxical insight, namely that the experience of liveness does not need spatio-temporal and/or corporeal co-presence any longer to be considered live; liveness is and can be 'more real' when it is mediated. Therefore, livecasting exemplifies that twenty-first-century British theatre is a theatre that is on the threshold; it does not come into being in an environment of mere simulation but a reality experienced *via* mediation and remediation the potential of which this book seeks to examine.

Part I

Spectacle and materiality

1

Old new media

The optionality of the theatre space and different forms of embodiment in early live theatre and music broadcasting

Many still have an objection to attending a public place of amusement, but none can complain of a concert brought to their own house, to their very bedrooms, if they wish. It is an excellent idea splendidly carried out.
(*Daily Picayune* 1899, 6)

The historical contextualization of the origins of livecasting begins in the late nineteenth century when first attempts were made to experience the communal art of theatre and concerts in places other than the theatre, namely in the privacy of one's home. The first experiment of the transmission of music via the electrophone (using telephone technology) took place at the Exposition Internationale d'Électricité in 1881, where '[w]ords spoken on the French coast were heard as distinctly at Dover as though no water had separated the speakers' (*The British Mercury* 1881, 2). In early accounts of this new technology there is a distinct awe and cautious scepticism, when the electrophone is described as a fashion and experiment, expected not to last too long. Indeed, the electrophone was a relatively short-lived phenomenon and superseded by the radio in the 1920s. Yet for roughly twenty-five years it did play a crucial role in the reception of music and performance. As this chapter shows, it was, perhaps counterintuitively, assessed in terms of the prevalent discourses privileging visuality and vision. The latter is particularly noteworthy as the electrophone, just like the gramophone and telephone, exemplified a kind of distinctly modern technology, which separated sounds from their sources. Pierre Schaeffer coined the term 'acousmatic' to describe this mismatch in perception. While it is not historically specific to hear something or somebody without seeing them at the same time it *is* a characteristic of modernity that such acousmatic listening proliferated and was the common denominator of several new inventions in the realm of music distribution and communication technologies at the time. Schaeffer argued that not seeing the source would amount to not being distracted by it, thus effectively making listeners more attentive (in Halliday 2013, 80). In my reading of electrophone technology I am shifting the focus to whether the acousmatic creates an experience of lack that is then compensated by listeners by reinstating the source of a given sound in verbal-visual terms. It is through the power of imagination and language that an auditory experience can create a spatial and embodied sensation.

In acousmatic settings where sound and the source of the sound are not side-by-side it is the listener who embodies the sound and in turn, as my readings of selected periodical accounts of the electrophone from the time in this chapter show, adds the sense of vision and especially a spatial dimension to the perception of 'mere' sound. What is striking when looking at accounts from the time on the electrophone is how they function as vehicles both for the imagination and (albeit often implicit) imaginative processes in which the listener's body is transported to the site of the spectacle. The accounts also ascribe to the technology a promise entailed in the future and even a healing power. As much as the history of instruments 'concerns not just the objects themselves but also what they promise, portend and make possible' (Patteson 2015, 4), the history of early broadcasting technologies must be read in a similar vein: as opening up entire worlds hitherto closed off to the majority of people.

There is an added value of looking at acousmatic proto-livecasting in the Victorian age for an understanding of twenty-first-century livecasting because it makes it possible to identify and trace ahistorical similarities despite the differences depending on the available technology. By contrasting different technologies used in theatre broadcasts, the way in which the technology shapes the production, texts and experience of theatre livecasting can be gauged in a more nuanced manner. Victorian acousmatic livecasts create an empowered perceiving/listening subject whose experience needs to be examined alongside that of the perceiving subject of scenic spectacle in theatre. As the experience becomes a primarily embodied one, the dimension of space and the necessity for theatre to be taken in on site acquires an optional quality. The question what happens when scenic spectacle is reincorporated in twenty-first-century livecasting is precisely the topic dealt with in the later chapters of this book. Then and now livecasting is a form of theatrical experience that reconciles the freedom of self-determined enjoyment and a form of enjoyment selected and distributed by a theatre. To focus on nineteenth-century accounts of journalists, critics and critics-as-audience-members means to turn to an archive of audience response, let it bear on the understanding of twenty-first-century livecasts and to trace the evolution of participatory culture.

A discussion of historical forms of broadcast music and theatre is also a discussion of the role of the visual versus the auditory in the nineteenth century and with that the role of the sense of vision versus the sense of hearing

– and more generally, a kind of aesthetic experience that was dependent on one's senses at all rather than transcending bodily capacities. This stands in contrast to the discourse of idealism at the time and works such as Grant Allen's *Physiological Aesthetics* (1877), where he argued that poetry was the 'highest' art as it was 'least obviously dependent on bodily capacities' (Halliday 2020, 37). The time in which the electrophone was used is thus bracketed by scientific positions that would a) emphasize the isolated functionality of each sense and b) privilege the sound of vision over the sense of sound. In line with this, Sophie Nield argues that 'the central story of the nineteenth-century stage is of technologically-driven scenic spectacle' (2019, 204). Thus, the example of the electrophone is actually untypical for the time: it suggests that by the end of the nineteenth century there was a (renewed) need for an experience of the auditory and a need that stood in friction with other prevalent modes of experience. Nield outlines how theatre at that time was both one of many visual and spectacular forms but also a form of resistance. It could produce a resistance to the dominant narrative of nineteenth-century visual culture, namely scenic spectacle, through the exploitation of technological innovation and the use of artificial darkness (see 2019, 205). Even though it had just become possible to have light and thus visibility on stage, not all theatrical plays followed that call. Rather, they employed the available new technologies to obscure and hide. One can argue that the electrophone theatre was also a form of resistance by relegating performance to the realm of audio-centred theatre and by introducing a discourse and kind of enjoyment that was, from one point of view, anachronistic and out-of-date, as it did not present a visual spectacle at a time that was also the beginning of cinema. From another point of view, in making use of new technologies and, for instance, 'chopping up' opera and plays, this form of theatre was in fact proto-Modernist. A fragment of an opera or play resembles a snippet from a conversation and is limited by the medium of transmission. In the vein of Filippo Tommaso Marinetti's (1914) *Manifesto del Futurismo* (see Tonini 2011) it is technology that makes or creates art in that the medium both makes the transmission possible and has an influence on the amount and length of the selection. This chapter, therefore, focuses on the role of audiences' experiences as related in contemporary periodical articles in investigating early theatre broadcasts, as both compensations and encounters with lack that are then turned into a multi-modal experience after all.

Early broadcasting technologies as substitutes[1]

The quotation at the beginning of this chapter is from an article published in the American newspaper *Daily Picayune* in 1899 about a visit at the office of the Electrophone Company in London, where musicians play concerts to an 'invisible audience [...] transmitted over wires to hundreds of homes, where, without stirring from comforting sofa or arm-chair, the weary may listen to the sweetest of sweet strains' (*Daily Picayune* 1899, 6). This is entertainment made for those who do not want to or cannot leave their homes. It is entertainment produced during 'the Mechanical Age [...] the Age of Machinery, in every outward and inward sense of that word' (Carlyle 1829, n.p.). Novels by Edward Bellamy (*Looking Backward: 2000-1887* [1888]) and H. G. Wells' *When the Sleeper Wakes* (1899) feature electrophone technology in the context of the notion of 'theatre for everyone', the motto at the heart of NT Live, and their protagonists utter their disbelief how one could have ever consumed theatre or music differently – now 'at a dinner one can skip the courses one does not care for' (67) and 'to live outside the range of the electric cables [would be] to live an isolated savage' (Wells 1899, 78). At the same time, however, it is a substitute, or a compensation. According to the author of a 1905 article in *Daniel Judy, or: The London Serio-Comic Journal*, '[i]f you cannot afford a fifteen-shilling dress circle at the Waldorf [...], you have still the Electrophone, do they call it? where you may take the Opera (with the diamonds left out) in tabloids of twenty minutes' (*Daniel Judy* 1905, 254), pointing to the bite-size and therefore more comfortable experience positions considerations of dis/comfort as characteristic for the broadcast theatre experience.[2]

An investigation of early forms of theatre broadcasting provokes a recalibration of the relation of place and theatrical event more generally and the ways in which (a) technological developments in the nineteenth century already played a significant part in this discourse and (b) such early forms of auditory broadcasts are actually linked to and overlap semantically with later theatrical discourses on the spectacular-visual: sound, indeed, is turned into something spatial and visual – something that can be switched *in* rather than switched *on*. As a consequence, I want to argue, the electrophone is part of a media ecology (see Tabbi/Wutz 1997) whose foundational *oikos* has been opened up in the nineteenth century. A look at this short-lived history is thus still relevant today in the context of sports events and their audiences (more on the connection between theatrical event and sports event in Chapter 2). When Gay McAuley talks about the social reality of the theatre experience, she, crucially, distinguishes between three spatial facts, two of which are relevant for this discussion: on the one hand, there is the performance space, which is the place constituted by the coming together of the audience and practitioner space, and the first spatial fact which is constitutive of and fundamental to theatre. On the other hand, there is the theatre space, that is, the building, its position within the urban space and also the kind of access it invites or denies, which is, however, an optional extra (McAuley 1999, 25–8). This stands in contrast to the history of theatre from the Renaissance. For instance, Jacques

Copeau holds that (a theatre's) architecture is at the heart of theatre aesthetics, dramaturgy and genre since 'a given dramatic conception postulates a certain stage design and just as much or even more: a given stage architecture calls forth, demands and gives rise to a certain dramatic conception and style of presentation' (Copeau 1990, 88); that is, architecture also produces drama by 'co-creating its meanings, conventions and aesthetics' (Rufford 2015, 2).

Both historical and present-day broadcasting technologies cast scenarios, in which there is no traditionally conceived auditorium, no actual stage with a backstage area or proscenium arch and both are mediated, thus transposing the social dimension and the dimension of proxemics into different spaces. The history of the electrophone shows that in the three decades before the advent of radio, 'an entire culture of audio transmission of drama entertainment had been established and funded by a subscriber system' (Crook 1999, 15). Early telephony and radio were most often found in the newly emerging spaces of middle-class culture, both for leisure and work (Sterne 2003, 191). The precursors to today's livecasting were the Telephon Hirómondo, the Théâtrophon and the Electrophone, operating in Budapest, Paris and London, respectively. Early users of the telephone employed it in different contexts that today would be called broadcasting and information exchange. The telephone, now merely a communication device, was in fact used as a broadcasting medium in Europe and the United States in the 1890s. A pioneer in this regard was the Hungarian Tivadar Puskás, who, after having worked with Thomas Edison in the United States, was one of the first to conceptualize a central telephone exchange. He then experimented with telephone broadcasting systems both in Paris and in Budapest.[3] Together with Clément Ader, they set up the Théâtrophon (sometimes also referred to as the théâtrephone in Victorian periodicals in the UK). The Théâtrophon Company of Paris was selling the equipment for home use with more than 1,500 subscribers by 1893 and an expanded repertoire that included the Parisian Opéra, the Opéra Comique and the Comédie Française. In these early concerts, probably the first stereophonic transmissions, four transmitters would be set up in different positions on the stage in order to transmit both the performers' voices and the orchestra's music (Sterne 2003, 194). Listeners held two earpieces, each of which transmitted the singing and the music, respectively. At the beginning, when using the service in a public space, such as the Paris International Exhibition of Electricity, one could not listen to entire concerts but was limited to two to five minutes because there was only a limited amount of earpieces available and many listeners had to be accommodated. The telephone concerts were later held for the president at the Elysée Palace, where they became the basis for a telephone broadcasting system ten years later (Sterne 2003, 194).

In London, on 10 January 1892, a room was set apart as a music room during the Electrical Exhibition at Crystal Palace and was fitted with the necessary appliances for the reception of music. The music of performances at the Lyric Theatre in London, and at theatres and concert rooms in Birmingham, Liverpool, Manchester and other places, was transmitted successfully and met with great interest. The music room at Crystal Palace remained in operation for six months and nearly 60,000 people were recorded as having listened to broadcasts in it (Baldwin 1925, 267). The Electrophone Company followed suit and was in operation from about 1895 until 1926 and by 1906, all the main London operetta theatres were available (Scott 2019, 200). Subscribers – among them Queen Victoria – were offered 'local' relays from theatres, churches and London's Royal Opera House (Hawes 1991, 24; see also Marvin 1988, 223).

The promise that new technologies created – to expand audience numbers in the late nineteenth and early twentieth centuries – has also been recognized in the foreword to the 2016 report, 'From Live-to-Digital', prepared by AEA Consulting for Arts Council England, UK Theatre and the Society of London Theatre (see Reidy et al. 2016). As the service became available to more people, comprehensive accounts such as the following were given in the periodical press of the 1890s to describe the workings of the electrophone system as used in the UK:

> The telephone system offers *several conveniences* to its subscribers [. . .] [T]he subscriber can sit *at his ease* and listen either to a play, a burlesque, an opera or concert, a popular preacher, High Church, Low Church, or Dissenter; and as a last resource, if it be a Saturday, one may ring up the Great Synagogue, and take a dose of Judaism.[4] [. . .] The electrophone gives both a clearer and a more distinct reproduction of sounds, and so far as the rendering of music goes, its achievement leaves little to be desired. [. . .] I have [. . .] enjoyed the performance at *half-a-dozen different theatres on the same evening*, the change from one to another being effected by merely ringing up the operator at the other end of the telephone wire. (Krausse 1897, 535–6, emphases added)

Several things are noticeably in this passage and they all demarcate more clearly the characteristics of the acousmatic experience created by the electrophone: first of all, it is an experience of comfort (the words used are 'convenience' and 'ease'). This creates the impression that the roles of culture consumption are turned around: the electrophone brings everything directly to the user, he or she does not have to go anywhere. Second, as Krausse's report shows, the fascination with this system oscillated between that of ease and excess, marvel and utility and the amazement in line with the time–space-compression – that David Harvey (1989) has identified for the Victorian perception in the context of the effects of the industrialization more generally – the electrophone afforded. It was not only possible to travel to more and more destinations by train, it was also possible to switch between several plays on the same night, regardless of the distances between the actual theatres. Such an overlap between time and space is also illustrated on the cover of the issue of *Invention* published on 1 February 1896 (Figure 1). The

Figure 1 Cover of the issue of *Invention* (Vol. XIX, No. 872) from 1 February 1896. © The British Library Board.

description of the electrophone in connection with the illustration creates strong resonances between normally separate spheres, both in temporal and spatial terms: the time and place of audience member and singer, of living room and music theatre, of producing music and listening to it collapse into one: this is global theatre in that it is all-encompassing, truly unfolding here, there and everywhere. That descriptions of travelling and indulging in theatrical entertainment overlapped semantically and the latter was described by verbs of movement, is a case in point and will be illustrated with a few examples in the next section.

Acousmatic livecasting in the nineteenth century: Visual landscapes

To take a historical perspective on the precursors of NT Live has the added value of understanding how and why theatre broadcasting is tied to (a) the optionality of theatre space (due to technology; technology as part of the broadcasting experience), (b) a different liveness and (c) new forms of conviviality and its general characteristics which take on historically specific guises. These three aspects are intertwined; the optionality of theatre space is the pre-condition for the emergence of a different liveness and differently perceived togetherness. When listening to a concert or opera at a distance enables the listener to have an individual embodied experience of it, this creates a sense of an *oikos* of media ecology that reverberates into today's media consumption practices.

One must note how a great deal of the Victorian fascination with electrophone technology stems from the fact that one can amass quantity (rather than quality), that is, *how* and *that* one can consume theatre rather than what kind of theatre it is. This, in connection with the detailed description of and fascination with the workings of broadcasting technology, can be connected to the general Victorian craving for material and details to rationalize and do away with anxieties in an age of radical shifts in all spheres of life (see Liedke 2018, 65–77). From a rhetorical perspective, Krausse's account earlier fits into this discourse with its hyperbolic dwelling on the materiality of this newly enhanced acousmatic theatrical experience.

Taking a look at its characteristics, it can be stated, first of all, that all sorts of fears were expressed on both sides of the Atlantic. A look at contemporary Victorian periodicals in the United States and the United Kingdom offers a more nuanced affective landscape. A historical discourse analysis draws our attention to how specific elements of the discourse on theatre broadcasting endure until today, especially concerning broadcasts as compensations. The added value of such an analysis is also a critical reading of this discourse in light of how theatre broadcasts are not 'merely' compensations; they contribute to the creation of mutually enriching texts. The accounts of the experience of the electrophone can be grouped into the following three categories: first, fear paired with wonder, second, palpable modernity and, third, comfort and care.

The American periodical press followed the developments in Europe – and how, for instance, Parisians booked their entertainment 'switches' ('The Drama and Stage' 1897, 13) weeks in advance – closely as the following selection of examples pertaining to Paris and London shows. Periodicals from Kansas, California, Wisconsin, Texas and Louisiana all commented on this new phenomenon by which Parisians would have 'the opera and drama laid on to their houses, like gas and water' – an information that was made more palpable by the fact that the cables would 'pass through the Parisian sewers' (*Atchison Globe* 1889, n.p.). The commentaries paid attention to all the details, including the limited slots that one could listen to ('five minutes') and the sum one had to pay for this (half a frank, or 5d) (*Daily Evening Bulletin* 1889, 4; *Milwaukee Journal* 1890, 3).

A phrase used in the *Daily Evening Bulletin* is noteworthy, since it describes the experience as being 'put into communication with a certain theatre' (*Daily Evening Bulletin* 1889, 4). There also seems to be a desire to be put into communication with the theatre *audience* and an ache for proximity that one is bereft of, as another article, describing the transmission of *The Nautch Girl* at the Savoy Theatre in London, points to the fact that the 'outbursts of applause in the house sounded a trifle more remote' which was 'no doubt owing to the fact that the receivers are on the stage inside the line of footlights'. Apart from that, everything could be heard very well with regard to the quality of the sound, so that there was 'certainly no appreciable difference between [the listener's] position and that of an occupant of a Savoy stall, at least as regards all that appeals to the ear' (*Milwaukee Daily Sentinel* 1891, 14).

Some artists begged to differ, however; the French opera singer M. Soulacroix started a movement among French singers and actors against the introduction of the Théâtrophon since the wire transmission greatly changed his voice 'for the worse' and pointed out that, when signing his contract, he had not signed up to sing to people outside the theatre 'after the manner of the gas water companies' and not receive any profit from it (*Milwaukee Daily Sentinel* 1892, 4) – an echo of today's copyright concerns that are one of the reasons why the NT, for instance, does not sell DVDs of its live theatre broadcasts after they are shown in cinemas. Similarly, from an economic point of view, it was feared that people would not want to go to the theatre anymore. Theatre managers refused to install the soundboards at first since they were worried that 'play and music "at home" would encourage people to stay in and discourage them from going to the theatre' (Grein 1923, 712). In fact, however, the exact opposite was the case as

> [t]he electrophone, instead of being a competitor, became an 'appetiser': people heard the tunes and voices, they were fascinated and wanted 'to see what they had heard'; so they decided to go to the theatre, which most likely they would not have done if the electrophone had not played the part of the piper of Hamelin. (Grein 1923, 712)[5]

The fear that a broadcast would cannibalize theatre is echoed over 100 years later by Nicholas Hytner, responsible for NT Live, and is countered with almost the same wording as earlier: 'NT Live will never replace the thing itself, nor does it discourage audiences from going to their local theatre: if anything, the cinema experience acts as a spur' (Hytner 2018, 273).

In the British periodical press the electrophone was also a popular topic in the late 1890s. In an article in 1895, for instance, the author, who enjoyed the electrophone at the Crystal Palace Exhibition, describes it as 'as marvellous and wonderful as anything'. The focus is then on the voice of the singer Marie Tempest in *An Artist's Model* at the Lyric Theatre:

> Heard her quite distinctly, quite as well as I would have done had I been at the Lyric myself. The only fault to be found with the electrophone is that while using it you can't keep your dignity. [. . .] You look foolish. You've got to put a couple of ear trumpets up to your ear, and there's a long handle sort of arrangement left in the region of your mouth. I caught myself in the glass for a moment, and I looked as though I were suddenly visited with some awful unnatural growths. (*Fun* 1895, 62)

The assertion that the singer's voice could be heard 'quite distinctly' is in line with the conviction held at the time that regarded 'distinctness' as the main criterion for a singer's or actor's success and was a staple feature of training texts for actors. When this feature receded into the background of acting training, Louis Calvert, among others, bemoaned this development in his *Problems of the Actor* (1919). In the earlier quotation the last phrase also offers a connection of two typically Victorian obsessions: that with innovation, on the one hand, and the monstrous and unknown. After all, this was the time of the discovery of species that had been unknown up to this point, thanks to the work of explorers and scientists such as Charles Darwin and Richard Owen in the 1840s.[6] Thus, to speak of the ear trumpet as an unnatural growth, presents the electrophone as something monstrous, as a somewhat worrying extension of the human body, and hints at complex questions regarding the supremacy of humans over other beings, not unlike contemporary debates surrounding the implantation of microchips into the human brain. The singer Ellaline Terriss felt similarly perturbed. In her autobiography she remembered what it was like to listen to *The Shop Girl* (1895) via electrophone: while it was 'wonderful', the majority of the description is concerned with the earphones 'on a kind of two-pronged metal rod' and the attachment which was 'like a stethoscope with little tubes which fitted in your ears' (Terriss 1955, 118).

Other articles describe the effects of the electrophone in spatial terms, when one can hear 'performances in Paris at your ease in London' (*The Magazine of Music* 1896, 607; see also *The Friend of India* 1896, 13). Paris and London can be mentioned in one sentence and one breath, thus the new technology compresses time and space into one. This geographical simultaneous zooming in and out is mirrored on the level of sensorial perception, too, when the effect of the auditory experience is such that details before unnoticed come to the fore and the theatrical experience is heightened in that it is dissected into its constitutive elements.

In contrast to the twenty-first century where, as broadcasting historian John Wyver has recently bemoaned (2019, 175; 2020), livecasts are given little to no journalistic attention – since they are not regarded as the outcome of a complicated and creative artistic process – this is not the case with regard to the electrophone broadcasts in the Victorian age. It is a combination of the content presented and the *way* in which it was presented that is at the centre of the reviewers' attention, thus creating a much more comprehensive narrative of the effects of acousmatic art consumption. In addition to being narratives, these reviews also play the role of recordings of performances and the ways in which they were received from a time before the existence of recording equipment.

Most articles highlight that comfort and care are increased through the introduction of the electrophone. In fact, the availability of theatre (mentioned in the same sentence with churches) is linked to mental and physical health when plans by the Electrophone Company to install their services in the major London hospitals are described as providing 'a source of pleasure and comfort to the thousands of sufferers who [...] are treated in these admirable institutions' (*Daily Picayune* 1893, 6). The Texas-based *Galveston Daily News* suggests that the 'effect of this system on London's mortality will be watched with interest' (1895, 4).

In *The Sporting Times* the author of 'Round the Town' writes about a variety of cultural activities, such as attending the Palace Theatre and the picture galleries at Suffolk Street and the Grafton Galleries and includes a report of attending a concert at the Queen's Hall 'through the medium of the electrophone. Sitting in an armchair in the smoking-room of a hospitable house, drinking my share of an unexceptional bottle of port, I heard Miss Palliser sing delightfully [. . .] and many selections, and a violin and clarinet solo' (*The Sporting Times* 1899, 2). The author of an article in *The Idler Magazine* from 1897 writes a satirical story about a millionaire called Mr Sims who would switch on the electrophone if a guest bored him (Lawrence 1897, 688–9).

On the one hand, at least at the beginning, to have such an item at home meant to be wealthy. Numerous articles point to how members of the royal family especially enjoyed using the service – the Prince of Wales, when confined to Marlborough House because of an injury, can attend 'performances at the Alhambra, Daly's, Empire, Gaiety, Prince of Wales's and several other theatres – per electrophone. Truly we live in stirring times . . .' (*The Outlook* 1898, 775). On the other hand, the mere fact that the electrophone was included casually in a list enumerating cultural activities shows how well known it was by the end of the nineteenth century. Indeed, it held the promise of a more egalitarian future in which the arts would be available to everyone. In a brief essay titled 'We Shall Be as Princes' in *The New Zealand Graphic and Ladies Journal*, the author also takes up the topic of the Prince of Wales' illness and how he relied on the electrophone during this time:

> But what is reserved for princes and potentates and powers to-day, will be ours tomorrow, if Science does not belie the high hopes she has taught us to entertain. [. . .] Now [. . .] we can have the talent of half-a-dozen kingdoms and continents sing to us, play to us, dance to us. [. . .] For though we are not heirs-apparent to the Throne of England, we are heirs of a still mightier Empire, the Empire of Science [. . .] Depend on it, the time will come when we too will have operatic and music hall music laid on to our houses just as we have gas and water now, and when we are sick we shall have the European stars to come and cheer us; and even if we should be in articulo mortis, who knows but that some modern Orpheus, more fortunate than the first gentleman of that ilk, might not win us back from the gloomy portals. (*The New Zealand Graphic and Ladies Journal* 1898, 162)

Crucially, science does not give answers to all unexplained phenomena – it portends a sense and a promise of what it may one day explain.[7]

Only five years later, in 1901, the author of an article when describing the electrophone does not distinguish between physical immobility and virtual mobility: instead, verbs of motion are used to describe his switching between different broadcasts on the switchboard: 'I *paused* to hear Suzanne Adams in Lalo's new opera *Le Roi d'Ys*, produced for the first time in this country at Covent Garden, and without *staying* for a selection from the Lyric *wended* my way towards the Western Gardens' (*The New Zealand Graphic and Ladies Journal* 1898, emphasis added). Other articles also describe the switching to other operas, for instance, as 'going' there (the cultural venue then is mentioned) (*Daniel Judy* 1902, 393). An author in *The Illustrated London News* concludes that one should not say that listeners were 'switched on' to Covent Garden but rather 'switched in', as 'one could hear the general "buzz" of an audience, including remarks and coughs, the tuning up by the orchestra' and at the end one could hear how 'the noise of hand-clapping rose to such volume that it could be likened to the sound of a waterfall' (W. H. S. 1923, 146). These descriptions illustrate how acousmatic livecasting hauls the visual-spatial into the realm of the listener's here and now and turns his or her perception process into a moment of embodied participation. One is *there*, and one is able to see what is only heard. As a consequence, this brings about the awareness, so central in the context of twenty-first-century performance studies, that live performance does not constitute 'a privileged site of temporary encounter' but rather 'yet another form of mediated interaction' with its 'texts, contexts, and artifacts' (Bay-Cheng 2012, 33).

To continue this thought: if it is not live performance that is a privileged site, what – or who – *is*? Looking at early forms of theatre and music broadcasting provides a thought-provoking discussion of how the optionality of theatre space gives rise to a different form of embodiment: one that makes recipients more aware of how they perceive the play. Such considerations are still valid when thinking about how both the spectacular framing and the visibility of theatrical material in the twenty-first-century context bring about distinct forms of embodiment. With regard to the theatrical experience in the nineteenth century, Nield argues that in the theatre and on the theatrical stage as 'a three-dimensional box, within which representation was able to be fully, and materially present' (Nield 2019, 225) a *dis*embodiment between spectators and illusion may have been brought to its most extreme. As she points out, theatre 'could not annihilate time and space, for the time and space of the audience are experienced' (Nield 2019, 225). The conclusion Nield draws from her analysis is that the nineteenth-century spectator is the model for the disembodied observer of 'an increasingly accelerating visually-driven culture' (2019, 226). With regard to auditory experiences, however, the earlier descriptions present instances of embodied experience. In the same moment, in which a spectator realizes they are is detached from the spectacle and its scope, they realize they have the capability to perceive all this and take it in.

When theatre is reduced to the auditory and merely listened to, as in the case of performances and snippets of performances that were broadcast via the electrophone, it is even more about those who listen to it and their perception.[8] With livecasts and broadcasts the perceiving subject precisely registers their act of perception.[9] The reviews from the periodicals from the time attest to this kind of self-affirmative thereness of the users of the electrophone; these technologies and innovations would be nought without the spectators and listeners operating them.

Not a substitute for the real thing – The NT's dip into broadcasting in the 1940s and 1950s

These nineteenth-century examples of displacing theatre and thus giving it a new space are precursors to instances of streamed and broadcast theatre that have emerged in the course of the twentieth century, both on the radio and on television, and today in cinemas. The National Theatre has, in fact, thought about a possible liaison with the BBC even before it was established, that is before 1963. From the outset, the stakes at establishing a National Theatre were high – as Kenneth Rae, the secretary to the National Theatre Board, put it in a TV interview on 21 January 1958, it was 'ridiculous that this country with the greatest dramatic heritage of all should be the only European country without the National Theatre'. Such a theatre was needed, since it was a matrix 'from which all inspiration springs' (Sir Donald Wolfit in 'Today – Morning Protest' on 4 December 1957).[10] The name 'national' theatre in itself posed a dilemma: on the one hand, it was expected to provide the 'best' in British theatre from the beginning; on the other hand, it could not be 'a nation-wide institution like a health service' (Elsom/Tomalin 1978, 136) – especially since drama was not 'that kind of mass-produced activity' anyway. In that sense, 'national' would from the outset not refer to 'of the people' or 'popular'. Perhaps it was for this reason that notions of how to link theatre to a more 'popular' form hovered in the background of the institution's inception process.

When it was still in its planning phase, questions were raised among members of the Shakespeare Memorial National Theatre Committee, the board of the Old Vic and the BBC about what kind of relationship theatre and broadcasting should have. On 29 April 1948 Norman Collins, a controller at the BBC had written to Lord Esher, then chairman of the Old Vic, and asked for a meeting 'to discuss the possibility of having incorporated in the architectural design of the theatre provision for Television [sic] cameras so that when the theatre is built, productions could be televised direct from the stage without in any way interfering with the comfort of the audience'. Already fifteen years before the actual theatre (the National Theatre) was opened, there were considerations concerning the broadcasting of its plays. In a handwritten note to Rae, Lord Esher wrote somewhat indignantly about his exchange with Collins that he had replied 'that at first sight it would seem that his viewers would sit comfortably at home and never set foot in the National Theatre'. On 6 May 1948, Collins replied to Esher, in an attempt to calm his worries:

> Most naturally the promoters of sporting events, as well as theatrical managements, have been more than ample to show that not only has the audience remained constant, but in many cases the audience has grown as a result of an introduction to the sports hall or theatre by means of the new medium.
>
> Moreover, in the case of the National Theatre, there will clearly be many people living too far away for a personal visit to be possible, except on the rare occasion when they are visiting London, and for such people it would seem highly desirable that the work of the National Theatre should be made known to them.
>
> Finally, I believe so strongly that no matter how well a play is televised it is not and can never be a substitute for the real thing, and I cannot believe that in making my suggestion I am doing the National Theatre a disservice.[11]

It seems as if the actual 'father' of NT Live was the BBC's Norman Collins, since the arguments he raises overlap with the motivations to launch NT Live in 2009, summarized by the head of the digital department at its inception, David Sabel, as 'access', – part of this being that the initiative 'encourages theatre going as a habit' – 'amplification' and 'innovation' (Groves 2012). Back in the 1940s and 1950s, the idea was dismissed, after the National Theatre Council had not approved of the facilities for the television cameras in view of the architect's objections. Yet letters from

1955 by Sidney L. Bernstein, a 'dynamic businessman' who was managing director of a chain of cinemas, the Granada Group, which he had also established (Elsom and Tomalin 1978, 75), indicate that he had been trying for a while to convince the Council otherwise. In a letter to Bronson Albery, director of the New Theatre, on 6 January 1956, Bernstein asks him 'to consider the possibility that the [National] Theatre may find new and vigorous forms of expression through these new tools at its disposal' and that 'there will be many occasions to which the Committee will want to admit a far greater audience than can be contained within four walls'. Indeed, three years later, Bronson from the NT Committee wrote to Bernstein to reconsider his resignation from collaborating with the theatre, emphasizing that he agreed with his view 'on the matter of cinema and television, provided that the theatre is not used as a cinema-theatre. [. . .] I cannot imagine that it would be right to use it in competition with the existing cinema circuits'.

The launch of NT Live[12]

The idea behind NT Live, then, was to solve a dilemma 'that had obtained since 1963: how best to make the National truly national, when it was funded by taxpayers throughout the country, but based in London, and its regional tours could reach only a tiny proportion of the population' (Rosenthal 2013, 793). Hytner referred to the unavailability of London theatre in his local cinemas in the 1960s, and NT Live was in a sense the realization of a childhood wish he had had (Rosenthal 2013, 793). In 2009, the NT's budget allowed for new ventures, and following the steps of the Royal Opera House, which had televised broadcasts of opera and ballet, and especially the Metropolitan Opera, which was the first institution to broadcast their shows to cinemas around the world in 2006, Hytner and Sabel (the National's first director of Broadcasts and the Digital) launched the initiative. Looking at Hytner's agenda for the theatre as a whole, the launch of NT Live was one of his 'balancing acts': the motivation was to attract new audiences while at the same time producing something that was as close as possible to the theatre visit. As Sabel relates in an interview at the beginning of the Covid-19 pandemic, looking back at the early days of NT Live, a main reason why it was easy to persuade both performers and audiences that the project was worth a try, was that it was in fact replicating so much of the theatrical experience: one had to choose a date, buy a ticket, go to the (cinema) venue (Sabel 2020). The set-up of any NT Live production consists of high-definition cameras and 5.1 audio systems combined with satellite distribution and digital cinema projection and the involvement of a television broadcaster is not necessary, making this a feasible scheme for a cultural institution to reach remote audiences (Wyver 2019, 169).

NT Live extends a tradition begun by early television broadcasts from American and London theatres in the 1960s, for instance, the technique of 'Electronovision', which used small, electronic cameras that functioned with only available stage lighting. For instance, black-and-white footage of *Hamlet* with Richard Burton in the title role was recorded at Broadway's Lunt-Fontanne Theatre, edited into a 'Theatrofilm' and, distributed by Warner Brothers, screened for four performances at 1,000 US cinemas in 35 mm format (cf. Wyver 2014a) – with a $1 million profit. Broadcasters such as the BBC also produced television versions of selected plays from theatres in London and elsewhere in the 1960s, 1970s and 1980s but it was yet to be determined how and whether to share producing responsibilities and whether the way to go was to produce recordings in sterile studios or live in front of rows of spectators 'to capture a vivid sense of theatre' (Morahan in Rosenthal 2013, 793–4). Christopher Morahan, who had directed *Bedroom Farce* for television in 1980, acknowledged that

> our work *is* accessible to large numbers of people and we MUST do something about this, or die. The bigger problem [. . .], is that if you just squirt a camera at a stage (the cheap option) it will always look clumsy and undernourished compared to TV drama. It can't ever be regarded as anything but a wholesale dilution of the theatrical original. [. . .] But maybe if it was a live event, a sort of outside broadcast, then it could work. (Rosenthal 2013, 793–4)

From the beginning, theatre and TV have seemed to be incompatible from an aesthetic perspective: if one does not do it right, filmed theatre will merely be a diluted version of the original as presented on stage. The danger here is that people who are already reluctant to go to the theatre would take such a diluted version as an additional demotivation for theatre-going. In this logic, theatre emerges as the genre that is in a position of lesser power and certainly lesser popularity than TV. The fact that actors and actresses appear both on screen and stage further complicates the emancipation of theatre films: in contrast to opera, which works on the (small) screen because its only point of reference is opera, spectators have to deal with unconscious prejudices when watching theatre on the screen, since the automatic points of reference are film and television and they tend to find it unusual when actors shout or break the fourth wall (see Hytner 2018, 270).

Presenting the other side of the equation, Wyver argues in his analysis of screen versions of Shakespeare that television must also prove itself against theatre: if it wants to stand on its own and 'be truly televisual, the medium must be liberated from aspects of and associations with the theatre' (Wyver 2014b). He takes up this argument to point to a tension that has accompanied the history of screened Shakespeare plays between theatrical elements on the one hand, and televisual and cinematic elements on the other – elements that are employed without precision. Wyver defines the theatrical elements as 'the components specific to the presentation on a stage, including the characteristics of continuous performances pitched to an auditorium and *the acknowledged presence of a live audience*' (Wyver 2014, my emphasis). This latter phrase is curious: for if acknowledging the presence of a live audience is key, then indeed NT Live broadcasts and their early auditory counterparts and predecessors from the nineteenth century were certainly theatrical – radio-theatrical versus cinematically theatrical.

The RSC had ventured into filming their productions for the cinema already in 1971 when John Glenister was behind an adaptation of *Miss Julie* (dir. Robin Phillips) which worked with cinema techniques such as framing, camera moves and the cutting of sequences. According to Wyver, this adaptation 'deserves to be recognized as a significant precursor of NT Live and RSC Live from Stratford-upon-Avon' and the reason why it is not sufficiently acknowledged may be its low-budget production (Wyver 2019, 103). In the late 1990s, the RSC kept experimenting with filming in front of an audience precisely to capture the essence of the theatrical, with Gregory Doran's *The Winter's Tale* that was filmed live by Robin Lough, later one of the main stage-to-screen directors for NT Live, at the Barbican on 22 and 23 April 1999 as a co-production with Heritage Theatre for straight-to-video release. Shots of the audience were established through wide shots at the beginning of each scene and the audience's response was heard throughout (see Greenhalgh 2018, 30).

The experience of both early and present-day forms of theatrical broadcasts has thus always been accompanied by (a) the tension or seeming incompatibility between the theatrical and cinematic and the doubt, uttered for instance by the then artistic director of the RSC, Michael Boyd, that it would 'be a long time before cinema can capture anything more than a pale reflection of the art form' (in Wyver 2019, 154), and (b) an oscillation between the freedom of enjoyment, that for many spectators comes along with sitting in a theatre and being able to choose what spot to look at on stage, and the notion of a supposedly more pre-shaped experience that comes with theatre that is filmed by cameras. As a consequence, these tensions can bring about a heightened preoccupation with the experience of watching or listening to theatre plays, as the discussion of nineteenth-century electrophone plays has shown.

In order to bridge the gap between then and now which will be taken up in the remainder of this book, a look to the 1930s proves illustrative. The 1930s were the beginning of televised plays: the first television drama, transmitted in 1930, was a short studio-produced presentation of Luigi Pirandello's *The Man with the Flower in his Mouth* and the first broadcast from a theatre took place in 1938 when J. B. Priestley's *When We Are Married* was transmitted by the BBC Television Service. When looking for accounts from a time from which one does not have actual recordings, it is again review writing that is a valuable source. One of the most prominent publications for reviews of all kinds but those of early television broadcasts in particular was *The Listener*, a weekly magazine that was established by the BBC and published between 1929 and 1991. It was well known as the medium which reproduced both radio and later television broadcast talks and (p)reviewed major new publications and musical and theatrical shows. One of the most sharp-tongued reviewers was Grace Wyndham Goldie, who made a career as a producer and executive for the BBC, pioneering many television formats that are now taken for granted in the UK. It is worth taking a look at one of her reviews of a performance of *Twelfth Night* televised live from the Phoenix Theatre on 2 January 1939 in order to see how, first, the experience of 'attending' a show is still dwelled on more than forty years after the advent of electrophone broadcasts and despite the change from auditory to visual, and second, how the aesthetic set-up of this hybrid new medium is negotiated.

Wyndham Goldie starts off by referring to her evening entertainment as '"straight from the theatre" stuff' about which she is sceptical. Interestingly, she spends a quarter of the review describing her expectations, the situation of watching a play on the TV at home and the expected aesthetics of the televised play, using phrases such as '[t]here was the actual feeling of being in a theatre', 'the *effect* of having a night out' (my emphasis) and '. . . it gives a curiously valuable sense of *shared enjoyment*, of being part of an audience and not an individual' (1929, 171, my emphasis). She also points to the incompatibility of television and theatre from an aesthetic point of view. The turn to an analysis of the actual play is initiated by a nonchalant 'What more is there? What about the play?' and Wyndham Goldie compares the experience to being forced to watch an entire play through opera glasses with one's 'vision cramped and irritatingly limited'. While the acting is praised, she concludes that the play 'seen in camera shots, made very little effect as a whole' because of the angle of vision for which it had been originally produced (a huge one) and the one in which it was shown now (a tiny one). What one can conclude from this is that 'people who care more for "going to the theatre"' than for the plays they see and who want to know something of the plays which are running and the actors and actresses who are being discussed will prefer the "televiews" from theatres in contrast to television studio plays which allow to focus on the plays 'neat', as Wyndham Goldie puts it (suggesting a more immediate experience). That is, Wyndham Goldie underlines the compensatory nature of televised plays; the focus on the experience of watching them is in fact quite reminiscent of the reviews of electrophone plays.

Then and now: The fifth auditorium

When Denys Lasdun, the architect of the building of the NT, designed it, he thought about the front-of-house spaces as the 'fourth auditorium' of the theatre, and those behind setting up the Digital and Broadcast Department many years later regarded the digital space as a kind of 'fifth auditorium' (Sabel 2020). Shortly before Hytner became the fifth artistic director of the National Theatre in 2003, he stated: 'As a nation we think we know who we were, but we need to find out what we're becoming, [. . .] so it's a tremendous time to be a national theatre' (Hytner 2018, 33). It is tremendous, yes, but especially after Brexit, a political decision that has created new (ideological) borders between the UK and the European continent, it is a responsibility, too. While the National has from the outset proclaimed to state the 'best of British theatre', such phrases strike a different chord now. What the National as *pars pro toto* for British cultural capital represents is a decisive part of Britain's soft power. It is therefore of especial importance to acknowledge what initiatives such as NT Live do with this power (an aspect that will come up in the discussion of *A Midsummer Night's Dream* in Chapter 2 which analyses how the production – of a Shakespeare play, thus representing British culture par excellence – was turned into a production with explicitly *global* appeal, as if to erase its Britishness).

Both in the nineteenth-century and in the present-day contexts of theatre broadcasting, the technologies employed play a central role and are in fact part of the media ecology of the events they transport. Today, while presenters of NT livecasts encourage spectators to ignore the cameras, those attending the recording of a performance, cannot *not* see the cameras – they are, like the microphones fitted on different spots on stages of theatres in London and Paris at the end of the nineteenth century, fixed to tracks in front of the stage. They are indeed like those 'monstrous' earpieces. In the nineteenth century, the earpieces – or unnatural growths – would be explicitly acknowledged as *part* of this new theatrical experience, as intimidating yet practical helpers. Crucially, nineteenth-century theatre broadcasting technology emphasizes and is positively self-conscious about its medium: the electrophone and the earphone are almost as much part of the play as the play itself.

A similar phenomenon can be observed when performances are broadcast into cinemas or streamed into people's homes as it has happened during the Covid-19 pandemic in 2020. In both settings, the medium is/was also consciously perceived; and especially so, when there are/were glitches (delays in the broadcast; wobbly internet connection). Therefore, rather than presenting merely a 'compensation' the broadcasting of theatre has presented and still presents a dissection of a cultural text into two mutually enriching texts – the actual performance and the transmediated experience around it, which includes both the broadcast and the imagination of what it was like 'on site'. With its roots in the late nineteenth century, this practice underscores the long history of the complexity of media ecology and audience experience in the cultural realm. In addition, this history attests to a changing history of documenting performance (see Sant 2017, 13), which is very different in our contemporary reality than it was towards the end of the nineteenth and in the first half of the twentieth century. No matter if it is turned into an auditory form or if it retains its visual components, then and now broadcasting or livecasting theatrical performance is a way of prolonging, displacing and shaking up the potential stasis surrounding in-situ performances. It is not only *there*; it is *everywhere, with* us. Processes of broadcasting performance do away with questions such as which sites of encountering plays are prioritized and which are those constituting conditions *sine quibus non*. The actual sites of encounter, where the plays take on a unique form, are within those listening or watching them. While this was always the case, now this experience is in competition with others because there are alternatives, which used to be not there. Thus, livecasting is a challenge for the genre of theatre.

2

Watching others having fun – livecasting as spectacle

> *Feeling so happy after seeing the @_bridgetheatre production of A Midsummer Night's Dream via @NTLive tonight. Such a spectacular performance! (@hvamitchell)*

The terms used by the National Theatre in particular to advertise their livecasts and those used by spectators to refer to their experience of them place livecasts in the conceptual and semantic field of spectacle.[1] While the visual plays a crucial role, livecasting affords a mediated, more varied type of spectacle that emotionally engages and stimulates spectators on several additional levels of sensory perception, namely the auditory and affective – both their own and others', when a livecast theatrical performance and its audience are watched on a cinema screen. Following the understanding of affect from the perspective of cultural theory, affect here is approached as an outcome of the interactive dynamics between multiple actors and actants in socio-material settings (Slaby, Mühlhoff, and Wüschner 2019, 3).[2] Affect is an effect of an affective arrangement, a concept introduced by Slaby, Mühlhoff and Wüschner to describe

> a material-discursive formation as part of which affect is patterned, channelled, and modulated in recurrent and repeatable ways. Key to such arrangements is that they bring multiple actors into a dynamic, orchestrated conjunction, so that these actors' mutual affecting and being affected is the central dimension of the arrangement from the start. (2019, 5)

Given the philosophical footing of this concept, this definition is both abstract and broad – as the authors readily admit, affective arrangements in this sense are 'ubiquitous in social life' (2019, 5). Yet shortly before this remark, the authors speak of 'thresholds of intensity' that give affective arrangements their 'contours' and describe affective arrangements as exerting a '"pull", a kind of active allure, potentially drawing individuals into their ambit by offering them occasions for immersion within a sphere of resonance and intensity' (2019, 5). Livecasts, as this chapter develops, are an illustration of what this 'pull' can look like when a live theatre performance is transported onto the screen and when one compares this experience with that of live theatre performances. In other words: the affective arrangement differs when one looks at livecasts versus live theatre performances because the thresholds of intensity characterizing both settings are crossed/played with differently.

Turning to the affective dimension of the spectacle in the second part of the chapter, I argue that in the livecasting context, the effect of the spectacular set-up creates a new manifestation of a global mediatized communitas. The term 'communitas' was popularized in performance studies by the anthropologist Victor Turner (1982). In order to grasp the effect of the mediatized performance on audiences, I am taking the cue from the Cluster of Excellence 'Temporal Communities' at Freie Universität Berlin, which conceptualizes 'global' in temporal rather than merely spatial terms. I understand global as an affordance that brings about resonances between different types of texts and directly impacts the reception of said texts by 'audiences' (a term I use to demarcate a specific type of communitas) across time. The global dimension of NT Live points outwardly, towards the recipients of the media, and aims to translate across as many (cultural, geographical, linguistic) borders as possible. This will be illustrated by a case study of Bridge Theatre's *A Midsummer Night's Dream* which ran from 3 June until 31 August 2019, was directed by Nicholas Hytner and filmed for NT Live by Ross MacGibbon. Not only during the show but also in its aftermath, the livecast afforded a multi-layered spectacle that was explicitly geared towards a global audience. It retained the 'layers of action'[3] of the original performance, and by relying on its paradocumentational brim, prompted spectators to access it not primarily through the text but through the experience of the performance.

The best of British theatre

In the *OED*, 'spectacle' is described as '[a] *thing* seen or capable of being seen; something presented to the view, esp. of a striking or unusual character; a sight' (2020, my emphasis). When something is referred to as a 'thing', this means that one cannot grasp what one is referring to. Notably, there is a parallel to this difficulty in describing a spectacle and attempts to define a livecast. For instance, the NT Live presenter Samira Ahmed, when introducing the live broadcast of *Antony and Cleopatra* in December 2018 to the audience used the phrase 'if you haven't been to one of *these things*', thus suggesting a certain uneasiness with regard to what term would describe the spectacle about to follow best.

The motivations behind the launch of NT Live can be thought of as a double-edged sword: on the one hand, it has the aim of making the NT, and other theatres involved, stay competitive in the face of a changing media landscape. In its current state, this hybrid theatrical form is still primarily enmeshed in institutional structures in that its major producers are theatres at the centre of cultural production. On the other hand, when thinking about the ways it makes many performances more accessible, one finds that the initiative reverberates with Arnoldian ideas. Matthew Arnold's claim in his 'The Function of Criticism at the Present Time', *Essays in Criticism* and *Culture and Anarchy*, is that the experience of culture endows one with an especially great spiritual condition:

> But what *is* greatness? – culture makes us ask. Greatness is a spiritual condition worthy to excite love, interest, and admiration; and the outward proof of possessing greatness is that we excite love, interest, and admiration. If England were swallowed up by the sea to-morrow, which of the two, a hundred years hence, would most excite the love, interest, and admiration of mankind,–would most, therefore, show the evidences of having possessed greatness,–the England of the last twenty years, or the England of Elizabeth, of a time of splendid spiritual effort, but when our coal, and our industrial operations depending on coal, were very little developed? (Arnold 2006, 38–9)

In the aftermath of Brexit asking what would show evidences of greatness if England were swallowed up by the sea tomorrow adds fuel to the fire. Focusing on a nation's cultural 'output', Arnold seems to suggest, actually gives one a true picture of the nation's spirit, rather than reducing it to its 'mechanical' endeavours. Culture's pursuit is to get to know 'the best that has been thought and known in the world' (Arnold 2006, 5), a superlative repeated in NT Live's slogan that 'National Theatre Live broadcasts live performances of the best of British theatre to cinemas in the UK around the world'. Certainly, the slogan is motivated by PR marketing hyperbole; but the impetus bears Arnoldian traces and the initiative deserves to be considered and approached as part of this wider discourse. I argue that livecasting is a specific form of theatrical spectacle that is aware of the fact that it is a substitute (for 'real' theatre) and makes up for this lack by working consciously towards establishing the frame of an affective arrangement – a frame within the frame of a screen.

Spectacle and theatre on screens – images and deception

In *Les Bijoux Indiscrets* (1748) Denis Diderot ridicules the notion of perfect illusion (see Burwick 1996, 145) in a dialogue between the Sultan's 'favourite' and Selim (1749, 60–7). According to Diderot, spectators are intelligent people who know that they are witnessing an illusion. Similarly, when one looks at the responses on social media one can see that most livecasting spectators are very much aware of the distance between what they are watching in the cinema and the theatre – they can only feel 'as if' they had been there, for instance, by thanking the theatres for making the given content available to them even though they live far away from London (in the case of NT Live) or missed one of the in-situ performances (see Reidy et al. 2016, 48). It is this 'as if' through which the awareness that one attends the compensation (see my related discussion in Chapter 1) of an experience is uttered and accepted.

Concerns about the institution and nature of the theatre as such have been reiterated after Guy Debord (1967), who conceptualized theatre and theatrical representation (specific representational, obscuring practices) as a code for capitalism.[4] For instance, for Baz Kershaw the theatre 'is a kind of social engine that helps to drive an unfair system of privilege' and 'performances in theatre buildings are deeply embedded in theatre as a *disciplinary system*' (Kershaw 1999, 31). For him, to be entertained within a theatre building is to succumb willingly to the forces of capitalism: theatre performances are commodities for which one buys tickets and that are part of a system of privilege. That is, it is not so much about the content one sees but about the fact that the place and type of spending one's leisure time are pre-determined and pre-organized. Would that mean that theatre when enjoyed outside its originary building, in a cinema space, is subversive and has escaped the shackles of capitalism, as in the case of livecasting?[5]

On the one hand, when it comes to the entertainment industry,[6] it is of course not the small fringe theatres that offer global broadcasting spectacles on cinema screens, but those theatre institutions that are already established. One must note that small theatres such as the Orange Tree Theatre or the Finborough Theatre do have active livecast programmes, but these happen online and not in cinemas and remain limited in their reach. In light of this, one can say critically that livecasts reproduce a theatrical discourse that is already dominant, there is no 'off' stage or fringe; they perpetuate the 'soft power' of this British cultural capital in the form of its National Theatre. The selected performances so far have aimed at maintaining an established status quo and represented 'safe bets' rather than bold ventures into experimental territory.[7] On the other hand, in the present-day society of screens, it seems logical to see performance and theatre broadcast in cinemas because in a mass-media society of spectacle, everything is commodified to the greatest extent. It is also not surprising that these developments are met with scepticism, especially within the academic discourse. Continuing Debord's line of thought, Dennis Kennedy argues that in today's world 'the incursions of electronic simulations are so pervasive that there is no substantial difference between watching and not watching. Citizens in the capitalist world have little choice but to be part of the spectacularization of life' (2009, 7). Both live theatre and livecasts are commodities, but theatre opens up spaces of resistance and agency whereas livecasts might be seen to fully succumb to an alienating commodity form. Therefore, it is particularly necessary to examine what mechanisms the livecast form can put into play in order to escape such a pigeonholing after all.

Enjoying 'a good night' still has its place in the 'post-dramatic age' (a term coined by Hans-Thies Lehmann (2006 [1999])), where performances do not rely on a dramatic text as a structuring device. Structure can also be achieved through the fostering of and relying on specific modes of representation, and through the framing of an event as being pleasurable. With regard to livecasting, the framing of the performances on social media plays an important role. A play or livecast is entertaining when it moves us on an affective level, when we get something out of crossing the threshold of intensity and when it manages to exert a pull on us, towards joy, sadness, anger or thoughtfulness, to name just a few emotional reactions. In lieu of or in addition to post-show chats with friends that one attended a show with, such affective responses can receive validation and unite spectators when shared afterwards on Twitter or Facebook. The phrases used to describe the experience of entertainment are from the semantic field of emotions since theatre 'traffics frequently and fundamentally in feeling in all its forms' (Hurley 2010, 4). In this light, it is possible to identify a conceptual proximity between entertainment, theatre and spectacle since they are united in their purpose to please.[8] If, however, 'the primary function of theatre is to entertain and give pleasure in any age, the nature of pleasure and entertainment nevertheless requires subtle redefinition from period to period' (Davis 2016, 47). These redefinitions and the proximity of both new and traditional forms of theatre to other forms of spectacle, especially sports, will be developed in the next sections.

Sports events, spectacle and NT Live

The following quotations from the 'NT Live FAQs' from February 2017 can be found on the NT's homepage and explain the main ideas behind the initiative:

> The approach to filming National Theatre Live broadcasts is to prioritise the audience in cinemas for that night. The camera director is given complete flexibility in choosing camera positions, so that the performance can be captured from the best seats in the house and with a sophisticated camera setup, involving tracking shots and, [. . .] when appropriate, a crane. The audience in the National Theatre are aware that cameras will be present, so the theatre is transformed into something of a live studio.
>
> We generally show a live introduction to convey the immediacy of the live event and the presence of the audience here in London.
>
> We are passionate about preserving the live, communal experience and the sense of event through these big screen exhibitions. (NT Live FAQ 2017)

What one notices here is an insistence on the dynamic, vibrant atmosphere (flexibility of the camera director, tracking shots, the theatre becomes a live studio), excitement (the idea is to broadcast the immediacy of the live event and presence of London audiences) and the spectacular quality that relies on the communal aspect – just like a sports event. Indeed, according to multi-camera director Ross MacGibbon, most camera operators who are involved in the production of live broadcasts have mostly filmed rugby games and other sports events, also major ones like the Olympics, because they require a certain similar skill: mental and physical flexibility (one needs to carry and move around with a camera for usually around two hours) and filmic choices such as mid-shots that are frequently used in both kinds of live broadcasting (MacGibbon 2019).

In 'Theatre as Sport' (1920) Bertolt Brecht establishes a black-and-white dichotomy between cinema and theatre, describing the latter as a sport. Cinema is a vending machine, that gives quick satisfaction, for instance, to see action or romance ([1920] 2015, 20). Theatre does not present anything on a platter; going to a play

> should be like attending a sporting event – not to watch wrestlers flexing their biceps but to witness subtler contests, ones fought with words.

There are always at least two people on the stage, and they are usually engaged in some kind of struggle. You have to watch closely to see who wins. [. . .] That's why those with more intelligence and subtlety need to go to the theatre, but they must treat it, as I have said, as if they were watching sport. (21)[9]

Livecasts shed a different light on this dichotomy: both their framing, the descriptions of the filming process and the experience of them present themselves as a sport and sporting event. Even though – or because – the livecast displaces a theatrical performance from the stage to the screen, it adds a peculiar pace to it through the use of cuts and camera movements. One cannot only watch contests fought with words but between images and frames.

As Alan Tomlinson and Christopher Young (2006) put it in their working definition of global sport spectacle, it is 'an event that has come to involve the majority of the nations of the world, that is transmitted globally, that foregrounds the sculptured and commodified body and orchestrates a physical display of the body politic, and that attracts large and regular followings of on-site spectators for the live context or event' (2006, 3). In comparison, the definition of NT Live in their FAQs from March 2018 reads:

> What particularly excited us about this concept was the fact that it was captured and broadcast live, and the shared experience of watching with an audience on a big screen. Whilst we could never replicate the experience of actually sitting in the theatre, the broadcasts retain something of the feeling of live performance and there is a real sense of event, with so many people around the world connected and sharing in the experience. [. . .] [O]ur biggest single broadcast to date is *Hamlet* with Benedict Cumberbatch which has been seen by more than 850,000 people. As of March 2018 the worldwide audience for National Theatre Live has reached almost 8 million people. (NT Live FAQs 2018)

Both sports events and NT Live are described in terms of their scale and their global reach; they are explicitly framed as orchestrated events that attract spectators.[10] Out of the over 2,000 cinemas around the world that show NT Live, 700 are in the UK (NT Annual Review 2018–19 and NT Live FAQs 2017). Most cinemas are in countries in Europe (Czech Republic, Denmark, Germany, Ireland, Sweden, United Kingdom) but cinemas in Australia, Cayman Islands, Chile, China, Hong Kong, Japan, Mexico, South Korea, Taiwan, UAE and the United States also participate (NT Live FAQs 2017). As Cochrane outlines, there are three ways for cinema audiences to experience a livecast: the simultaneous experience, that is 'cinema audiences watching the theatrical performance at the same time as the theatrical performance', the delayed experience, that is, watching the livecast at a later date but on its first showing and often elsewhere in the world, and the 'encore', which are repeat screenings of the original broadcast (Cochrane 2018, 345). The past years have shown that livecasts of plays with a famous lead actor or actress are special audience magnets – a tendency that has also been reflected in the popularity of the plays shown as part of NT At Home on YouTube during the Covid-19 pandemic: for instance, *One Man, Two Guvnors* with Jamie Cordon in the title role had the most viewings with 671,133 views (the total number of times a video is watched, including multiple watches by the same people, see Markwell 2020). Around 34 per cent of the viewers watched the performance on the premier date, that is on the first night on which it was shown (Buckeridge 2020). In comparison, looking at all the performances broadcast as part of NT At Home, on average 25 per cent of viewers tuned in on a show's premiere date, with 16 per cent across all titles watching in premiere mode (Buckeridge 2020).[11]

In fact, sports, theatre and spectacle have been united in the context of broadcasting from the very beginning (see Chapter 1). It makes sense to think of spectacle as 'a performative genre in its own right, engaged in a complex dialectical and functional dynamics with the other master genres, and not just as a loose, imperial trope for everything dubious about the contemporary world', as John J. MacAloon (2006, 15), influential theorist of spectacle and researcher of the modern Olympic Movement, puts it. The term 'spectacle' is still used today as a master metaphor for every conceivable manufacturing of power. In light of the growth of the Olympic Games since the 1960s and 1970s, the term 'mega-event' has been added to this vocabulary of the spectacular (16), and the NT Live takes up this mega-mentality.[12] Even MacAloon, who initially doubted that to watch (a transmission of an event on) television could be a true spectacle experience, has updated his position and claimed that the televising of games or rites can very well 'call into being a large group subject to a real festival or spectacle experience' (26) that can also manifest itself via watching events together on video boards and other attendant electronic technologies.

While the spectacle abounds around us, and still poses the danger to dehumanize culture, performance studies witness a (new) spectatorial turn.[13] For the purposes of this chapter, in order to think about spectators of theatre events versus sports events in contemporary culture, Kennedy's comparison proves particularly fruitful. In 'Sports and Shows: Spectators in Contemporary Culture', he postulates from the outset that theatre spectators give up part of their agency when they agree to assist at the spectacle.[14] Kennedy's main argument is that soccer spectators enjoy more playful freedom than theatre spectators, for three reasons: first, they can choose from a wide range of options of how to create a relationship with other spectators they do not know (2001, 278); second, they have a greater freedom to condemn the outcome of the 'performance' – 'fans know better than the coach' (279); and third, they are free to vary the purpose of their presence whereas theatre goers cannot 'write themselves into the performance event' (279) in the current setting.

If we are to define theatre as needing live audiences who, in their role as audiences, assist at the theatrical event, this means that without those assistants the event would not exist or at least not run its smooth course (the soccer games in empty stadiums during the Covid-19 pandemic in 2020–1 prove this point). For the livecasting spectator, the viewing situation is an in-between and can be described as a combination or reconciliation between Kennedy's classification of theatre versus sports spectators and Brecht's dismissal of the cinema. Livecasting spectators are physically in a cinema but to some extent given a similar agency to that of sports spectators. To what extent is this an illusion of power and are livecasting spectators puppets for the theatre institutions who need and use their social media response? Or are they indeed reinstating their power-as-audience through other means?

Framing livecasting: Mediated spectacle and communitas

When one looks at the NT's press releases describing or advertising upcoming livecasts over the course of the initiative's young history, one notices a change in the verbs and nouns that are used to describe them. Between 2009 and June 2014 there is a change from 'see' and 'played to' to 'experience' the work or theatre, and 'see' the broadcast to 'experience' the broadcast, which is a phrase used for the first time in June 2014. Occasionally, the phrase 'broadcasts are/have been seen' is still used, whereas 'the work of National Theatre Live' is continually referred to as being 'experienced'. Notably, when describing the livecast of *Frankenstein* and the Encores, it is the broadcast that is referred to as 'an international sensation' and not the play or the production.[15]

In the tweets both by the NT and spectators about livecasts, there is a link established between the productions and the notion of the spectacular. Between 29 June 2010 and 27 August 2019 #ntlive in combination with 'spectacular' comes up forty-three times[16] and @NTLive in combination with 'spectacular' sixty-two times, between 17 February 2010 and 12 November 2019. It is used with regard to about thirty-one different productions,[17] and

A Midsummer Night's Dream most often (8 times). While these numbers are not great in themselves, it is noteworthy that the adjective 'spectacular' is repeatedly chosen to describe the experience, but also the specific effect of the NT Live broadcasting aesthetics, as in the following description of the livecast of *Fleabag*.[18] The technique is described as being 'spectacular' since it makes it possible to forget that one is at a cinema. This suggests that only the in-situ performance can be spectacular and livecasting can compensate for this (Figure 2).

Livecasting is a multi-layered spectacle because of its convergent nature, incorporating and combining the aesthetics of theatre, cinema and television. With regard to cinema more generally, paratextual elements are all kinds of marketing material such as trailers, posters and merchandise and extend to the institutions' social media accounts (see also Atkinson 2019, 307). In livecasting, this paradocumentational brim is supplemented by tweets of the livecast attendees and, as part of that, other ways by which they express their experience, for instance through GIFs. Henry Jenkins, Sarah Atkinson and especially Jonathan Gray insist that these seemingly

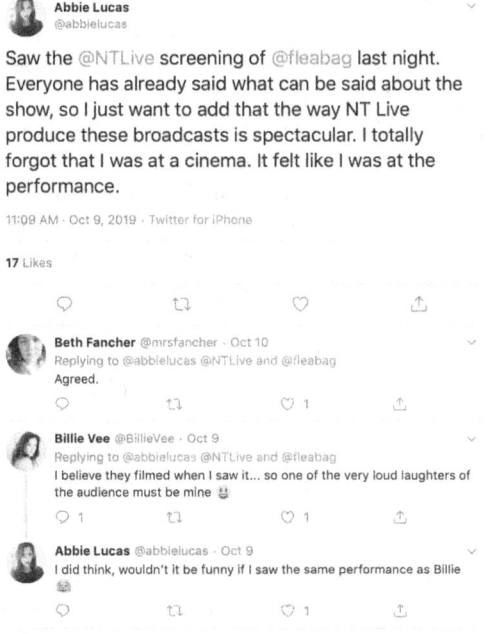

Figure 2 Screen capture of Twitter account of @abbielucas on 9 October 2019.

supplementary materials must be given attention, too, as they 'are as intrinsic a part of a text's DNA as are the films and television programs' (Gray 2010, 221).

Livecasting frames performance and the experience of it as a spectacle and is much more invested than live theatre in making individuals become part of its affective arrangement by luring them 'into their positions by providing opportunities for attachment' (Slaby, Mühlhoff and Wüschner 2019, 9). With regard to the role of the spectator, mediation has taken on an even greater role in the last two decades. When Kennedy argues that we are all mediatized spectators now – something that he seems to align with being metaphorically imprisoned – he suggests that to be physically present at an event has acquired an even greater value than it had before the twentieth century (2001, 282). In the livecasting context, this 'prison' of being a mediatized spectator is also manufactured into the livecast machinery but at the same time re-defined because one is experiencing this mediatized liveness *with others*, which generates a new form of authenticity. In other words: shared and communal feelings are an anchor point for what is coded as authentic. Livecasting suggests that one cannot only assist at something that is immediate but also something that is mediated. Such new forms of authenticity hinge on the sharing of emotions and on emotional contagion that is transported visually by seeing others on a screen, as the case study later in this chapter will illustrate.

As I outlined in the Introduction, livecasting emerges out of an environment in which theatres are reinventing themselves as multi-media companies.[19] The trailer produced by the NT to mark the tenth anniversary of NT Live, which is available on YouTube and was shown before livecasts in cinemas during the year of 2019, gives an idea of how the theatre emerges as a part of the multi-media industry and how the expectations for a spectacular theatre event are built up. In the 1:34-minute trailer we first see a shot of St Paul's Cathedral and its surrounding area, that is, the view that one would have when standing at the Southbank to the left from the National Theatre building. To joyous violin chords there is a mix of brief phrases ('From 21 stages – To 3,500 cinema screens around the world – 10 years of the best of British theatre – Watched by nearly 9 million people in cinemas – This is theatre for everyone – The best of British theatre. On a cinema screen near you. Find your venue on ntlive.com.') interspersed with shots from the Olivier auditorium and backstage shots. This then overlaps with a woman's voiceover, saying 'Counting to show: 10, 9, 8 . . .', and when the countdown ends, in an eruption, both auditory and visual, a rapid succession of impressions from different NT livecasts from the last ten years is shown, in no particular chronological or thematic order, to triumphant music. The description of the trailer below the video reads: 'Whether you come along to one of the live broadcasts, or catch one of our many Encore screenings, you'll have the best seats in the house. And you'll be part of something much bigger; an audience thousands strong, watching from around the world – sharing every gasp, every laugh and every dramatic moment, with you.' One YouTube user (Kristin Doe) sums this up with the comment 'This trailer gives me chills'. Indeed, the chill-inducing, spectacular event of the best of British theatre in the specific location of London superimposes itself on the drama as such; what matters is the effect produced (National Theatre 2019).

When it comes to creating a relationship between audience members and audience and the spectacle, the (in contrast to the theatre) more informal setting of the cinema affords a communal framework. One is not only unified with others in an act of something akin to voyeurism but a sense of communitas can also manifest itself through being there and *not* in the theatre. If theatre audiences are participatory publics, then livecasting audiences are quasi-theatre audiences. As Jill Dolan elaborates, communitas is used to describe

> the moments in a theater event or a ritual in which audiences or participants feel themselves become part of the whole in an organic, nearly spiritual way; spectators' individuality becomes finely attuned to those around them, and a cohesive if fleeting feeling of belonging to the group bathes the audience. (2005, 11)

Victor Turner, who coined the term, describes communitas as spontaneous and immediate; crucially, it 'preserves individual distinctiveness' (1982, 46). It allows a momentary giving up of the various roles (statuses, classes, etc.) and breaking away from the norm-sets people have been conditioned to play and follow in order to conform to the 'social structure'. While some 'human essence' is involved in these played roles, '*full* human capacity is locked out of these somewhat narrow, stuffy rooms' (46). When communitas, such as in the theatre, manifests itself, it is a 'total confrontation of human identities' (47).

For Turner, any social world 'is a world in becoming, not a world of being' (Dolan 2005, 14). For this reason, he theorizes communitas as 'anti-structural' and most evident in 'liminality' (Turner 1982, 44–5), that is any condition outside or on the peripheries of everyday life, including performance. Communitas is non-conformative, it exists a priori to social agreements and its very existence 'puts all social structural rules in question and suggests new possibilities' (Dolan 2005, 14). Dolan makes a connection between communitas and utopian performatives, but it can be applied to the context of livecasting as well: most notably, in these settings, the spectators already are *outside the theatre*, and still – or because of that – the experience of theatre plays can affect them and let them enjoy these instances of communitas with others.[20] The National Theatre enforces such manifestations because there are no plans to make broadcasts available on DVD, both 'due to [their] rights agreements with [their] artists and [their] current [*sic*] focus on building the live, *communal* experience in cinemas'.[21] And precisely because of the mediated nature of the livecasting spectacle and its reliance on social media, its spectators can very well write themselves into the event, by their comments on Twitter (after all, spectators' tweets are often used on the NT's Twitter page to sum up a given livecast), and thus inscribing themselves on the paradocumentational brim.

The rhetoric of NT Live explicitly invites a coming together of spectators, urging them to tweet 'from where they will be watching' or, in the case of Encore screenings, asking where they had watched a given livecast, which users answer quite willingly, often adding with whom they have watched it. For instance, on 27 December 2019 the NT Live Twitter page, in looking back on one of the most 'spectacular' performances of the past year, namely the livecast of *All About Eve* (on 4 April 2019, which had also been shown in Encores), asked its followers to recapitulate where they had watched it from, a call that was re-tweeted forty-one times, received 227 likes and twenty-seven replies (as of 6 February 2020). Most of the answers name two locations and users such as @KristenArchule4 also mention with whom they went to see the livecast, thus creating a communal transgeographical web (Figure 3).

The livecasting spectacle dismantles the divide between more and less affective forms of performance; the spectacular atmosphere created around it actually puts to the fore that theatre is something like a '"feeling-machine", an apparatus designed to stimulate [and simulate?] feelings through triggers such as lighting, sound, movement, mise-en-scène, pacing, structure, characterization, human proximity and more' (Harvie and Allain 2006, 149). Livecasting as an affective arrangement not only puts affect at its core by luring spectators in through various medial and communicative means but *needs* this orchestration of affect to make up for the proxemics typical for live theatre. As a consequence, the affective dynamics – which can be relatively contained in the context of live theatre – are intensely processual, that is, adapting anew to each livecast, as will be illustrated in the remaining part of this chapter.

Figure 3 Screen captures of @NTLive Twitter account on 27 December 2019.

Livecasting as affective spectacle: *A Midsummer Night's Dream* (Bridge Theatre/NT Live)

As Kershaw points out,

> the commonly human, the person, the subject – as much as any object or thing – can be [...] at the heart of spectacle. This is especially interesting because the magnitudes of power at play in spectacle tend to expel the merely human, to objectify it, to replace it with emblems, ciphers, symbols and other types of abstraction. (2007, 209)

London's Bridge Theatre precisely put the commonly human at the heart of its 2019 summer production, Shakespeare's *A Midsummer Night's Dream*. There were experiences in the in-situ performance that one would think difficult to capture in the subsequent NT livecast. Yet the effect of the spectacular set-up managed to cross the real-digital divide and created a manifestation of mediatized communitas. The performance and the NT Live recording of it can be characterized as projects that were centred on coordinating and manoeuvring energy, and extending invitations to participate. One must note that two of the main people behind NT Live, Nicholas Hytner and David Sabel, were responsible for the foundation of the Bridge Theatre in 2017, and one of them (Hytner) directed *A Midsummer Night's Dream*. It was thus from the outset conceived of as a 'balancing act' and supposed to appeal to global audiences both as an in-situ performance and as a livecast.

A play about love, illusion and the fragile boundaries between dream and reality seems like a well-suited canvas on which to play out the experience of the spectacle. With a stage design by Bunny Christie, the play ran from 3 June to 31 August 2019 and was staged in the theatre's promenade format.[22] In an email sent out to all subscribers to the theatre's newsletter, which had the function of a countdown until opening night, future audience members were assured that 'summer is coming' and sent rehearsal pictures and a link to the appearance of Gwendoline Christie (who played Titania) in *The Graham Norton Show* on BBC One. The email also included a section titled 'Choose how to experience it', which read: 'The special thing about our production is that *you* can choose how to experience it – sit wrapped around the action or follow it on foot with immersive tickets. There are perks to both depending on what tickles your fancy' (Bridge Theatre 2019a, emphases in original). When clicking on 'immersive tickets' one was forwarded to the theatre's homepage and got the additional information that:

The theatre becomes the forest – a dream world of flying fairies, contagious fogs and moonlight revels. The seating is wrapped around the action while the immersive tickets allow the story to be followed on foot. [. . .] Standing tickets: To be immersed in the action you should select 'pit' when booking tickets. This will mean you will stand for the performance and move around as the story develops around you. There may be elements of participation for those with these tickets (but don't worry, you won't have a speaking role!). (Bridge Theatre Homepage n.d.)

In addition, the email already included the 'NT Live announcement': 'We're so thrilled to announce that NT Live will be streaming a recording of *A Midsummer Night's Dream* on 17 October [2019] to cinemas around the world. Perfect for those who can't make it to London this summer or who want to see the show again from a whole new perspective' (Bridge Theatre 2019a). Further email updates included new trailers of the show while it was already running and included several sequences in which audience members were the heart of the spectacle.

An email sent out on 15 June 2019 to mark the production's half-time stated that 'we are certainly feeling the love from our audiences and reviewers alike', notably putting the audience first. Throughout the show's run, the affective quality of it was emphasized by describing it as wrapping itself around 'you' (personalized), taking place in the summer (associated with warmth) and how it created a feeling of love among audience members. There were no comments on the content of the play, only on individual actors' performances and the effect it achieved (Bridge Theatre 2019b). Before the final performance, an email summed up the highlights from '*The Dream*' (the abbreviation creating a familiar atmosphere, as if the play was an old friend) and encouraging prospective audience members to come and see the play ('Need more convincing by people that aren't just us?'), using tweets by spectators referred to as 'the stream of love' (Bridge Theatre 2019c).

The production itself playfully blurred the boundaries between illusion and theatrical artifice. When I attended the show at the Bridge Theatre on 15 June 2019 with my partner, we were indeed part of the forest in which the plot unfolded since we had standing tickets in the pit. The actors and actresses would rush past us or, as in the case of the actor playing Puck (David Moorst), engage in eye contact and perhaps even utter impatient outbursts to fellow spectators that were off (Shakespeare's) script, such as 'Out of my way!' followed by a contemptuous 'Londoners . . .', when there were too many people in his way, or 'I like your dungarees!' to a woman in the audience (see Figure 4).[23] At the end of the first part, right before the intermission, there was an extended party scene celebrating the love between Oberon and Bottom-

Figure 4 'I like your dungarees!' – Screen capture of a scene from *A Midsummer Night's Dream* directed by Nicholas Hytner, directed for the screen by Ross MacGibbon © NT At Home Collection 2019. All rights reserved.

as-Ass. The actors and actresses playing the 'Rude Mechanicals' turned to the audience members, grabbed a few by the hands and manoeuvred us dancing in a big circle in the pit, around the stage islands. When the music stopped after a couple of minutes to signal the beginning of the intermission, we found ourselves dancing with strangers in a liminal space (and time) between performance and intermission – for those audience members in the pit, the illusion was dispersed. What is more, we found ourselves performing ourselves, or rather 'performing "audience"' (White 2013, 5) as we were watching the performance. There was an awareness of being part of an audience as both a socially constructed practice and a position taken through being a spectator to the world around us, 'our own actions in it as well as those of other people' (White 2013, 5).

Throughout the performance there were breaks in the experience of immersion and illusion because we were repeatedly gently pushed around and guided by the stage hands positioned around the stage islands making sure that the action could unfold as planned. Being shoved around like this and bumping into fellow spectators made it hard to allow for an all-encompassing manifestation of an illusion; one can say that not only the fourth wall[24] was broken but also the fifth wall between audience members.

As mentioned, the play was pitched to audiences as an immersive experience. Put simply, to immerse oneself in a performance means to change one's perspective. As Gareth White elaborates, '[t]he term [immersive] designates audience experiences of proximity, flexibility and interaction [...] We are invited to "join in", to "be a part of it", to "take part"' (169–70). What White points to here, and what reminds us of Kennedy's terminology when he speaks of spectators assisting at a spectacle, is that to accept the invitation to plunge into the spectacle, as in the case of *A Midsummer Night's Dream*, is to become an integral part of it. In the marketing emails prior to the performances, future spectators were indeed invited to let the story develop around them and the experience of the pit was characterized by an atmosphere of proximity, flexibility and interaction. The performance of *A Midsummer Night's Dream* presented the two sides of what an immersion inside the experiential space of being a spectator can be like: a gentle plunge into a world that had not much in common with the busy atmosphere on London Bridge just a few metres outside the theatre building; and at the same time a constant reminder of the bodies of other temporary theatre visitors around us. In the following I will shed light on how the notions of proximity, flexibility and interaction were transported into the supposedly less immersive space of watching the production on a cinema screen.

The play was chosen to mark a decade of NT Live, an ambitious decision, given that 1,200 scripted shots for seven cameras were necessary in a 2.20-hour show to capture 'not just theater in the round' but 'theater in the round with an audience smack in the middle' (Valentini 2019; see also MacGibbon 2019). It was first shown in cinemas on 17 October 2019 as a 'filmed live screening' (there was a slide including that specification when one entered the cinema auditorium) since the 'capture' of it had happened in the final week of its run for scheduling reasons (Buckeridge 2019).

On entering the foyer of the Barbican before the NT Live show on 17 October 2019, I was confronted with quite a different 'pit' than that in the Bridge Theatre, namely the sign leading to the front rows in the Barbican's Cinema 1. There were, as is often the case, 'Who's Who' slides shown before the show and the presenter Samira Ahmed greeted the cinema audience at the 'NT Live recording [. . .] while the audience continues to arrive here in the pit' (where she was), suggesting a temporal simultaneity between the viewing situation in the cinemas and the theatre in the same sentence in which she was making clear that this was not the case. For those cinema audience members unfamiliar with the NT Live terminology, the distinction would not have been so obvious, that is, that 'recording' meant 'not live', while 'broadcast' meant 'live'.

A striking feature of the livecast was that it demystified the theatrical illusion by laying bare the work that went into creating it and included metatheatrical comments on its production context and its materiality. This, however, did not seem to spoil the magic of watching the filmed performance. For instance, when seen on the screen the crew with their headsets seemed to be part of the show – not only because they ushered spectators and ascertained the smooth goings on of the production but because they were so close to the stage, at the same time reacting and watching the events unfold very enthusiastically and closely.

During the entire play, but especially in the second half, the atmosphere in the cinema was equally joyful, many people were laughing and a few even applauded at the end. The main reason why the livecast transported the immersive experience of the play onto a screen was technical and the sheer skill of the multi-camera director. As a former dancer at the Royal Ballet, Ross MacGibbon[25] in his work as a filmmaker focuses on filming (he avoids the term 'capture' because it suggests stasis) the energy of human bodies in motion. When confronted with a rather untypical format such as that of the promenade, the task is especially complex. The spectator in the cinema cannot build a story on their own but has to rely on the screen director to tell that story (see Champagne 2018).

When preparing for his filming of the show, MacGibbon did not go to the rehearsals because in his experience it sometimes 'confuses things' and waited until the show was in production. He saw the show twice, one time from the promenades and one time from the audience, and relatively late in the run since it would then come closest to the show that he would shoot. For a screen director doing a livecast of a theatre show, the first question always is how many cameras their team will have (usually six to seven). Something that was noticeable when watching the livecast of *A Midsummer Night's Dream* was the intuitive and dynamic approach to filming. It did not seem as if the cameras were shutting some part of the stage off, even though because of the promenade format there was no actual centre. MacGibbon worked with a scratch tape, filmed in one wide shot from that spot in the Bridge Theatre where people naturally assume that this is where the front is, combined with his own, as he said, 'gut feelings' from watching the show (he had already prepared his camera script directly on the play text). In several scenes, the camera captured moments that only lasted for the blink of an eye; all of these, however, were moments of planned improvisation.

For instance, in one scene that also served as a metatheatrical comment on the production context, Bottom grabs a phone from an audience member to consult a calendar and find out what the date of the Midsummer festivities is. The Rude Mechanicals then take a selfie with this phone and the camera captures this moment in such a way that the shot of the group on the phone screen is visible for two seconds – a small screen within a bigger screen (Figure 5).

This had been arranged – or impro-planned – beforehand, since MacGibbon instructed the actor to be roughly in this area so that he could

Figure 5 'Portrait!' – Screen capture of a scene from *A Midsummer Night's Dream* directed by Nicholas Hytner, directed for the screen by Ross MacGibbon © NT At Home Collection/Ross MacGibbon 2019. All rights reserved.

have a camera nearby and film the moment accordingly. These are instances of planned improvisation and of self-control, a characteristic of an actor that already Diderot found indispensable and discussed in his *The Paradox of Acting*.[26] Analogously, what is required of the involved cameramen is both the physical presence and the skill to be courageous and spontaneous; the screen director choreographs them as well while the show is happening, sometimes telling them what to shoot in the last second. None of this can be theorized or planned in advance in its entirety, an element of risk is crucial.

The reason to film many scenes with a handheld camera was twofold: first of all, MacGibbon did not want the livecast 'to be just observational' but 'to be anticipatory, like the production was' to render the excitement of audience members, who had been in the pit. Second, the screen director wanted to transport the three dimensions of the performance onto the screen, that is, a mixture of foreground, centerground and background. In order to do this, many slightly wider shots, with the camera slightly lower than the eye line were used to frame the layers of action and the visceral depth of the production by taking into account a mix of angles, and for instance, shoot the low foreground, the centerground where the action was happening on one of the 'stage islands' and the trapeze on top in the background all in one frame (Figure 6).

Figure 6 Screen capture of a scene from *A Midsummer Night's Dream* directed by Nicholas Hytner, directed for the screen by Ross MacGibbon © NT At Home Collection/Ross MacGibbon 2019. All rights reserved.

This artistic vision has also been influenced by MacGibbon's background as a dancer: the camera is not primarily a framing device but a motor, which has a direct influence on the pace and depth of a performance:

> Dancing influences my filming in terms of fluidity. I tend to be on the brave side, rather than the boring. [. . .] I enjoy the pace and rhythm of a production. I like to deliberately slow down and speed up scenes. [. . .] Cameras can change scenes that appear flat on the stage.
>
> [. . .]
>
> For me the important thing above all is to keep it visceral, entertaining, imaginative, and honest to production. So that people see the production and not your kind of whacky interpretation. It *is* your interpretation, but it is done with the best possible motives. (MacGibbon 2019)

The filming team of the livecast was therefore far from just 'shooting' the show – under the instruction of MacGibbon their labour was a highly creative and alert process that required a great amount of focused attention that still left a leeway for enjoyment. While some theatre companies often think that the filming of a performance for livecasting purposes happens as one goes along, it is an intricate process of script and camera work and improvisation within parameters.

When watching the livecast, another noteworthy aspect from the perspective of the cinema audience was the enjoyment of mediatized communitas, that is, watching others having fun. Those audience members at the Bridge Theatre who were there on the night of the livecast played

Watching Others Having Fun – Livecasting as Spectacle   67

Heather Mitchell
@hvamitchell

Feeling so happy after seeing the @_bridgetheatre production of A Midsummer Night's Dream via @NTLive tonight. Such a spectacular performance! Tear-inducingly funny and, at times, enchantingly dark. I can't recommend it enough 😊

12:06 am · 18 Oct 2019 · Twitter for iPhone

3 Likes

Lorna Good #TVTTagTeam
@GozzaGood

Well, that was spectacular! @NTLive I truly believe if Shakespeare was alive today he'd have absolutely loved Nicholas Hytner's interpretation of A Midsummer Night's Dream; I bloomin did. Best show I've seen in a long time. From performances to production: perfect. #BridgeDteam

11:16 pm · 17 Oct 2019 · Twitter for iPhone

12 Likes

Figure 7 Screen capture of the Twitter accounts of @GozzaGood and @hvamitchell, showing posts from the night of the NT Live broadcast of *A Midsummer Night's Dream* on 17 October 2019.

the part of the carriers of affect for those audiences watching them in their cinema. After the livecast, when I was cramped with fellow cinema spectators in the elevator in the Barbican one woman said to another: 'I wonder what it would have been like for people in the seats – watching everybody having fun.' A selection of responses on Twitter reflects in what ways the livecast was perceived, namely as a spectacle and a primarily affective experience (Figures 7 and 8).

One user described the atmosphere in the cinema as '@NTLive that was incredible! The whole cinema was crying with laughter at the rude mechanicals and the staging and direction was magical. A truly wonderful experience. #BridgeDream' (Rebecca @Becci_Nembs27, 17 October 2019), and another wishes they could have immersed themselves in a literal way when they say, 'Oh WOW. @NTLive. I can't remember a better night out in ages. I wanted to climb into the screen and join you all at the Bridge. Just JOYOUS [followed by nine emojis depicting a cone full of confetti]' (Sarah

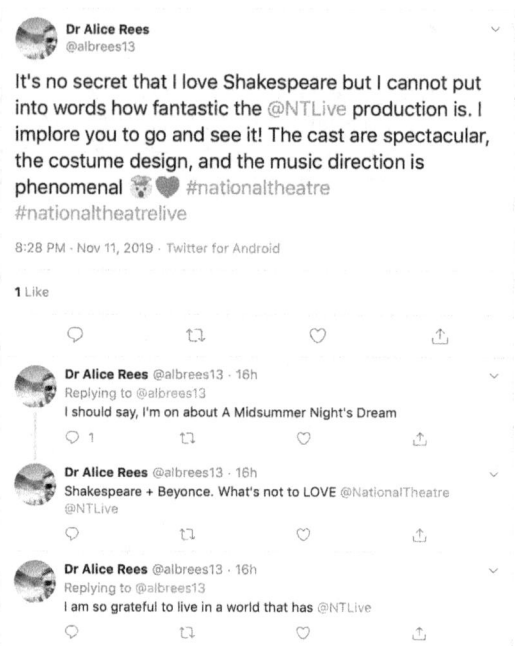

Figure 8 Screen capture of the Twitter account of @albrees13 on 11 November 2019.

Todd Taylor @scraphamster, 17 October 2019). Another user tellingly calls this their 'favourite theatre' that they have watched this year, suggesting that there is no distinction between the particular place where a theatrical performance is watched.[27] In a review, the immersive experience was described as being 'palpable even via live broadcast' (Hatfull 2019, n. p.).

What contributed to this palpability was that in several shots there was one of the cameras visible, as if it were a spectator, too, recording/watching the performance. This was complemented by seeing many audience members wear purple floral head decorations after the intermission. MacGibbon refers to these shots, when somebody seems to be in the foreground by accident, as 'dirty' shots, that increase the dynamism of a performance and contribute to a participatory and communal feeling (MacGibbon 2019). Watched from the cinema, there was no clear hierarchy between performers and spectators; while the performers were on elevated stage islands, the spectators formed the majority and thus filled most of the screen. The dramatic space appeared in an extended form, with the roles blurred – who was merely watching and who was part of the play that the cinema audience was watching? There

Watching Others Having Fun – Livecasting as Spectacle

Figure 9 Puck jumps into the audience – Screen capture of a scene from *A Midsummer Night's Dream* directed by Nicholas Hytner directed for the screen by Ross MacGibbon © NT At Home Collection/Ross MacGibbon 2019. All rights reserved.

were several moments in which it turned into an increasingly slippery affair to distinguish between who was playing what role. This slipperiness was created through watching the entire space laid out on the screen: watching how the fourth wall was broken increased the awareness that the idea of a mimetic illusionist theatre was blown apart. When Puck dashed off to fulfil Titania's request to put the love potion onto Lysander's eyes, his impatience was energetically captured by the actor playing him, David Moorst, who simply jumped off the stage, seemingly into nothingness. When I watched the performance at the Bridge Theatre, from my standpoint this was what it looked like. In the livecast, however, there was a perfectly timed shot of how Puck was caught by six crew members wearing headsets. For a moment, therefore, Puck was both Puck and an actor and the crew members were both crew members (or quite literally stagehands) and assistant performers catching a fictional character. Such a framing introduced the layer of work and perfectly timed precision into a scene that, on a fictional level, represents a moment of magic in which a fairy can simply fly away. In the livecast, both the fictional and factual layer merged and overlapped – to see the stagehands catching the actor playing Puck coincided with seeing the character of Puck fly off the stage and disappear into an invisible web (Figure 9).

In another actual piercing of the fourth wall, the actor Jermaine Freeman, who was playing an actor playing 'Moon' in the Rude Mechanicals' rendering of *Pyramus and Thisbe*, shone his torch right into the camera, thus blinding the cinema audiences (there was an audible flinching in the Barbican cinema) in the same way in which the actors on stage were blinded. This seemingly simple trick also laid bare the 'work' that went into the performance, as for a second the cinema audience could experience the same pain that the performers on stage felt when being blinded on stage.

Apart from the enjoyment it induced in audiences around the world to watch people just like them be put first, the use of pop music in particular contributed to a prolonged affective engagement with the show and let the performance appeal to global audiences in particular. Both the live theatre production and the livecasting event were connected through the featured songs and the Spotify playlists made available after the events. Typically, when a play is over, strangers shuffle out of the venue, in moments that Richard Schechner calls '"cool down," so reminiscent of when the lights come up after last call in a bar to reveal the tired, too human, sweaty flesh of ordinary people who'd been transformed only a moment ago by flashing lights and a persistent, irresistible beat' (Dolan 2005, 19). *A Midsummer Night's Dream* indeed ended with an extended scene in which audience members were encouraged to hold hands and walk around the scene islands, after having danced to Dizzee Rascal's song 'Bonkers'. Thus, after the play was over, it was like the awakening from a dream, usually, as Bert O. States puts it in his 'Phenomenology of the Curtain Call' 'an abrupt fall into the mundane, fraught with the nostalgia of exile' (1981, 374). Yet the production managed to ease this cooling down by providing a Spotify playlist to the production, which was made up of the show's five theme songs.

In recent years, directors of Shakespearean productions have sought to connect with their audiences by incorporating popular music in their plays.[28] Hytner for this production focused on three main pop songs to 'lodge specific moments in the audience's memory' after it was over, namely Dizzee Rascal's 'Bonkers' (2009), Beyoncé's 'Love on Top' (2011) and Florence + The Machine's 'Only If For A Night' (2011) (Hatfull 2019, n. p.), each of which encapsulating a pivotal scene in the play. 'Love on Top', one of Beyoncé's most upbeat tracks, escalates over the course of four and a half minutes due to the four ascending key changes and thus functions as an enhancing meaning carrier to describe Oberon's (in this version it is not Titania) sudden and powerful infatuation with Bottom. Their first scene together becomes an act of erotic celebration that is both hilarious and sexy. This scene was scripted roughly by MacGibbon, who called the shots while watching the action, comparing this method to the filming of a rock show. The cameras were mostly improvised, the handheld camera would follow Oberon and Bottom all the time but everything was controlled, thus another instance of planned improvisation.

The lyrics to 'Bonkers' acted as a plot synopsis to the wider play – a link the Bridge social media team encouraged Twitter followers to make: 'I wake up everyday it's a daydream / Everythin' in my life ain't what it seems' (post on 6 August 2019 – 'A synopsis of #BridgeDream by @DizzeeRascal') And Florence + The Machine's 'Only If For A Night' functioned as a meta-commentary on the entire play.

When comparing the livecast with the live performance one sees that the thresholds of intensity of these two affective arrangements differ: in the case of the livecast, these thresholds are lowered and expanded, to make up for the in-situ intensity absent in the mediated production and to prolong the affective attachment to it. Because of the promenade format of the show and the invitation to become part and walk through the dreamland, spectators of the in-situ performance, after they had accepted the invitation, were a vital part of the affective arrangement. In the case of the live theatre event (not only *A Midsummer Night's Dream*), this arrangement could be experienced as relatively self-sufficient and structured both by the stagehands and the experience of the play itself.

The affective arrangement of the livecast was more permeable: in its default position, a livecast presents itself as a recording of other people's participation in an affective arrangement; cinema audiences are onlookers and at first excluded from this. As a consequence, the threshold to cross in order to re-enact the intense theatrical experience is low, it does not seem to address one directly. The effect of the affective arrangement is dispersed and can be localized in different places: it is contained within the cinema screen, as one watches its manifestation in the actual theatre; it spills over into the cinema auditorium; and it is prolonged and further dispersed in comments on social media. This means that, in contrast to its stability in the context of in-situ performance, the arrangement is not there *a priori*; it is (re)created while the broadcast is being watched and spilling over into the cinema.

Livecasts are just as immersive as live theatre, but the manifestations of immersion in comparison to the live theatre event setting differ. Figure 10, which provides a visualization and model to think about the difference between live theatre events and livecasts in general, illustrates this line of thought.

In contrast to live theatre, with its long tradition of theatre-going and adhering etiquette, the response to the fairly new phenomenon of livecasting entails drawing on different generic frames, namely theatrical, televisual and cinematic, to orientate and familiarize oneself with this hybrid material-discursive formation. A key difference in how affect is patterned in the

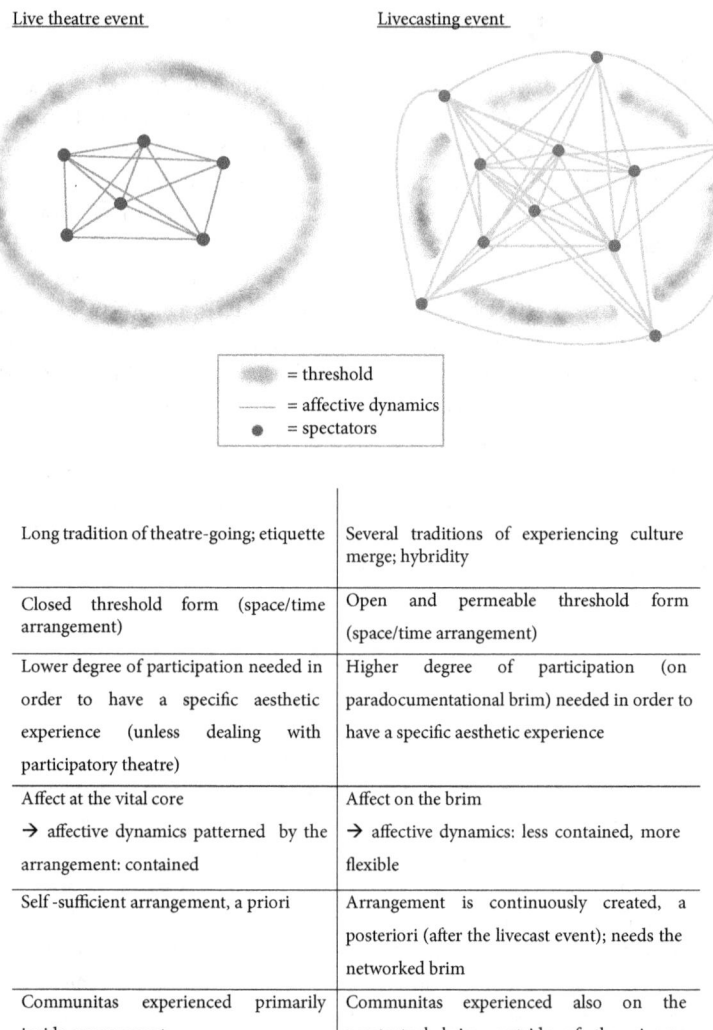

Figure 10 The affective arrangement of live theatre events versus livecasts.

livecast is that its arrangement is characterized by a more open and permeable threshold form because the paradocumentational brim is a constitutive element. This in turn also means that the amount of energy and effort that needs to be invested to have the full aesthetic experience of a livecast is comparatively higher than that of non-participatory live theatre because spectators are encouraged to participate in the event by posting contributions about the livecast on social media.

The manifestation of communitas is especially noteworthy: in the live theatre event communitas is experienced primarily at the theatre venue and during the performance because of the 'closed' space/time arrangement, that is, a specific start and end time and only one specific location. In the livecasting event, this lack of bodily (static) presence needs to be compensated for. This happens through the affordances of the arrangement and the paradocumentational brim: on the one hand, communitas is experienced in the cinema because of its more informal setting and generally smaller numbers of attendees. On the other hand, it is also experienced outside of the cinema and after the livecasting event, namely with the perceived audience at the live theatre event – for instance facilitated by 'dirty shots' that increase the dynamism of a performance and contribute to a participatory and communal feeling – and with other people who are tweeting about the livecast after its broadcast. Hence, communitas here can be experienced both in a closed and open space/time arrangement.

In conclusion, livecasting is on the one hand firmly enmeshed in centralized structures of entertainment and marketing hyperboles and thus may well be perceived to present a dangerous form of spectacle, as described by Debord, in that it superimposes a pre-shaped kind of looking onto the consumption of theatre. Yet on the other hand, – as a theatrical spectacle that is part of a complex media ecology – it inherently possesses the capacity to foreground the theatricality behind all spectacle and to tease out different experiential dimensions. The effect this can have when (re)visiting a performance that one has either seen in situ or is seeing for the first time is comparable to the effect of the introduction of the use of artificial light in theatres in the early nineteenth century. Advances in technology coincided with new models of vision and added meaning to productions. In 1822, when Samuel Taylor Coleridge attended a performance of the actor Edmund Kean which used technologically advanced illumination, he was prompted to say: 'To see him act is like reading Shakespeare by flashes of lightning' (in Rowell 1978, 24).

A livecast can precisely be the flash of lighting on a performance, both bringing it to life (differently, anew) and teasing out experiential dimensions not there at first. In that sense, it takes part in the developments which began in the twentieth century, the age of post-dramatic theatre, which challenge the primacy of textual production over other forms of representation. As my analysis of *A Midsummer Night's Dream* has shown, the pleasure evoked by these livecast spectacles that are not merely visual but also auditory and affective (if only by looking at other fellow spectators immerse themselves) plays a central role, and the joy of experiencing theatre together with others. In addition, livecasts indeed demystify the theatrical image: they expose the made-ness behind all theatrical production (see next chapter) and introduce a greater dimension of play.

In order to understand the appeal of livecasts, it is therefore necessary to see this kind of twenty-first-century spectacle as part of the affective turn, which has 'has shifted credit for meaning-making *from* features and practices which focus on semiotic systems, representations, sense-making and interpretation *onto* bodily experience, feelings and emotions' (Harvie and Allain 2006, 149). The livecast of a theatrical performance becomes an event in Bakhtin's sense, namely that which is 'about individuality and potentiality coming together to produce a radical form of presence and present-ness' (see Sullivan 2018, 61–2), an affective spectacle.

The pull which the NT Livecast of *A Midsummer Night's Dream* managed to exert into its affective arrangement extended, in fact, into the domestic sphere, when the livecast was watched during the Covid-19 pandemic. It encapsulated the ache for proximity that was created by an almost historic sense of watching a play, increased by the 'archival framing' through the screen, that created a joyful, convivial atmosphere at a time when that was still possible.[29]

3

Capturing the atmosphere

The material-theatrical

When Nicholas Hytner attended the first NT Live broadcast at the BFI Cinema (*Phèdre*), right next to the building where it was filmed, it was the possibility of risk, of possible glitches, which transported the livecast's theatricality and which was for him encapsulated by Helen Mirren skipping one line that night – forever now archived in that recording (Hytner 2018, 272). Theatricality, indeed, hinges on contingency, risk and spontaneity – all three of which become porous when a glitch occurs. In other words: glitches make the theatricality of any performance visible. The conceptual triad of this book – spectacle, materiality, engagement – points to these three central characteristics of theatricality and in turning to the aspect of materiality in this chapter, I want to connect it to the glitch. As Brandon Hunter puts it, 'theatricality is an expected and in some cases conventionally ascribed attribute of the work' (2021, xvii). The material can precisely accentuate the potential of a (mediated) performance to circumvent the expected. When theatricality is conceived of denoting that a performance is always already ephemeral *and* archived, that is, still-there and not-there-any-more, the material indeed is the hyphen in these compounds.

There are some key parameters when one thinks of the practicalities of attending what one might call a regular theatre performance. At its core, a theatre attendance is an experience of heightened and guided hearing and looking – the words used to describe the attendees, audience (from Latin *audire*, to hear) and spectators (from *spectare*, to look/watch) underline this. Especially the dimension of vision and visuality has undergone quite a change with the commercial introduction of electric power in England in 1887. With those new visual possibilities not only a more comfortable viewing situation was created in the nineteenth century, but also 'a freeing up of vision' (Crary 1990, 24). According to Dominic Johnson, this produced 'amplified affective responses in audiences, such as laughter, discomfort, and fear' (Johnson 2012, 37). With the further development of technologies and the combination with digital technologies and diverse media, this amplification of affective responses can be, I argue, multiplied, and the heterotopic quality of theatre can be expanded. As Michel Foucault has defined it, the theatre is heterotopic in that it juxtaposes several incompatible sites/spaces in a single real (mostly rectangular) space; curiously for the purposes of this chapter, Foucault in the same sentence mentions the cinema that is also a heterotopia, 'a very odd rectangular room, at the end of which, on a two-dimensional screen, one sees the projection of a three-dimensional space' (1986, 25). With regard to cinema and the cinematic space one can also speak of spheres that invite musings of different spaces. The film scholar Stanley Cavell (1979, 39) has referred to films on screens as magically arisen reproductions of the world. What we see in a cinema in many cases goes beyond people's everyday experience. Recent scholarship on cinematic space incorporates its material and immaterial histories.[1] As Thomas Elsaesser defines it, the cinematic space is made up of two spaces that are each other's opposites, the screen space and the auditorium space. In contrast to theatre, where stage and auditorium are physically connected, the two spaces are completely separated from each other; both the widening of the screen and the use of Dolby-stereo and surround sound aim at a bridging of this divide, to create a fuller sense of unity (2002, 75). For Elsaesser it is detrimental that cinema audiences now have to remain seated and concentrate on the screen as opposed to the setting in early Nickelodeons, where there were no rows of seats; a seating order implies regulation and a forcing into order of the audience (2002, 75).

My analysis in this chapter combines my experience of attending selected livecasts in cinemas and the productions these livecasts were based on in the theatre. While the theatrical and the cinematic space are two separate spheres, it is an essential part of the hybrid form of livecasting that on the side of reception, a merging of these two spaces occurs which necessitates a side-by-side discussion of both 'in-situ' and 'mediated' performance. The effect created is that of a multi-experiential space that is characterized 'by an interplay of remediated theatrical, televisual and cinematic concepts and conventions' (Wyver 2014b, 104). Livecasts are theatrical as they relay a performance in its entirety and render them (apart from Encore screenings) live; they are televisual as they involve multi-camera directing and live editing; and they are cinematic as they are created with the reception on big cinema screens in mind (see also Aebischer, Greenhalgh and Osborne 2018, 6). In my readings, I use the idea of the glitch and audience dis/comfort to focus on the materiality of livecasting.

A word on wires, screens and electricians from a Brechtian perspective

It is a rainy afternoon in early December 2018. I am in the Olivier Theatre to watch the matinee-cum-camera-rehearsal of *Antony and Cleopatra* that is open to the ticket-holding public. With me and the other audience members, there are seven cameras in the middle part of the stalls: one in the front in the second row, five cameras two rows behind that, one on a crane on a platform in the centre of the stalls. Before the performance begins, a presenter comes onto the stage and explains that this matinee performance is being filmed ahead of the NT Live broadcast the next day. She also urges us to ignore the cameras (even though they are, as mentioned, impossible not to see) and turn off our mobile devices so as not to interfere with the broadcast equipment. At this point, my mobile phone is still lying in my lap and an audience member sitting next to me urges me to 'turn it OFF. OFF'. Technical equipment and other kinds of electronic devices dominate the situation yet they are either supposed to be 'ignored'; the theatrical experience does not begin with a step into an auditorium filled with excited chatter and with a view of a stage already lit and prepared prior to the performance but with hands-on business. This kind of theatre is cluttered with equipment.

This chapter discusses how in the livecasting setting the material conditions of production are almost grotesquely emphasized: the livecast is positioned on the spectrum between film and theatre (performance) and, while incorporating especially cinematic aesthetics, is the hub for a new kind of theatricality. I am calling this mode of theatricality the material-theatrical as it creates or emphasizes a kind of theatre that manifests itself through objects. It is here that I see a parallel to Bertolt Brecht's dramaturgical theory. In his analytical essays, he inserts economic and technological vocabulary into his discussion of dramaturgy, viewing opera and theatre as 'Produktionsapparate', revealing the artists and writers not to be in control of the apparatus but rather the economically motivated apparatus to be in control of their work. They resemble suppliers that do not create but produce something that needs to be utilizable for the apparatus and not the other way round (cf. in Ostmeier 2001, 240). In two of his poems, 'The Curtains' and 'The Lighting', too, the focus is not primarily on the works of art or plays that are staged but rather on what they are made of and how theatre is made possible through processes of labour. More precisely, what makes the stagings (referring both to the mise-en-scène and to scaffolding more generally) work and what the plays are composed of takes up more space in the two poems. 'The Curtains' approaches Picasso's peace dove painted on a curtain not via what it symbolizes but via what it is made of – the first word of the poem is 'Paint'. It continues: 'Stretch *the cord of wire* behind / And there hang / *The screen that gently flutters* / With its two overlapping waves of gauze: / *The screen that lets* / The working woman disappear / Handing out her leaflets, / And Galileo disappear / Recanting' (Brecht 1961, 12, emphases added). The poem 'The Lighting' begins with an incantation: 'Electrician / Give us light on our stage. / How can we disclose / We playwrights and actors / Images to the world in semi-darkness? [. . .] Therefore flood full on / *What we have made with work* / *That the watcher may see* / The indignant peasant / Sit down upon the soil of Tavastland / As though it were her own' (Brecht 1961, 14, emphases added).

'The Curtains' is a celebration of the screen – it takes on its own life as it flutters gently, obscuring what is behind it, only to make entire worlds appear afterwards. Without it, neither suspense nor expectation would be created because the captions are projected onto it. The poem is a reminder to the speaker's friends – those working in the theatre, backstage – that the spectator must see and take in that the wires (as in: the intestines of theatre) are showing. All of this, the theatrical world, does not appear out of nowhere; it is made, and it is made through work. 'The Lighting', too, addresses the profanity of the magic of theatre in a prosaic tone. The electrician's help is needed to create images and whatever version of 'night' is to be evoked, it will be made of lamps and moons (again, object and signified are put side-by-side).

Brecht's two poems initiate my line of thought in this chapter which is concerned with unearthing the crucial role of the material and props in making theatre and their role in the context of livecasting more specifically. In the following I want to provide a few illustrations of 'unruly' objects, that is, objects that leave the peripheries and contribute to the text of the performance as well. It has become a common trope in contemporary theorizations of materiality that materiality resists representation.[2] Is it possible to approach this force and make it more palpable? In what areas does it become more manifest? To think of livecasting as a specific aesthetic form that puts the made-ness of performance (you see the wires, the cords) to the fore stands in contrast to the rhetoric surrounding livecasts which occludes the idea that, in the filming, a selection and heightening process of a given performance takes place. Wyver also critically speaks of the 'myth of non-mediation' around livecasts that evokes an 'outside broadcast fairy' that captures the performances (2014b, 109). This suggests that mediation and/or technologies are inherently detrimental to what many consider to be the purity of performance.

To deconstruct this binary, one needs to take on the perspective of the objects involved. This approach is informed by calls within theatre scholarship to study and acknowledge the role of objects, props and (backstage) craft more generally 'to understand the complete theatre event'(Monks 2014, 176). In 'In Defense of Craft', inspired by Walter Gropius' Bauhaus manifesto, Aoife Monks outlines the three main areas of scholarship in the study of costume that need to complement the study of directors, writers and actors: first, scholarship on performing and costume, and especially the costume's role in 'producing character and affect, its function as a ground for the possibilities of the body, tracing out the emotional and economic vulnerability that underlies the actor's relationship to stuff'(177); second, scholarship on labour relations, and third, on the ethics and values of practice, including considerations of the role of the archivist and curator in the afterlives of costume. Monks' claims about costumes refer to stage props more generally as well and have also been theorized by Andrew Sofer (2003) and Bert O. States. According to States, objects used on stage 'are always in danger of slipping from their semiotic moorings and piercing the image onstage with the assertion of their own claims to agency and subjectivity' (Monks 2013, 53).[3] As States puts it:

> Theater ingests the world of objects and signs only to bring images to life. In the image, a defamiliarized and desymbolized object is 'uplifted to the view' where we see it as being phenomenally heavy with itself. (1985, 37)

Considered thus, to use an object as part of an image is reductive; objects are always objects and, in the context of theatre, symbols. It is precisely in settings where theatre wants to create the most perfect illusion, however, where the objects' 'shudder' is most palpable. Hence my contention is that it is crucial to complement an analysis of the aesthetics of livecasting with what the technique does to the material(s) it is made of and how they – rather than being ingested by the workings of the spectacular livecasting set-up – refuse to settle into this setting and draw attention to themselves.

Brecht, too, saw a liberating potential in film technology to undermine the stupefying mimetism of the bourgeois novel, drama and film and this paves the way from a discussion of theatre per se to livecasting. He coined the term 'neue Apparate' ('new types of apparatus') with regard to film technology to distinguish 'the inventive capacity of the camera from its reactionary use by the ignorant entertainment industry' (Ostmeier 2001, 241). In his argumentation, film undermines the concept of an omniscient narrator typical for bourgeois art and provides an external perspective on characters, one that has an influence on both epic and dramatic forms. Reality is explicitly constructed; it is artificial and staged. 'Neue Apparate' refers to what a camera/camera work can achieve when it creates a film that is not veered towards mere entertainment. According to Brecht, the best film techniques are those which are least likely to produce an imitation of reality, thus making visible the functions of the apparatus. Film technology, read in this light, can be understood as a magnifier of what theatre does or can do. In Brecht's thinking, to praise the potential of certain film technologies is to see their potential as means to critique capitalism and its structures. Here the analogy between Brecht's view of the potential effect of laying bare the functions of the apparatus in the mid-twentieth century and livecasting in the twenty-first century does not work as well: with regard to livecasting, one may well hold that it perpetuates capitalistic structures and spectacularizes performance (see my discussion in the first part of Chapter 2). Yet there is a crucial difference between what function the form *could* have and the function and effect it *actually* has. When the form draws attention to itself, it precisely has the potential to, if not change then at least, temporarily suspend hierarchical structures.

There is another convergence between theatre and technologies in Brecht's thinking, as Walter Benjamin assesses:

> The forms of epic theatre correspond to the new technical forms – cinema and radio. [. . .] In film, the theory has become more and more accepted that the audience should be able to 'come in' at any point [. . .] For radio, with its public which can freely switch on or off at any moment, this becomes a strict necessity. Epic theatre introduces the same practice on stage. For epic theatre, as a matter of principle, there is no such thing as a latecomer. (1998, 6)

Of course, epic theatre is quite different from livecasting; yet the position of both forms in relation to technologies and new media is a similar one. To invoke Brecht here shows that livecasting is a continuation of a kind of theatre that relies on film technologies and their capacity to distort but also perfect. It is a kind of theatre that can expose the workings of the theatre (industry). In addition, it is a kind of theatre that is more prone to being 'consumed' as it is more consumer-friendly by being available to audiences closer to their homes in cinemas. It also does not leave anybody behind. Quite literally, nobody is left outside as, in contrast to the situation in the theatre, one does not have to wait until a scene change to be let into the auditorium of the cinema. This theatricality of livecasting, which is dependent on the material, invokes the following characteristics, concepts and practices:

   a) It invokes a synthesis between theatrical and cinematic modes that is conditioned by the presence of editing and filming techniques and that can be understood against the background of the aesthetics and history of filmed theatre as conceptualized by André Bazin in the 1960s, whose theories can be applied in a fruitful way to reflect on livecasting.[4]

b) It comprises and is a consequence of the 'spatially extended atmosphere' (Aebischer 2018, 122) that is created by the involved theatre institutions and that shifts our understanding of the materiality of the theatrical space on a macro- and micro-level. The stage work is only a part of 'an extended engagement with the play' (Bay-Cheng 2012, 33). Indeed, spectators are invited to pay more attention to the elements that the livecast production is comprised of.

c) Since this new theatrical form relies so much on technologies, there is a higher risk of glitches which can create awkwardness and make the experience of theatre porous; the realms of the reality of the production and the reality of watching it in a cinema bleed into each other. As a consequence, livecast-theatricality is tied to different dimensions of dis/comfort.

After introducing André Bazin's foundational writing on film versus theatre, this chapter further conceptualizes and illustrates these three dimensions of the material-theatrical by referring to recent NT Live productions (from 2018 to 2019) of *All My Sons*, *Small Island*, *Antony and Cleopatra*, *Julie* and *The Madness of King George III*. The examples illustrate the three different ways in which the televisual/cinematic[5] frame of the livecast can (or cannot) enhance the theatrical quality of the play: first, when the framing relies too much on cinematic and televisual effects, this disturbs the theatrical quality of the play (*All My Sons* and *The Madness of King George III*). Second, the foregrounding of props as props and the artificiality of the mise-en-scène can enhance the theatricality of the play when the audience's awareness is raised to 'what makes theatre theatre', such as the labour that goes into the theatrical production of space (*Small Island* and *Antony and Cleopatra*). Third, the peculiarities of the cinematic livecasting frame can create the effect of structural similarities between the experiences of the protagonist of a play and that of the audience (*Small Island*, *Julie*).

Theatrical and cinematic modes – filmed theatre

As Thomas Postlewait and Tracy C. Davis point out, 'the idea of theatricality has achieved an extraordinary range of meanings, making it everything from an act to an attitude, a style to a semiotic system, a medium to a message.

It is a sign empty of meaning; it is the meaning of all signs' (2003, 1). The concept 'can be abstracted from the theatre itself and then applied to any and all aspects of human life', either as a mode of representation or as a style of behaviour or an interpretative model/theoretical concept to describe identities, ceremonies or spectacles (1). I use 'theatricality' to describe the characteristics of the theatrical event, that is, how the interplay of (the labour of) producers, performers, spectators and the material creates the event.

Theatre has been criticized since antiquity for displaying diverse characteristics: it can be both excessive and empty, offer more (than reality? everyday life?) and less. Put negatively, it tends to be deceptive and affected, and at the same time it 'conceals or masks an inner emptiness, a deficiency or absence of that to which it refers' (Postlewait and Davis 2003, 5). The claim that theatricality can be applied to other aspects of human life as well is, conversely, repeated by André Bazin, a highly influential figure in the development of film theory and criticism in the 1940s and 1950s, when he distinguishes between dramatic and theatrical reality. He writes of drama as 'the soul of the theater [. . .] [which] sometimes inhabits other bodies' (Bazin 1967a, 81). Theatre would not exist if it was not dramatic, while other texts do not need this quality. Still, the dramatic has an influence on all branches of the arts and especially cinema. Bazin even argues that 'half of literature and three quarters of the existing films are branches of theater' (1967a, 82). With such a statement Bazin anticipates the role of theatre and drama in the current media society, indeed their capacity to generate 'some of the master models and metaphors' of this day and age (Voigts-Virchow 2000, 7). Voigts refers to Willems' term 'Inszenierungsgesellschaften' (1998, best translated into English as 'societies of dramatization') and Bourdieu's characterization of television as relying on dramatization as 'it puts an event on stage, puts it in images. In doing so, it exaggerates the importance of that event, its seriousness, and its dramatic, even tragic character' (Bourdieu 1996, 19). In the last decades of the twentieth century, especially the mass media 'have provided outlets for drama derivatives (post-theatrical drama)' (Voigts-Virchow 2000, 7) and, in turn, different media forms have provided the material and context in/for performances, a development described as post-dramatic theatre (Lehmann 1999, 28–39). In other words: the dramatic does not need the theatre and still can find its way into narratives, be they literary or everyday societal narratives.

What Bazin sees as a complication is that the theatrical text synthesizes the dramatic and the theatrical in such a way that it is impossible to extract one from the other. For this reason, novels can be and are often dramatized while it does not happen often that a novel is made from a play: 'It is as if the theater stood at the end of an irreversible process of aesthetic refinement'

(Bazin 1967a, 83). Would livecasting, then, make theatre less refined in pushing it one notch down on the ladder of aesthetic refinement? Susan Sontag's question whether cinema is 'the successor, the rival, or the revivifier of the theatre' (1966, 33) still resonates today, especially when read in the context of Auslander's claim that 'at the level of cultural economy, theatre (and live performance generally) and the mass media are rivals, not partners' (2008, 1). Livecasts, too, are embedded in this discourse and form a kind of bridge between mass-media forms and theatre. Yet one might need to think about them as complements that create a new mode and adaptive instantiation. Livecasting is, as is often the case with new trends, not undisputed, both among academics and actors. For instance, the actor Rory Kinnear was among the first to utter his scepticism when the initiative was launched at the National Theatre and his fear that actors would prioritize the screened performance since it would reach more people (in Rosenthal 2013, 795). Similarly, Michelle Terry, who played Helena in Marianne Elliott's production of *All's Well That Ends Well*, which was the second NT Livecast in 2009, said that she was, as most people, 'wary: "How are we going to maintain what is inherently theatrical?"' (Rosenthal 2013, 795).

Bazin is helpful in this context to get a historical perspective. When theorizing the merits of filmed theatre – a phrase that had at the time he was writing been used mostly deprecatingly (1967a, 81) – he uses the example of Charlie Chaplin to argue that cinema can actually relieve theatre of its imperfections by going beyond it. For instance, he says about the gag that, when performed on stage, it is directed by the kinds and amount of laughs that it provokes and to which the performer has to adjust, thus potentially altering the pace he or she initially had in mind, and usually making them exaggerate for greater effect. On screen, Chaplin could attain 'mathematical perfection of situation and gesture whereby the maximum effect is obtained in the minimum of time' (79). Bazin then constructs the analogy that theatre is like an organism that contains a set of dramatic facts and situations that have been stopped and left unrealized – 'congenitally atrophied' (79) – until the appearance of cinema.

The choice of an adjective relating to vision is noteworthy here and relevant for the livecasting context: in the same way that film helps theatre recover from a condition of incomplete vision, the idea of a gaze that is directed in a supportive way is central to the marketing of livecasts. They offer 'the best seat in the house', one in which there are no restricted views. As Alison Stone points out, '[c]lose shots create some of the intimacy of television, while an "eye of God" aerial shot or a sweeping crane shot is more cinematic' (2016, 632). She is right in emphasizing, however, that material edited in such a way 'exceeds the fixed viewpoint from any one seat, including aerial shots unavailable to the house audience' (2016, 632). A new gaze is created, one that while being comprised of several different shots, presents a new totality normally unavailable to spectators.

Bazin also speaks of cinema's capacity to defy restrictions of time and space that are in a sense limiting to theatrical action and argues that if

> by cinema we understand liberty of action in regard to space, and freedom to choose your angle of approach to the action, then filming a play should give the setting a breadth and reality unattainable on the stage. It would also free the spectator from his seat and by varying the shots give an added quality to the acting. (Bazin 1967a, 86)

That is, a good example of filmed theatre would create a mutually beneficial synthesis of cinematic and theatrical characteristics. Bazin then presents a successful and an unsuccessful example of filmed theatre, both of which provide strikingly fitting points of comparison for recent NT Live productions. His negative example is *Le Médecin Malgré Lui* (he refers to the version from 1934, directed by Pierre Weil[6]), with which he found fault due to its inharmonious combination of cinematic and theatrical elements:

> The dramatic primacy of the word is thrown off center by the additional dramatization that the camera gives to the setting. Finally and above all, a certain artificiality, an exaggerated transformation of the décor, is totally incompatible with that realism which is of the essence of the cinema. (Bazin 1967a, 86)

What Bazin means with the 'dramatization' that the camera gives to the setting can be explained in Bourdieu's terms, namely that scenes are put into images and thus exaggerated (see Bourdieu 1996, 19). Bazin is even more specific in his disdain for this version of *Le Médecin Malgré Lui* and describes the opening shots of the film: the camera takes in several bits of a forest ('une *vraie* forêt' [Bazin 1951, 898]) and somewhat unnecessarily aims to capture the effect the sunrays have on the leaves of the trees. These shots are followed by the first dialogue of the play between the character Sganarelle and his wife, who wear theatre costumes, which give them a grotesque appearance ('le malheureux Sganarelle et sa femme dont les costumes de théâtre ont ici l'air de déguisement grotesques', [Bazin 1951, 899]). It is, therefore, the yoking together of seemingly *real* and blatantly *artificial* elements that does not work in this instance. The costumes are theatre costumes and appear out of place within the frame of a cinema screen.

The viewing experience is belittled because, one is neither watching a play nor a film – what such a statement refers to is actually a fear still surrounding livecasts that was articulated by Nicholas Hytner when he attended the livecast of *Phèdre*: 'I watched it in the BFI cinema, next door to the National. I had kept from everybody a residual fear that it would look like a bad movie. But you almost forgot you were in a cinema' (Hytner 2018, 272). A 'bad movie' here would mean that there is a 'rough cut' feel to it or a mismatch between the theatrical acting and the limits of the screen. When the framing relies too much on cinematic and televisual effects, this disturbs the theatrical quality of the play. This could be seen in the NT Live production of *All My Sons* that ran at the Old Vic from 20 April to 8 June 2019 and was broadcast live on 14 May 2019. On the one hand, this livecast promised what Bazin singles out as central to cinema, perhaps apart from there being 'plenty of action' (typical for Arthur Miller, the conflicts are negotiated and related in dialogues, the action of the play covers a few days and the setting is Kate and Joe Keller's house): the camera could take in the elaborate décor of the stage and the main actors – Bill Pullman and Sally Field – are both 'a somebody', primarily known for their work acting in Hollywood movies. Impressions of the realistic stage design that blended in with the Old Vic's interior were already presented ahead of the livecast, together with a shot of the camera equipment (Figure 11). It is telling that the page listing camera prompts and the camera itself take up most of the picture and the auditorium and bits of the stage recede into the background; one can only see the stage in its entirety on the camera screen in a miniature version. What is implied here is that the camera has – quite literally – a grip on the performance; this tweet introduces a show that can only be seen

Figure 11 Screen capture of @NTLive Twitter account showing the filming equipment being set up in the Old Vic Theatre a few hours before the start of the NT Live broadcast of *All My Sons* on 14 May 2019.

via a fixed frame, and in this case a high-quality filming apparatus. The tweet illustrates what Bazin has called cinema's 'inferiority complex in the presence of an older and more literary art, for which the cinema proceeds to overcompensate by the "superiority" of its technique – which in turn is mistaken for aesthetic superiority' (1967a, 87).

In the case of the *All My Sons* livecast, the high resolution of the cameras is detrimental to the presentation of the stage design, which is supposed to be warm and autumnal (an atmosphere that is well captured in the in-situ performance and can be taken in even from the severely restricted bench in Lilian Baylis Circle, where I was seated on 15 May 2019). But in the screen/cinema version it resembles a cheap TV aesthetic as seen in sitcoms, enhanced by the fact that, as mentioned, the entire action takes place in front of the Kellers' house, with the characters either sitting on a bench, the porch steps or next to them. Because of the resolution, it is impossible not to see that the lawn the characters are walking on is synthetic – the effect that is created is cold and fake. While Billington in his review of the play praised it for perfectly fitting into an age 'of flux and fakery when lies masquerade as truth' (2019a), he was referring to the content; on a formal level, the fakery of the situation is exposed in an uncomfortable way. Certain audio-visual techniques 'work' for live relays; others do not, depending on the degree of naturalism evinced and on what the human eye is being able to replicate (Cochrane and Bonner 2014, 128), that is an impression of artificiality vs. naturalism.

At the Hackney Picturehouse, where I attended the livecast, this fakery was also enhanced by a technical glitch: the sound level was too low and the volume was only turned up after about thirty minutes. In two scenes that were particularly noteworthy, the TV aesthetic brought about a comic effect, which – although corresponding with the content of the scenes – added a decidedly slapstick quality to the film that is untypical for theatre. When Katie asked Annie – who was first in a relationship with Chris' brother, who died in the war – if she was going out, this exchange was presented in a mid-angle shot showing Chris in the background on the porch steps right in the middle between the two women anxiously awaiting the response (Figure 12).

The audience knew that he was about to propose to Katie – something his mother was not aware of – and the shot framed his impatience. The audience was 'in on the joke' whereas Katie was not; this particular framing captured Chris' facial expression squeezed in between the two women. In another scene, when the Kellers' neighbour suggested to Annie her Dad, who was falsely accused of committing a crime in the war, was lucky not to have been executed in the first place, there was a reaction shot of Bill Pullman as Joe making an awkward face that created many laughs in the cinema. Such an

Figure 12 'You Go Out Much?' – Screen capture of a scene from *All My Sons* directed by Jeremy Herrin, directed for the screen by Ross MacGibbon © NT At Home Collection 2019. All rights reserved.

effect of laughter was even more out of place since it was later revealed that it had been Joe who knowingly shipped defective aircraft engine cylinder heads, and not his partner (Annie's father). In general, reaction shots like these are often used and, while certainly providing comic relief or increasing a moment that was meant to be funny in the first place, they do resemble the aesthetics of TV shows such as *The Office*, where the camera zooms into one of the characters' faces to bring home mostly feelings of awkwardness or conspiracy between spectators and characters. With regard to capturing the overall stage design of *All My Sons*, there was a clash between the aforementioned blatant artificiality of the homey setting and the elegant and old interior architecture of the Old Vic. While in the theatre performance, the green of the stage blended in organically with the green of the theatre's balconies, on-screen the impression that the stage was a box that had been violently planted there was increased.

The livecast, therefore, was uneven in that the dialectic between theatrical conventions and cinematic realism was not resolved. Something similar happened with *The Madness of King George III* which was livecast from the Nottingham Playhouse as part of NT Live on 20 November 2018. The production was focused on Mark Gatiss, known to many because of his appearance in the BBC's *Sherlock* series, who played the main part, but the amount of reaction shots of the King was grotesque. There was an attempt to imitate a stylistic device that occasionally works in TV or cinema films, namely slow-motion shots. These shots were employed in scenes where a dialogue took place downstage and the other characters 'froze' in the background. When filmed, the two groups of characters were equally visible: the camera also showed the frozen characters closer-up, which undermined the 'freezing' as a strategy of foregrounding the 'unfrozen' characters.

What is happening in these examples is that techniques from the cinema are layered over theatrical aesthetics, creating an incongruous clash. Bazin refers to a successful instance of filmed theatre that does one crucial thing differently, namely Laurence Olivier's *Henry V* (1944), which does not pretend that it is merely a movie that is superior to the play, but a film of a performance of a play. In the beginning, a travelling shot that lasts more than two minutes places the viewers in the courtyard of an Elizabethan inn, which is firmly within the conventions of the theatre: 'Never for one moment is *Henry V* called "filmed theater." The film exists so to speak side by side with the theatrical presentation, in front of and behind the stage' (Bazin 1967a, 89).

Since the beginning of the production of screen versions of theatre plays, and especially Shakespeare plays (see Wyver 2014b), there has been a tension between what are characterized as, on the one hand, the theatrical elements of a broadcast and, on the other hand, the televisual and cinematic elements. The televisual and cinematic are primarily grounded in close-ups, especially during a dialogue between two characters (Sullivan 2014) whereas the theatrical is 'more open, contingent, unpredictable' (Sullivan 2014), that is, relying on an interplay of camera angles and shots that take the 'stage scape' into account.

As a consequence, when watching a theatre livecast in a cinema, audiences 'expect things to move', as Matthew Amos has put it. He directed *Julie* for the screen in 2018, a play about a manic, lonely, upper-class London woman, adapted by Polly Stenham from August Strindberg's *Miss Julie*, and the camera script and filming added an additional structural layer of meaning onto Carrie Cracknell's dramaturgy. Indeed, the livecast illustrates the effect of what happens when things do not move and how the cinematic can foreground the material of a production. As Amos put it in an interview with me:

> I think of cinema in a language of television, which means that people expect things to move. It can be quite disconcerting if they don't. So to take that decision, especially at the end of *Julie*, to be able to just go [hand gesture 'wide']. [. . .] Because if I do cut to it, then I'm imposing what I think people should be looking at. Whereas if it's left like that then the decision is left up to the viewer, the same as if they are in the theatre, there they are making that decision themselves, rather than me making it for them. [. . .] [T]here was a lot of thought that went into it, and it did feel like cutting away from it was gonna be hard. (2022)

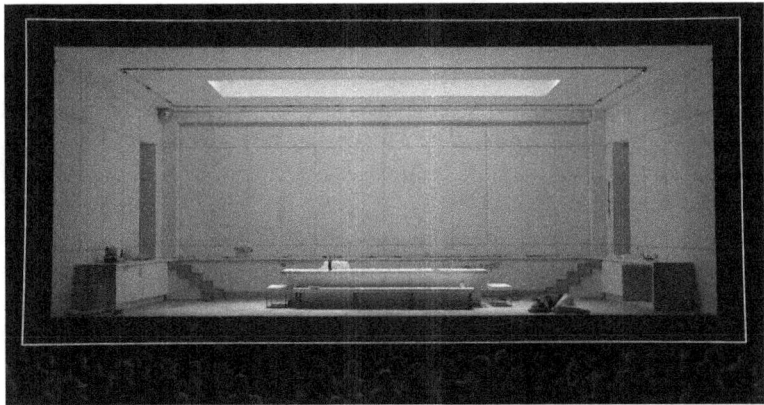

Figure 13 Screen capture of the final scene from *Julie* directed by Carrie Cracknell, directed for the screen by Matthew Amos © NT At Home collection 2018. All rights reserved.

For Amos it is of crucial importance to think about how things look through a lens, within a frame and what their position within the frame does to the viewer. In the case of the final scene, which lasts for five minutes, the frame of the set is doubled by the frame of the camera, and into the final minutes of the scene even tripled by an additional frame of a bright light around the set (Figure 13). In its stillness and disconcerting calmness it both leaves the freedom of where to look to the viewers and also aesthetically emphasizes the despair and loneliness of the protagonist to take her life. It also highlights the presence of the stage and the in-situ audience who can be clearly seen in the shot.

That the tension or competition between the cinematic and theatrical is a mutually beneficial relationship, can also be seen in the *Small Island* livecast first shown in cinemas on 27 June 2018. Much like Olivier's *Henry V*, it does not hide the theatrical conventions at play but embeds them in the frame provided by the film genre's aesthetics. The foregrounding of props as props and the artificiality of the mise-en-scène can enhance the theatricality of the play and focus, for instance, on the importance of a trained actor's voice and on the labour that goes into the theatrical production of space. *Small Island* was adapted from Andrea Levy's novel for the stage by Helen Edmundson and has been called 'one of the most important plays of the year' (Billington 2019b). The story of first-generation Jamaican immigrants in post-war Britain is a tumultuous polyphonic novel and the adaptation captures its hurtling (and hurting) energy: it shows theatre exercising a truly national function. From page to stage to screen, the livecast, too, captures this energy by employing a varied mix of cinematic and theatrical elements. In analogy to Sarah Bay-Cheng's (2012) statement that live performance is not 'a privileged site of temporary encounter' (33) but another form of mediated interaction with its texts, contexts and artefacts, the *Small Island* livecast is framed with texts – a detailed schedule at the Curzon Bloomsbury where I watched it, several 'Who's Who' slides before the show – and with its own artefacts from within.

Cinema techniques can make us more aware of the boundaries and the materiality of the stage and enhance the theatrical effect and thus a play's made-ness, that is the sense of being constructed of different parts. The use of microphones, for instance, draws our attention to the enunciation and articulation of the actors/characters that we can effortlessly hear. In the case of *Small Island*, the Jamaican English spoken by several of the play's protagonists heightens the immersion into the world they are about to leave behind. As Brandon Hunter observes with regard to the RSC's livecast of *Hamlet* (2016) and Paapa Essiedu's eponymous role (and his diction and control of breath, among other things),

> the elements broadcast crews endeavour to preserve – like the particular qualities of actors' vocal production – indicate aspects of theatrical stage production understood as key to its translation into a new form, effectively emphasizing, clarifying, and reifying the properties that qualify as constitutive of virtuosic theatrical production. (Hunter 2021, 15)

When the sound is mixed and balanced in such a way as to 'provide an optimum experience for the broadcast audience', the way actors control their breath, how their voices resonate and how clear their diction is actually 'implies the significance and specificity of that kind of virtuosic production to the theatre itself' (Hunter 2019, 22). The awareness of the importance of actors' virtuosic speech for successful theatrical performance is the key criterion. In other words, here the form of the film conversely enhances the theatrical quality of the play. The specific cinematic technology and materiality actually puts the focus on the theatrical, rather than superimposing a filmic or cinematic layer onto it.

In Act One, Scene Two of *Small Island*, Queenie tells the audience about her upbringing and her parents, who come from a long tradition of butchers:

> I don't come from a place where you do much imagining. Growing up, I knew just one thing – that I didn't want to spend my whole life

on that stinking farm, with my dad butchering the animals in the shed, helping my mother with the meat pies, swilling out the blood from my brothers' overalls. (Edmundson, 2019, I.2, 29)

What is at stake here is Queenie's complete rejection of the future her parents have envisioned for her – she dreams of a life far away from the village of Lincolnshire where one's hands are constantly covered in animal blood. Her parents do not seem to notice this anymore. There is a gigantic pig in the centre of the stage and Queenie's mother swings about the pig's intestines like a lasso. As opposed to what is normally the case in a film where things seem realistic and do not draw attention to themselves, the extremely high resolution of the livecast cameras changes the experience of the production: a true sensation of being disgusted does not occur for the spectators in the cinemas because the thingness and artificiality of the props are so blatant. The livecasting techniques shatter the illusion and in this particular case create a similar distance between the spectators and the artificiality of the play as there is a distance between Queenie and the life of her parents. The peculiarities of the cinematic livecasting frame can, therefore, create the effect of structural similarities between the experiences of the protagonist of a play and that of the audience.

The second example of enhanced theatricality occurs right at the end of the first act. As Hunter has emphasized (see 2019, 22), a livecast includes the moments before and after a production to capture a sense of the spatial reality of the theatre. The final scene in *Small Island* before the break is one of the most powerful moments in the play: Hortense has agreed to marry Gilbert and give him enough money to be able to go to England. Once he has settled in, he promises to send after her. This is a purely pragmatic transaction. Yet the poetic set design by Katrina Lindsay endows the moment of parting with solemnity and gravitas: we see the silhouettes and shadows of those embarking on the Windrush, with Hortense standing right in front of it, with her back to the audience. Right before Gilbert is about to disappear out of sight, he lifts his hat in a gesture of goodbye – and Hortense, whom we have encountered to be rather reserved and controlled in her gestures and facial expressions, breaks out in a violent wave that shakes up her entire body. Her gaze is firmly directed towards this ship on a canvas that signifies all the longing for a better future that is bottled up inside of her. A few seconds later, this is what we see (Figure 14): The powerful canvas crumbles; it is no longer a signifier but material, and the stage in front of it is vacuum-cleaned. Hortense's dream is echoed in the spectators' memory of the theatrical bombast witnessed moments before. What is suggested in this production, when the material takes on centre stage, when scene changes within the play

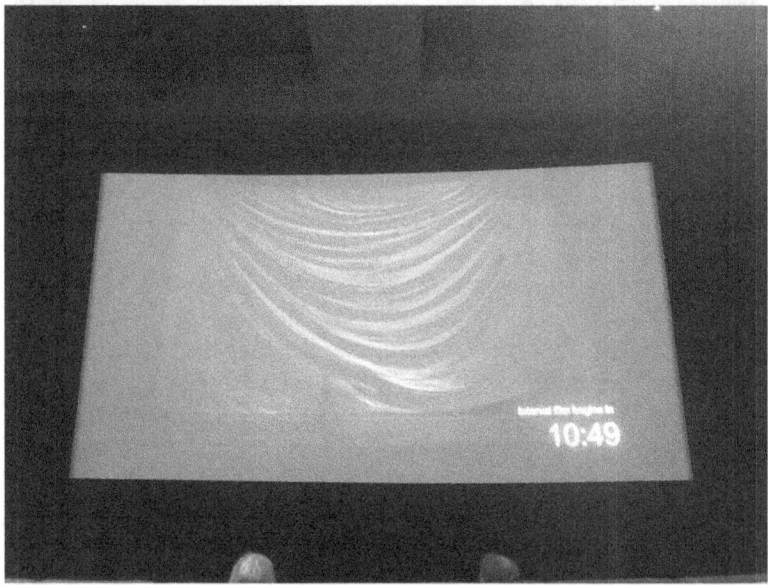

Figure 14 First picture: Screen capture of Leah Harvey as Hortense in *Small Island*, directed by Rufus Norris, directed for the screen by Tony Grech-Smith © NT At Home Collection 2019. All rights reserved. Second picture: Crumbling Canvas – the screen in the Bloomsbury Curzon Cinema, London, during the NT Live broadcast of *Small Island*, taken during the intermission on 14 July 2019 by the author.

are as visible as the scene work itself in the interval, is the significance and meaning of the space(s) between scenes and the ways in which material and technologies create the transitions; the cinematic space and cinema screen becomes the stage for the workings of theatrical production. The theatrical skeleton is laid bare, and to use a Marxist phrasing, the material conditions of production are exposed and the 'theatrical image is understood as the effect of workaday processes – fundraising, rehearsal, blocking, directing, and so on' (Johnson 2012, 52).

For the livecast audience, the crumbling canvas and the fact that the stage is being vacuum-cleaned appear on the same screen which a few moments before showed the mise-en-scène of the play. Since there is no intermission film, this shot of the canvas being taken down is the filler between the two acts. The livecast therefore enhances theatricality because it foregrounds what we see as a theatrical production. On the one hand, sitting in the front row of a live theatre production may make spectators as aware of the equipment involved. On the other hand, and this is the crucial difference, a live theatre broadcast presents sequences of a performance, cuts it down into images to be dissected. In the cinema setting, even the cleaning of the stage and the canvas being taken down is presented within a frame – the same frame that a second ago only contained the text of the play. Thus, a slight recontextualization of what is central to the narrative occurs (see Wyver 2020). Most importantly, this ending to the first act of the play does not hide the theatrical conventions at play but embeds them in the frame provided by cinematic aesthetics. Livecasting thus offers a perspective on the material theatre is made of and shifts our gaze from the centre to the periphery that encompasses not only the play's story that is told but the story of theatrical labour within which this story is embedded.

Spatially extended atmospheres: The materiality of the theatrical space shifts

As Kate McLuskie and Kate Rumbold argue, theatre institutions such as the NT, the RSC and the Globe, actually use new technologies to heighten the materiality of their physical sites by, for instance, making it possible for audiences to gain virtual access to their sites (2014, 203). Yet Diana Taylor's remark that concepts such as 'site', 'presence' and with that the ephemeral and embodiment need to be recalibrated in the digital age (cf. Taylor 2003, 4–5) is apt. Indeed, new technologies and livecasting especially do create 'spatially extended atmospheres' (Aebischer 2018, 122) – a formerly single-medium space, the stage, becomes 'a hybrid space accommodating multiple media' (Greenhalgh 2018, 35) and being watched and commented upon via multiple media. At the same time, by being so present in and central to these productions, the technologies employed bring back a new awareness for the sites themselves and the constitutive material elements involved in making a theatre play come into place.

There is a certain irony in looking at livecasts from the perspective of the equipment involved. Indeed, one gets the impression that the theatre companies that produce livecasts want them to be transparent – that is, to deny the fact of mediatization as much as possible. As Jay Bolter and Richard Grusin put it, 'a transparent interface is one that erases itself, so that the user would no longer be aware of confronting a medium, but instead would stand in an immediate relationship to the contents of the medium' (1996, 318). Susanne Greenhalgh notes that the 'care taken to remove technical equipment from view is a notable feature of all the films so far' (2014, 259). Regular NT Live broadcast director Robin Lough believes that 'the broadcast process should, as far as was feasible, remain invisible and unacknowledged' (in Wyver 2015, 296). That the livecasts are 'not making a movie' is also a 'mantra' for RSC Live (Wyver 2015, 290). This clashes with the insight that these productions – much like television's adaptations of previously staged performances, especially of Shakespeare since the 1930s – are examples of mediated theatre that Bay-Cheng, to reiterate, defines as 'any theatrical performance originally created for live performance [. . .] and subsequently recorded onto any visually reproducible medium including film, videotape, or digital formats, presented as two-dimensional moving images on screen' (2007, 37). Indeed, even conventionally live theatre is 'largely activated by and within mediated networks', in which the stage work itself comprises only a part of 'an extended engagement with the play' (Bay-Cheng 2012, 33). Staging, set design, cuts to a text are the products of mediation: of the director's interpretation of a given playtext. Livecasts are doubly mediated, as the interpretation of the play director is interpreted a second time by the multi-camera director of the broadcast: in this sense, camera shots can inform the broadcast audience of the relationship between performer and in-house audience, thus providing a commentary about theatre, and about the text and one's place within the other network.

At the beginning of this chapter, I described the situation before the camera rehearsal of *Antony and Cleopatra*, which illustrates how the materiality of the theatrical space shifts in the livecasting context. Even though all audience members had to switch off their mobile phones so that there were no disturbing sounds and lights, one could not help but see two very piercing lights coming from two of the cameras in the auditorium.

Capturing the Atmosphere 95

While they were indeed very quiet, there was a swift swooshing sound coming from them when they moved on their rails, which must be quite audible to the people sitting directly next to or behind them. When the play started, it was like being at a film set and the presence of the equipment made it impossible to immerse oneself even for a minute in an illusion of the reality of theatre. Instead, a very strong sense of the reality of acting was created – paradoxically, the presence of equipment created higher levels of familiarity with the production because it was clear that this was (a) play. Crucially, while the fourth wall would normally only (occasionally) be broken by the actors, here it seemed to be the other way round: when the camera that was fixed to the crane moved closer and closer to the stage (visibly casting a shadow onto the stairs on stage), there was something coming from within the auditorium that smashed this distance between actors and spectators (Figure 15).

Many audience members observed what the cameras were doing and watched the team operating them providing another performance. Both the actors and the spectators had signed the unwritten agreement that they were ignoring that the theatrical space was invaded – 'please ignore the cameras, as we want you to enjoy the production'. And yet, by being intruded upon, by being told to pretend that everything was the same even though it was impossible

Figure 15 A sketch of the stage of *Antony and Cleopatra* directed by Simon Godwin in the National Theatre's Olivier Theatre during the camera rehearsal performance for NT Live on 5 December 2018, as imagined by Stella Toonen in a conversation with the author.

not to see the cameras, a new kind of proxemics, as referring to the role that physical distance plays in face-to-face communication, could materialize: one in which the cameras reminded us of the playfulness of the theatrical situation. There were two groups of people, one sitting, one mostly standing, facing each other, both pretending they were not actually aware of the others (actual bodies that were very close) apart from their roles as performers/spectators, while this awareness formed a main part of the reason both groups were there in the first place. There were almost didactic moments when the camera on the crane zoomed close to the stage and then back again, making the audience aware of the fact that *this* was a particularly crucial moment in the play.

But rather than estranging audiences from actors I argue that to watch a performance in the presence of camera equipment and with the awareness that what you are watching is filmed from different angles makes it even more theatrical than if no equipment was there. When there is no intrusion or interruption (if only in the way one's gaze is directed), it is easier to fall into a sort of lull and willingly go along with the illusion that is being created. Yet watching the performance side-by-side with at least seven cameras relativizes one's own status of being a spectator and perhaps even the perceived monopoly on exclusivity ('This is for me!'). The equipment enhances the liveness of the situation because this liveness is simultaneously being contested and exposed as fragile and arbitrary. While we turn off our devices, bigger ones next to us are turned on. In his poem 'Weigel's Props' Brecht describes how each item is 'picked by hand, / The buckle, pewter box, strap and bullet pouch [. . .] Everything is chosen / According to age / Uses / And beauty / By knowing eyes and her / Net-making bread-baking / Soup-cooking hands / At home with reality' (Brecht 1961, 22). NT Live's bullet pouches and ammunition are satellites, cameras, cables and cranes – all of these are objects that function as second-level props. Most importantly, they are essential parts of this particular form of mediation.

The performance that I saw was livecast the next night. Without an announcement in the auditorium, the presenter started reading from a teleprompter (on a camera on a crane); she did not have a microphone but stood in the first row up in the circle with a spotlight on her. There was an awkward silence in the auditorium, several people giggled and pointed to the cameras. When she was finished, some people clapped. While the cinema audiences were shown the introductory film (Simon Godwin talking about staging the play), the presenter turned directly to the audience in the Olivier and asked us – in case we had never been to 'one of these things'– to not be afraid to show our feelings and react as we would if there were no cameras. Only then would the cinema audiences be able to pick up on the atmosphere in the theatre. This was followed by urgent reminders to make sure no sounds or lights from any mobile devices interfered with the broadcast equipment.

Thus, in fact, the livecast experience, both in the theatre on the night it is filmed and in the cinema, makes it impossible to perceive the technologies as invisible. With reference to the myth of non-mediation one would assume that livecasts feed into the claims of film apparatus theory, as introduced by Jean-Louis Baudry, which problematizes the highly mediated form of the cinema and demystifies the cinematic spectacle as part of a larger ideological framework. According to this theory, the physical layout of the theatre space produces a spectatorship that falsely identifies with the onscreen subject – the spectator is unaware of the apparatus producing the filmic image (Baudry 1986). Yet when theatre is pushed from stage to screen, a shift occurs from the potential of an all-enveloping mimetic setting to a setting in which the dwelling of the overall set-up on the material creates an anti-mimetic atmosphere. As the preceding analysis has shown, this applies both to the atmospheric space in the theatre and the cinema.

According to Bazin, the fundamental difference between theatre and cinema is that they are based on different approaches to the organization of space. In the theatre, the stage is marked out as a materially enclosed area, whereas the cinema 'denies any frontiers to action' (1967b, 105). As we are incited to imagine the off-screen space as well, Wyver (2014b, 118) insists that it is necessary to conserve these theatrical characteristics in screen adaptations of stagings because they contribute to an understanding of the space of the theatre. One is reminded here of Olivier's *Henry V* and the fact that usually in livecasts both the stage and the first rows of spectators are visible. The two groups of spectators (in the theatre and the cinema), and the question whether they are visible or not, also play an important role in reconfiguring and expanding the theatrical space as part of the livecast. Seeing the theatre audience from one's seat in the cinema can, but does not have to, emphasize distance. As Parker-Starbuck puts it, livecasts combine audience bodies and performer bodies with an object technology; crucially,

> the transmission via satellite [. . .] masks itself as cinematic while also representing a live feed. The show would still go on without the technology, but only for those in the theatrical, not the cinematic, spaces. [. . .] [F]or cinematic viewers the bodies remain distanced and fixed on their screens. This fixity or capture within the technological apparatus resonates throughout this category, especially in relation to the need to expand the commercial audiences across the distances. (2015, 72–3)

While this argument insists on separation and a kind of disconnection between two groups of spectators that is caused by the involved technologies, in the livecasting context the technologies contribute to an extension of the theatrical space. They create an idea of the stage that goes beyond its initially laid out boundaries, bringing about a revision of even relatively recent definitions of theatrical space.

Making the theatrical experience porous: Stuttering screens

Thinking about livecasting through materiality also means thinking about it through the practices it turns inside out. Shifting the focus from specificities of the genres of film and theatre to the notion of space, in its final section this chapter thinks about materiality in the livecasting context in connection with the effects of an increased reliance on technologies in performance which brings about a higher risk of glitches that can create awkwardness and make the experience of theatre porous. Paul and Levy define the term 'glitch' as referring to 'images and objects that have been tampered with' or 'corrupted' and outline that this quality can be created 'by using machines or digital tools in methods different from their normative modalities' (2015, 31). Betancourt argues that a 'glitch aesthetic' brings to the centre the peripheral and 'superficial flaws' we experience in encounters with the digital (2017, 7) and has the capacity to re-materialize, disrupt and disturb 'the aura of the digital' as 'a self-productive domain, infinite, capable of creating value without expenditure' (15). When glitches occur during both regular performances but even more so livecasts which rely first and foremost on functioning screens, these moments bring about different dimensions of dis/comfort, the latter of which being a central marker of the contemporary theatre-going experience.[7]

In all kinds of performance, moments where technologies fail cannot be programmed or planned; they are loaded with potential and risk (of failure). Of course, every time when any production relies on the use of technical equipment there is the risk of failure; in fact, in the case of livecasts glitches happen relatively rarely, as there is an entire team of camera operators and vision mixers who are alert and can adjust, as Amos has described it. When a glitch occurs, he says, 'There's nothing you can do about it! Part of it, for me, [is] that obviously, it's live, and hopefully, people who are watching it go "Woo! Woops!" and they understand it's a live thing. [. . .] Sometimes things go wrong, I think it's just the way it goes' (Amos 2022).

Typical technical glitches include slight delays in the transmission or interruptions in the video and/or audio played. For instance, during the first part of the livecast of *The Madness of King George III* at the Barbican on 20

November 2018 there was a slight mismatch between audio and video. A few audience members found this so distressing that they complained about it to members of staff after the show. Three days later, the Barbican sent an email to all those visitors who had shared their address when booking a ticket, apologizing for the 'technical difficulties' that made the viewing experience 'frustrating' and caused 'disappointment and inconvenience' and issued refunds to everybody. The apology also included the additional explanation that 'While we do our utmost to deliver the highest standard of cinema projection, there are times when technical issues occur and, rarely, we are unable to resolve these in real time' (Barbican 2018), which also drew attention to the additional pressure that was exerted on those operating the equipment since editing was not possible in a live situation. Why can glitches be so unsettling? As Baudry puts it, film 'lives on the denial of difference' (1986, 290); it consists of a succession of images that are different from each other, but the existence of this succession is ignored, forgotten or simply 'not seen'. When there happens 'a breakdown in the recreation of movement, when the spectator is brought abruptly back to discontinuity', the effects are disturbing because all of a sudden the technical apparatus can no longer be forgotten (1986, 291). In the livecasting setting, thus, such a throwback onto the imperfections of screen performance emphasizes the lack that cinema audiences are confronted with in contrast to theatre audiences and the distance to the actual performance; it brings about the awkward awareness that one is missing out on something. And it also puts the materiality of the mediated performance to the fore.

Figure 16 is a typical example of a situation where the experience of comfort is endangered and how it is resolved. This indeed reads like a live chat more commonly associated with a ticket booking website or an online shop. The event attended is nothing 'magical' but a product to be consumed; if there is a flaw, the NT Live team is immediately there to *fix* it. The NT seems to take responsibility for the experience of all spectators, also those at the cinemas – it becomes clear that they are invested in ensuring comfort by responding to complaints quickly via social media. As this virtual exchange shows, the concept of presence is transferred from theatre to cinema. Through this, there is a sense of liveness even though one is longer present and even though there is also distance through mediation. Mediation connects three groups of people: those in the cinema, those in charge of maintaining the Twitter account and those in the theatre. Spatial and – in the case of Encore broadcasts, that is broadcasts that are transmitted on later nights than the one when they were filmed – temporal co-presence is re-defined in the NT Live scenario.

Most importantly, to have signed up to this 'contemporary audience membership' (Kershaw 2001, 149) also means to perform. As Heim has

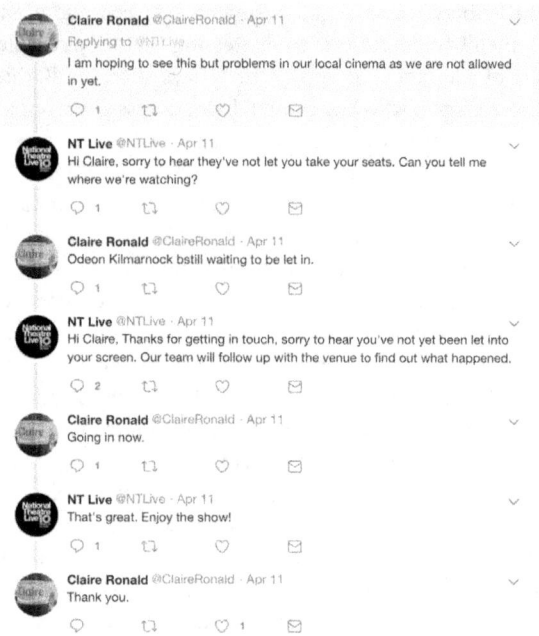

Figure 16 Screen capture of @NTLive Twitter account and exchange with @ClaireRonald on the evening of the livecast of *All About Eve*, 11 April 2019.

argued, not only the actors are performing; spectators are, too. Attending a play comes with a set of (implicit) rules and 'its own idiosyncrasies, prescribed gestures and spontaneous expressions' (2016, 2) that come into play in the encounter between actors and audience members, creating an 'electricity of co-creation' (2016, 2). Heim also holds that the twenty-first century has brought about an expansion of the audience's repertoire of action and that, for instance, spectators' tweeting their responses to the production during a performance is an example of what it means to perform as an audience now. New technologies bring about new opportunities for the audience to perform (3). Yet she excludes the space of the cinema as a site where (a) the aforementioned encounters can happen and (b) where the performance of being a spectator plays a role.

Within the live broadcasting context, I want to speak about the unifying power of glitches and distractions and think about spectatorship, especially as a relational model, based on attention on that which is contemplated, an acknowledging of other spectators' presence and a mediated engagement with the contemplated. As I will show in Chapters 4 and 5, 'distractions' in the form of tweets are in fact verbalizations of affective engagements. While being certainly performative, they are not disruptions of the flow (of attention), but rather a prolongation or extension of this attention; the rules of attention are dispersed – distraction and attention can stand in a mutual loop of exchange.

Livecasting provides a frame for a peculiar kind of theatricality, that, being dependent on the material, not only invokes a hybrid cultural product combining theatrical and cinematic modes but also shifts spectators' understanding of the theatrical space and makes the theatrical experience porous. Resisting the idea of a polished or 'removed' theatre, livecasting relies on technologies and props that can be unruly. When these peripheral objects move centre stage, this form brings about a shift of the spectators' perspective, too: in analogy to Brecht's poems quoted at the beginning of this chapter, theatre, also in this form, can be defamiliarizing. Screens or canvases, props and scenery can take on their own life and draw attention to the narrative within the theatrical and cinematic frames and sometimes even enhance their meanings. It is not only 'OK' if the wires show (see Kushner 1995, 11), it is necessary and beneficial for a more comprehensive understanding, if only implicitly, of the workings and processes of theatre. The mediated and the material come into close contact and thus, the new form that is created captures the atmosphere in the theatre in a newly palpable way and transports it to the cinematic screen and space.

The mediated and the material crucially come into contact with spectators who are engaged by them in multiple ways. In the next part I use the term 'engagement' as a central concept to denote scalable levels of involvement in the livecasting context (Chapters 4 and 5) and in recently emerged instances of Covidian theatre (Chapter 6). 'Engagement' is understood as a hailing of spectators as 'feeling I's enabled by the digital environment of the livecast and as an enacted sense of being part of a communitas of watcher-participants which also brings about verbalizations of quasi-expertise. New processes of engagement with a theatrical event are decisively shaped by livecasting as a new form of mediation of liveness, and even more personalized forms of mediation as they have become apparent during the Covid-19 pandemic.

Part II

Engagement

4

Livecasting, liveness and the feeling I

I never want to analyse the thing while I'm watching the thing.
(@cathusmax, 18 October 2019)

In the context of twenty-first-century cultural production and reception, social media plays an analogous role to that of newspapers in the nineteenth and twentieth centuries in making spectators aware of their fellow spectators.[1] As this and the next chapter elaborate, the online space is the new toilet queue (Blackwell 2018, 103) and can function as a substitute for post-show chatter. In other words: when one does not attend a theatre play in situ and cannot participate in conversations with friends or strangers afterwards, if in line for the cloakroom or toilet, social media can take over. The discourses created there both give rise to new forms of spectator-centrism and expand prevalent discourses on expertise and cultural criticism.

Livecasts in particular extend audiences (and income streams), they diminish feelings of cultural isolation (one does not have to live in London to get to see the NT's productions) and create notional communities (local, national and international). As Cochrane and Bonner point out, they are 'a valuable addition to global performance culture' and, as I have argued throughout this book, a distinct phenomenon rather than one characterized by sameness (to the in-situ performance) and simultaneity (cf. Cochrane and Bonner 2014, n. p.). When the livecast as such is a hybrid form, bringing together both different generic conventions and the connected practices of experiencing those genres, this, crucially, also reflects on the practices of spectatorship, which 'respond to the hybridity of the contexts of reception' (Aebischer, Greenhalgh and Osborne 2018, 13). But what happens to the social dimension of theatre when there is no auditorium and no actual stage and therefore the dimension of proxemics, that is the relationship of body and space, is altered? Or do the conventions of theatre-going always already save us from any (social) involvement with fellow theatregoers or commitment, as Alan Read (see 2014, 13) observes polemically?

Against this backdrop, a number of questions gain new pertinence: do we, on the one hand, live in a Rancièrian epoch of emancipated spectatorship

(2007) with its 'potential for democratic alliance, somehow in *excess* of the stage spectacle, always somehow more independent than reception theory would have us believe' (Read 2014, 12, emphasis in original)? Or do we live in an age of growing immunization and alienation? How do livecasting technologies respond to these issues? What contribution do they make to thinking about ways of engagement? Are they manifestations of what Rancière describes, do they bear the potential for democratic alliances and a critical examination of performance and theatre by individuals, or do they bring about an egocentric inward turn of the spectator that eschews critical engagement with cultural production? And, linked to that, how do they influence the perceived liveness of the performances that are being witnessed?

This chapter investigates these questions by drawing on concepts from the fields of adaptation studies, performance philosophy and audience studies. I argue that, on the one hand, livecasting opens up new possibilities for audience participation and fosters a multi-modal (see Kress 2010) engagement with the 'translated' sources. In keeping with an age of user-submitted web content, livecasts allow their audiences (the feeling of) a key role in determining its shape, and theatres reach out to audiences to engage with their shows on social media. As I have argued in Chapter 2, certain livecasts are especially successful at bringing about communitas, depending on the calls to kinds of involvement enacted by the livecasts and their affective arrangement. On the other hand, this new paradigm of spectatorship, with its emphasis on what Eglinton calls 'first-person experiences' (2010) in the context of immersive theatre, may come at the expense of more traditional constructions of 'liveness' which prioritize community and identification with the performance and the other audience members (Oddey and White 2009, 8). Many livecasts seem to particularly foster and enhance the manifestation of the 'feeling I', one's own and personal position with regard to the cultural product witnessed and particularly one's emotional rather than critical (i.e. more rational, reflected) response. Even though Erin Hurley in her concise *Theatre & Feeling* emphasizes that 'in addition to being theatre's reason for being, feeling is what is most consequential about theatre' as it 'draws us into the symbolic universe of the theatrical performance by connecting us emotionally with its characters [...] and hooking us with its moving narrative structure' (2010, 9–10), the feeling spectator who feels the need to share their (to others perhaps banal) feelings has not yet been given enough attention in a scholarly context.

As I suggested in the Introduction, one can examine livecasts through a Bakhtinian lens and understand them as living utterances that have taken shape and meaning in the context of post-2009 livecasting technologies and medial developments in the realm of performance and that brush up against dialogic threads such as the theatre's PR campaigns and the social media responses on the paradocumentational brim. When thinking about livecasts and the tweets surrounding them, one sees that these hybrid forms of theatre and film have the potential to enhance the experience of theatre – they suggest a movement towards a humanization of cultural perception (Cutchins 2017, 85), that is, a decreasing of the distance between a cultural product and the recipient. This is a humanization both in the sense of a democratization of access and in the sense that the tweets and livecasts prolong the liveness of a performance with the help of every(wo)men's voices. They can remind us that texts are not dead things (Bakhtin 1981, 252–3). At the same time, one sees the limits of a Bakhtinian reading and must ask critically whether the potential of this multi-modal complexity – at least in the present moment – is not complemented with and pushed off the stage by experiential simplicity and the manifestation of the 'feeling I'.

Spectator-centric theatre and modes of engagement with livecasts

The wooing of audiences by major theatre institutions such as the NT, the RSC or the Old Vic (which produces livecasts in cooperation with NT Live) via email newsletters and social media to attend – and, most importantly, share their experiences of – their shows and livecasts belong to the wider shift towards spectator-centrism in recent years in theatre and performance. Several scholars have encircled this development towards a spectator-centric theatre with new terminologies. Andy Lavender detects a shift from mise-en-scène to mise-en-sensibilité in twenty-first-century performance in general, and especially, but not only, immersive performance. In new theatre, the play no longer takes place 'over there' (on the stage) but 'with us inside it'. This (re)arrangement of affect

> implicates the *matter* of theatre – what it is about, deals with, dramatizes – with its *mediation*. When we are within mediation, as participants or immersants, we are differently response-able. [. . .] The power at stake here is a mixture of agency, authentic feeling, witness from within and – not least – the power to withdraw, not to participate. (Lavender 2016, 100, emphasis in original)

How is this different from immersive theatre throughout the twentieth century and what does 'being within the mediation' and 'being a witness from within' entail? First, the availability and addition of interrelated media have shaped this development and had the effect that '[t]heater has become more than itself, a compound of media' or even 'something other than an encounter between actors, or between actor and audience' (Lavender 2016, 9). A crucial difference to the (late) twentieth century is that while the former was to some extent already mediatized it was still pre-digital, and it is precisely the digital realm of new media and digital communication technologies that contributes to *mise-en-sensibilité* in the twenty-first century. To define theatre as a compound of media also points to how theatre, now more than before, creates an entire environment within which spectators do not only watch but simultaneously embody and experience. Second, then, and this is why I want to apply Lavender's conceptual thrust to my analysis of feeling spectators of livecasts, precisely because of the engagement via the digital – that is, a practice that people in the twenty-first century are familiar with on an everyday basis – this hailing of spectators to become witnesses from within occurs in an almost imperceptible, swift manner. Their feelings become feelings about and *of* a given show.

The term 'response-ability' needs to be unravelled: for to be response-able means to matter and be an important and central element of a performance. One has the ability to participate. When one thinks of the consequences of such a status/position, one can link this to Keren Zaiontz's concept of 'narcissistic spectatorship' (2014), which is developed along similar lines as Lavender's, yet more directly focused on the physical engagement and felt experience, and how spectators in a way implicitly compete with each other for 'better' experiences.

Combining Lavender and Zaiontz's approaches, Adam Alston coins the term 'narcissistic participation' for a similar phenomenon occurring in the context of immersive performances and describes it as being made up of 'two mutually reinforcing parts: the participant's internal experience *and* his or her participation (or *potential participation*) with the objects, spaces and people that shape that experience' (Spence and Benford 2018, 5, emphasis added). These parts, taken together, create an 'affective experience' and as a consequence 'affect then implicates the audience not just as a judgmental and potentially empathetic observer of a fictive world and its inhabitants but as an essential part and co-producer of that world' (Alston 2016, 36). Thus, narcissistic participation consists of both 'affectively perceived co-production' and 'physically embodied co-production' (Spence and Benford 2018, 5). In other words: the spectator needs others and their (bodily) presence and the participation in that group combined with the internal experience in order to participate narcissistically. This experience is always shaped by what the spectator 'brings to the stage' – that is their autobiographies. Spence and Benford add a further element here:

We believe that relationships with others must contribute to the autobiography that may profoundly impact a spectator's affect and therefore his or her experience. Rather than existing as a physically co-present or digitally conjured 'actor' taking part in each performance (and as such part of the performance environment), the people with whom a participant has an emotionally powerful relationship *may exist solely within the mind of that participant at that time*, but mentally conjuring their relationship involves far more than a dry act of cognition. (2018, 5, emphasis added)

While Spence and Benford speak of (existing) relationships that, when conjured up, can form part of the event itself, I argue that the *implied* presence of other spectators can have a similar effect on the individual spectator-as-centre: it can fuel the wish to articulate one's part of the event, even if only on its paradocumentational brim, even if only in one's own eyes. Thus, the earlier considerations can be applied as well when examining the reactions to livecasts which are explicitly advertised as inviting a direct response from audiences via social media and enabling them to participate in this event from their 'local venue' (each post announcing a new livecast ends with the appeal 'Check your local venue for dates and times' and a link with further information).

The notion of engagement is usually discussed from the viewpoint of the audience as a form of connectedness with media texts, as one of many 'psychological orientations to the world and to the artifacts within it' (Corner 2017, 3). These processes are so complex that scholars such as Annette Hill usefully speak of a 'spectrum of engagement' to describe the 'dynamic movement across the cognitive and affective work of audiences, highlighting the different positions and intensities of engagement' (Hill 2017, 7).[2] Building on my argument from Chapter 2 about the workings of the affective arrangement of a livecast on the spectatorial experience, I conceive of engagement in this context as specific effects of mediation – both aesthetic and involving the role of the audience on screen that the livecast audience sees – that exert a 'pull' of livecasts audiences into the event. I use the term 'engagement' as a general term to denote scalable levels of involvement: being pulled into the livecasting event entails specific cognitive and affective and communicative/medial work of audiences. First, this pull is therefore an active allure to describe a series of calls to kinds of involvement enacted both by a live theatrical event and also differently in its livecast counterpart. Second, engagement is used to describe an enacted sense of being part of a communitas of watcher-participants, enabled by the ways in which the livecast is filmed (see Chapters 2 and 3), or a hailing of spectators as 'feeling

I's' as orchestrated by the digital/medial environment of the livecast (as will be developed in this chapter). As a consequence, and facilitated by the presence of the paradocumentational brim, the livecasting frame affords the dominance of the 'feeling' spectator. This can be feeling either as part of a community or feeling as an individual 'I', but in both scenarios the experiential manifestations hinge on the affective.

A productive way of having audiences engage with a performance is to, quite simply, give them the opportunity to talk (with others) about it. There are different ways in which this can be done. In her study of twenty-first-century etiquette, Kirsty Sedgman holds that the central question today concerning audiences is 'which kinds of attention afford more democratic experiences by promoting productive collaborative engagements both with others in the audience, as well as with the wider world' (2018a, 36). Sullivan applies this to audiences of streamed theatre as well and argues that to encourage such audiences 'to talk about a performance with one another, while it occurs, is arguably one step towards more inclusive and enriching encounters' (2020, 106–7). As Lynne Conner suggests, talking about performance 'increases both the enjoyment and critical understanding audiences gain from them' (2020, 107). For example, some companies and/or artistic directors even encourage their audiences to participate in simultaneous discussion via Twitter: Tim Etchells, the artistic director of the Sheffield-based theatre company Forced Entertainment, promoted such discussions when the company streamed their *The Complete Works: Table Top Shakespeare* by tweeting during the stream and taking up other spectators' suggestions. Reflecting on his experimental theatrical work, Etchells has emphasized how he wants both his productions and his audiences to 'take their time' in relation to one another, creating an environment in which performances can 'flow, morph and stretch' and spectators can produce a 'parallel social track' in which they are able to discuss what they're watching (2015). This idea of a 'parallel social track' is similar to my notion of the paradocumentational brim; since a 'track' suggests a side-by-sideness and an optional quality (as in a soundtrack or voiceover that one can but does not have to turn on), I prefer 'brim' to explicitly include the idea that the event surrounded by it is also held together by it.

Etchells has put his ideas about 'stretching performances' into practice since the early 1990s, but more recently he has suggested that they 'have only found their true and proper moment now, in the layering of Twitter conversation and screen grabbing', and in the navigation of 'the dynamics of split attention and the conversational chorus of social media' (in Sullivan 2020, 107). These developments should be understood as enhancements of the theatrical experience as they depict and respond to the reality of 'multimedia, multi-tasking audiences' (Sullivan 2020, 107). In order to keep spectators engaged, therefore, it is vital to expand the frame of the event, something that livecasts manage to do.

Livecasts, liveness and 'we'

The immediacy conjured up in the context of livecasts to a great extent relies on placing viewers in relation to the event they are witnessing. Coming from the field of spatial theory, Robert T. Tally refers to the reassuring power of a '"You are here" arrow or dot or other marker [which] provides the point of reference from which we can both imagine and navigate the space' (2013, 2), and this is what is provided here as well. But the broadcasts themselves also 'construct a sense of place at a distance' (Sullivan 2017, 629): both before the beginning of a screening, when cinema audiences can only see the in-house audience and hear their excited pre-show chatter (635), and also during the broadcasts themselves, which 'use different shot compositions, editing paces, and camera views to produce forms of spectatorship that can vary dramatically in their theatricality' (629).

We get a new sense of what constitutes liveness here: while according to Auslander, live performance describes 'the kind of performance in which the performers and the audience are both *physically* and *temporally* co-present to one another' (2012, 5, emphasis added), live broadcasting, as Auslander also points out, 'meet[s] only one of the basic conditions', namely the temporal one. Livecasts do, however, invoke a sense of place through various strategies, which can be summed up in the formula 'place + communitas = liveness'. The sense of place relates to communitas in such a way that a connection is established between, on the one hand, the production context, the production history and the in-house audiences, and, on the other hand, remote audiences. Through this, the livecast can be placed both on a geographical and social plane.

Taking the example of the RSC Live broadcast of *Romeo and Juliet* (that I attended at the Barbican in London on 18 July 2018), the sense of place was highlighted on three levels: first, in the pre-show interview with the director Erica Whyman, who outlined how central the idea of having young *British* people in the play (as the chorus) was for her. That way, audiences could make a connection to the topics of love and violence important to those youths normally unheard and visible 'also *on UK streets*'. Second, pictures of previous RSC productions of *Romeo and Juliet* were displayed on the screen, showing well-known dramatic actors as the famous couple, such as Zena Walker and Laurence Harvey, and Sia Brook and Matthew Rhys, among others, thus placing this new production in relation to its predecessors and within a long line of other performers. In the interval, a film was shown that again emphasized the involvement of young people from all over the UK and their diversity at a point in history where the UK has to redefine itself as a nation (post-Brexit), thus linking back to Whyman's words. With regard to NT Live, Peter Kirwan has critically referred to these extras as attempts 'to ensure interpretation is as homogeneous as possible' (2014, 276) – when looking at the reception, however, such a problematic homogeneity does not occur, as Kirwan points out later.

Third, the creation of place during the broadcast itself was established through a balance of medium shots and close-ups and many scenes where one could see the in-house audience watching the play, thus creating 'a steady awareness of the space surrounding' the actors (Sullivan 2017, 639). This aesthetic is typical for the RSC's productions and also brought about by the layout of the apron stage, something the Barbican partly imitated for this production, which makes it harder to avoid capturing audience members than in the NT theatres that feature proscenium stages. Therefore, there is a threefold placing process going on: geographically, paratextually and through cinematic means.

As a consequence, a fabric of different senses of space is evoked for the livecasting audience. Despite the distance, it is the communal experience *both* the in-situ and livecasting audience are sharing. While their situatedness is different, the experience is similar, and, for the purposes of this argument, one can conceive of liveness as primarily enabling the experience of a 'we' (Zahavi 2014), of making the social dimension of a cultural event palpable. According to Dan Zahavi,

> experiential sharing isn't merely individual experience plus reciprocal knowledge; rather, what we are after is a situation in which the experiences of the individuals are co-regulated and constitutively bound together, that is, where the individuals only have the experiences they have in virtue of their reciprocal relation to each other. (2014, 245)

In the livecasting context, even though a viewer attending a livecast, say, at the Barbican in London will never actually know the vast majority of other viewers all around the world, experiential sharing can manifest itself with – or between – these people. After all, at the same time, one is aware that they – or rather we – are all shown the same prompts before, during and after the show. This comes close to a sort of collective 'thinking assignment', a co-regulation of expectation and experience. One can tie this back to Spence and Benford's argument and their focus on the role of relationships: one has to single out the role of [implied] relationships as (a) establishing the feeling of liveness by combining the evocation of a community with a fabric of places and, paradoxically, (b) increasing spectator-centrism and thus upholding the balance between similarity with and difference from others. Livecasting attendees all around the world potentially share the same encounter with a performance they all would normally not be able to see at the actual theatre venue. A tap of a finger on the smartphone screen and a look at the social media feeds, however, suffices as a reminder that one is thrown back onto one's very own viewing situation.

Similarly, in their introduction to *Modes of Spectating* Alison Oddey and Christine White ask, 'What is radically different about how we spectate now?' (2009, 8) and outline how in a live spectatorship setting the viewing situation fluctuates between that of relating one's self to what is being viewed and the perceived impression of being 'the nullified being' that is just one individual in an anonymous crowd. Liveness, in this day and age, indeed seems to have become to some extent 'a mode of entering the live event; a means of display' (8), as, for instance, screens on stage and auditoriums proliferate (for a thorough discussion of liveness and mediality, see Georgi 2014). According to Oddey and White, the 'new mode of spectating' is the event itself (2009, 10), and the activities of the 'audience' (as a group of people *listening* to something) and 'spectators' (as individuals *watching* an event) collide in the twenty-first century (12). 'The new definition of spectatorship', they continue,

> is interactivity. It is the combination of hearing and observation and it has fewer of the negative connotations of the late twentieth century ideas of passive viewing, which have led to an uninformed binary of passive and active, valuable and non-valid cultural activities [. . .] *Inter* [is] a prefix to the senses, as is all twenty-first century spectatorship. (Oddey and White 2009, 13, emphasis in original)

Crucially, with regard to livecasts, the senses are already prefixed with an 'inter' before the actual spectating starts in the space for the engagement and 'luring' of audiences, namely the paradocumentational brim surrounding the broadcast (still present when the show is over). This brim is particularly constructed on Twitter, but also on Instagram and Facebook. The specific responses can be conceived of as 'tactics' in de Certeau's sense, that is, actions that enable the spectators to create a place for themselves within the 'strategies' set out by the theatre institutions. As Rachael Nicholas discusses, in the livecasting context, the relationship between 'strategies' and 'tactics' can shift. For instance, tactics can become part of the 'strategies' of theatre companies when tweets are co-opted as part of their publicity campaigns (2018, 79).

Yet crucially, the tweets are audience performances which 'constitute tactics that operate within, and sometimes disturb, power structures and cultural hierarchies' (90).

This interplay between 'strategies' and 'tactics' occurs to a great extent within the paradocumentational brim of Twitter. For instance, in the days and hours leading up to the live broadcast of *The Merry Wives of Windsor* on 12 September 2018, the RSC Twitter page (@TheRSC) encouraged viewers to 'head to our Instagram @TheRSC and check out our Costume and Wigs takeover as we get ready for our live broadcast of Merry Wives happening tonight' followed by two emojis of a dancing woman and a pink lipstick and a video loop of one of the actresses in the makeup room. Another post read, 'Shut up! Merry Wives is broadcasting at my local cinema? Tonight?! Don't miss it, find your nearest screening here [followed by a link]' and included a GIF of David Troughton as Sir John Falstaff captured with an expression of disbelief.[3]

The NT also regularly posts intimate 'behind the scenes' features. On 6 September 2018, for instance, when *Julie* (dir. Carrie Cracknell) was livecast, the actress portraying Christine, Thalissa Teixeira (@thalteixeira), took over the NT Live Twitter account (@NTLive) for an hour and shared pictures from rehearsals, blurring the boundaries between fact and fiction, but also creating a feeling of virtual intimacy by giving those following the Twitter feed the impression that their experience was closer to the real thing than for regular theatregoers. In these instances, prospective livecast viewers are given intimate insights into the performances, as if the shows were made specifically for them; but to make the best out of it, they have to jump between several social media platforms – they have to prefix their auditory and visual senses with an 'inter'.

This new definition of spectatorship, that is, the idea that the mode of spectating (on different media) is the event itself, demands quite a bit of (unpaid[4]) labour from its spectators since – as is always the case when there are many options available – one constantly runs the risk of missing out on a particular extra. It can feel a bit like having to do one's homework first before being able to have the (quantitatively and qualitatively) enhanced experience of the livecast. Yet the presence of the paradocumentational brim and the availability of the resources described earlier do offer the potential for a truly multi-modal engagement. As defined by Gunther Kress, a mode 'is a socially shaped and culturally given semiotic resource for making meaning' (2010, 79) and navigating between multiple literacies within one medium is in fact characteristic of all communication. In the livecasting context, multi-modality is foregrounded and attains a playful mode. It thus contributes to a timely and more permeable understanding of what a medium is or can be. It enables spectators, at least potentially, to arrive at a more rounded, informed impression and opinion of a given cultural event, and they are given room to become a (speaking, writing) part of it.

Bakhtinian and Benjaminian traces – fabrics of engagement

In order to better understand how twenty-first-century spectatorship is constituted by an 'inter', it is helpful to briefly zoom out of the field encircling the spectator and give that which is being spectated its space. There is a certain potential latent in the livecasting phenomenon, the potential for a more human encounter with a given text when it is no longer there 'merely' as an original, but rather wandering between original and copy.[5]

This suggests that one needs to rethink Walter Benjamin's concept of 'aura' as a mobile and flexible one that can also manifest itself in a different shape in the encounter with something that is not the 'original'. Crucially, the experience of the aura of an artwork is a highly individual one. In his discussion in 'The Work of Art in the Age of Its Technological Reproducibility', Benjamin does not focus explicitly on the part and experience of the 'receiver' but roots the aura firmly with the artwork, which has to be experienced in its entirety. Through technological reproduction and/or mediation certain features of the photographed or filmed are enlarged, potentially enhanced and thus irrevocably altered.

A similar development can be observed when a theatre production is reproduced in a livecast. As already the discussions in the previous chapters have shown, livecasts put aspects of a theatre play centre stage that would normally either not be there, be not as present to the audience or be aspects among many others. This singling out of given aspects happens in particular through camera frames and angles. In the livecasting context one can say that the artwork – the original performance – and its aura are 'shattered' through mediation (in the livecast). However, I argue that from the side of the experiencers of the livecasts, a re-assessment of the status of the aura is necessary: in reimagining themselves into the place of the in-situ performance, in seeing the audiences on site, in articulating their feelings à propos the livecast performance, spectators precisely are re-creating something similar to the aura. In other words: Benjamin's assessment of the role of 1920 and 1930s technologies on the decay of an artwork's aura can be applied analogously to the impact of the technologies employed in the livecasting context and the consequential processes. But in contrast and in addition to what he is describing, on the part of the recipients this does not bring about a rejection of the 'original' or a disinterest in authenticity. In the moment in which the livecast is perceived to be special and creating a special experience for the spectator, it seems authentic.[6] One can therefore place a greater trust in the role of the spectators and their yearning for auratic experiences (with manifestations in experiences of communitas, for instance). The fact that livecasts foster a multi-modal engagement with the adapted source text/performance means that they can be understood as part of a new 'emotional turn' that prioritizes personal experience.

While it would be amiss to use the term 'experiential', as defined by Aleks Sierz as 'work that provokes, usually in a violent manner, its audiences to *feel* as opposed to *think*' (in Wallace 2010, 88, emphases added), in this specific context as well, it does point into a direction in which livecasts may be classified. The centrism on feelings in livecasts is also reflected in the wording of the questions in online questionnaires following some of the RSC's livecasts. After the aforementioned livecast of *Romeo and Juliet*, for instance, there was the possibility to take part in such a survey. There was a set of statements, explicitly regarding 'attending *Romeo & Juliet* in a cinema' with which one could 'strongly disagree' or 'strongly agree' (with five gradations in total). These statements were (all emphases are mine):

- 'I felt *real excitement* because I knew that the performance was live.'
- 'Being in the cinema was a *very different experience* from attending a live performance.'
- 'It was *totally absorbing*.'
- 'I *felt* an *emotional response* to the performance.'
- 'Watching the performance on screen gave me a good sense of what *experiencing* it live in a theatre would be like.'
- 'Being in the cinema was *more engaging* than if I had been there live in the theatre audience.'
- 'I would recommend the *experience* of attending *Romeo & Juliet* in a cinema to other people.'[7]

What is noticeable here is that there is a strong focus on the somatic and emotional component of attending a livecast already instigated on the part of the theatre institution itself. There are no questions about the acting or thoughts on the production but instead a clear focus on how it was experienced. It is not only one's opinion that matters but also especially one's emotions – something everybody can relate to and something that one does not, for instance, need to have a particular educational background for to understand. In the aforementioned audience survey, 69 per cent of respondents found the livecast 'totally absorbing' and 71 per cent felt an emotional response to it. Some of the reactions on Twitter regarding *Macbeth* (collected on the @NTLive page as 'Moments') are similar in their focus on the somatic and physiological: the livecast is described as 'Blimey @NTLive my heart is hammering out of my chest #Macbeth #NTLive' by @scrufflove and all @Jenstra1 can write is 'OMFG Goosebumps #macbeth @NTLive'.

Thus, livecasting, with its inherent – and, as I claim, *constitutive* – invitation to audiences to be a part of it and to *feel* it, can remind us that texts are not dead things. As Bakhtin put it with regard to translations, a discourse that has also been made fruitful in the realm of adaptation theory, 'beginning with any text – and sometimes passing through a lengthy series of mediating links – we always arrive, in the final analysis, at the human voice, which is to say we come up against the human being' (Bakhtin 1981, 252–3). With their appeals to follow and comment on their livecasts and contribute to their paratexts, the involved theatres do encourage something like a slight shift with regard to 'who has the say': of course, the audiences do not (yet) have a say in choosing which show staged in the NT, the RSC or other theatres[8] will be livecast. Yet in entering and participating in this space on social media created for them, the spectators in a way have the final word. This is an emancipation that demands activity on the part of the spectator and provides visibility. Quite importantly, this activity is purely self-regulated; while, during the RSC's livecast of *Romeo and Juliet* in July 2018, the presenter Suzy Klein repeatedly reminded the audience to fill in the online questionnaire after the show, this was entirely voluntary, and not, as Lauren Wingenroth has aptly problematized, an instance of 'non-consensual audience participation' (2018). This is precisely where the potential lies: the spectator has the option to engage in and share both one's opinion of the play and simply the experience of being there.

I feel, therefore I am (a spectator)

There is, however, a problem with the possibilities livecasts offer with regard to providing a space for spectators in which they can share their impressions and opinions: as much as they can create an atmosphere of being part of a whole, they also increase levels of subjectivity and foster first-person experiences that valorize solely *one's own* position and feelings with regard to the cultural event witnessed over that of a given community's, however broadly the latter is understood. There is still a cognitive awareness of the presence of others and thus the sense of belonging to a wider group of watchers, but through this sense of belonging the need arises to articulate one's individual viewing response.

What may seem obvious but is noteworthy about both the tweets and the follow-ups to NT Live shows – such as, for instance, a post on the NT Live Twitter page on 30 December 2019 asking followers and notably those spectators who had seen the livecast of *A Midsummer Night's Dream*, for their favourite line (or insult) from the play – is that they were posted in such a point in time as not to interrupt the watching experience. While theatre-makers such as Tim Etchells find it necessary to foster simultaneous responses to the shows, it is again crucial to leave this option open to spectators and think about extended forms of engagement also on a temporal scale. Posting about a play at one's own discretion – especially in lieu of a post-show chat with fellow theatre or cinemagoers – does not limit one's freedom as a spectator. Follow-up posts several months after the initial screening of a production can elicit memories of this performance. This is different in the case of other ways in which NT Live tries to engage audiences, namely the interval features during the show, a typical 'bonus' of NT Live. In the case of *A Midsummer Night's Dream*, several spectators were critical towards them and posted their dismay on Twitter. @cathusmax left in the interval because the interval feature spoiled that Oberon would fall for Bottom:

> @cathusmax (18 Oct 2019): 'I had to leave halfway. Please don't put any more analysis content in intervals. It totally took me out of the show which was wonderful. I never want to analyse the thing while I'm watching the thing. Also presenter spoiled things at the start. Usually such a fan of NTlive.'

To which @ironwrites replied the same day:

> Seconded. Those of us who know the story didn't need the alterations spoiled for us (after the cast were so tight-lipped and cautious over them too) and those of us who were new to the theatre did not need the plot told to us before or during the interval. Very poor judgement imho.

The verbs used here about the features were that they 'took [the spectator] out' and 'spoiled' the show, and, most importantly, they suggested a set role for the spectator, namely the person 'analysing the thing', associated with labour rather than freedom. To say that something 'spoiled' the show suggests a strong affective connection to it – the spectators are frustrated because they feel betrayed, as their engagement with the show has been interrupted. There is a parallel here to a phenomenon Rita Felski takes up in her study

Hooked when one feels personally offended when somebody does not like a book or movie that one loves (2020, 1): if a person either takes a (perceived) disturbance or someone else's reaction to a cultural product as an offence this suggests that there are affective ties in place in both scenarios.

The experiential dimension of the 'feeling I' dominates responses on social media to livecasts. When answering the call by NT Live on its Facebook page on the question which livecasts from 2017 were the favourites among the audiences, those spectators giving more detailed answers tended to insert *themselves* into their answers: who they were watching the livecast with, from where, but especially what it felt like (for instance, to have the 'intimacy of the theatre' transported onto the 'big screen'). The call for opinions posted on 25 December 2017, received 344 likes, and what is striking is the length of the responses (certainly motivated by the fact that there was a chance 'to win [a] bundle of signed goodies'). As of 12 July 2019, the post had received 406 comments. Most users began with naming the livecast they had liked most, followed by an appraisal of the actors and often a comment on how they (the commentators) would not have been able to play such an emotional/demanding part every night. While there were several comments on the atmosphere in the cinema, there was no interaction between the respective users, apart from occasional likes of what others had posted. Instead, in about one out of four comments, people explicitly related *their own emotional state* with regard to the favourite play.[9]

The responses that are given do not focus on specific scenes or detailed references to a given play's content but relate quite extensive descriptions of the commentator's emotional state of mind during or after a show. With regard to *Yerma*, for instance, such phrases included 'I felt like I was living a life and not just watching a show. Billie Piper was absolutely phenomenal, I couldn't believe someone's acting could actually make me feel such a spectrum of emotions' (Alexandra Bonita) and 'Thoroughly engrossing, provocative and affecting production with an extraordinary central performance from Billie Piper. . . . Absolutely loved the modern, innovative stage design. . . . Won't forget' (Matthew Floyd). Regarding *Angels in America*, Sophie Elizabeth felt taken back to her 'uni days' and reminded of why she loved 'Drama', and for Lynda Fogg, it was such a joy 'to watch the very talented actors that [she] didn't want it to end'. Similarly, Amber Bytheway reported being left 'aghast with amazement and vulnerability and hope' and, after watching *Millennium Approaches* (the first part of *Angels in America*), Kit Rafe Heyam wondered how they were 'going to emotionally get through the next week'. Several commentators would also insert biographical information and detailed context for how they came to watch their favourite livecast (a sibling's birthday; parents were ill but friends took care of them so the person could go to the cinema) and, in the case of *Angels in America*, several spectators identifying as LGBTQ* reported being especially grateful to have seen the play. The following list shows more examples of observations made:

> Angels in America was an incredible feat of emotional theatre. It took you through a rollercoaster and left you almost breathless. I could only imagine what it was to be there in person soaking it all up in the theatre – the cinema was a good second best. (Lizzy Balmain)
>
> Angels in America. [...] A [sic] amazing 8 hours, I laughed, I cried I was 100% emotionally involved with the character's [sic]. Can't even describe the 'electricity' in the audience watching it, it was a shared experience that can't properly be explained unless you've seen it. (Sara Griffin)
>
> Overall, the experience of nt live has always been good to us. [...] That day made us feel like we were in the right place at the right time. (Peter Malmquist)
>
> I was completely blown away by Follies. [...] Lots of laughter & tears – I was emotionally wrung out and exhilarated by the end. Saw it in Munich with a lovely bunch of girlfriends. (Dagmar Burnett-Godfree)
>
> Angels in America, without a doubt! [...] It took me to places I didn't know existed and I don't think there'll ever be another play to affect me so profoundly. (Chloe Bisset)
>
> It changed my life. (Laura Jane Northmore)
>
> You completely forget that you aren't in the original audience. (Jenny Angel)[10]

When surveying these responses one can detect a superimposing of the spectators' own (feeling, sensitive) selves onto the production: the NT Live's prompt was to name the favourite production and say why and *not* how it had made them feel, but this for the majority seemed to be synonymous. Is this because of the specific technological format the responses are solicited in and the fact they can only be given from one's personal computer or smartphone? Such a collection of statements that are not interconnected but run in parallel to each other is certainly not what is meant when the phrase 'socially interdependent' is used. Harvie has perhaps phrased the most poignant critique of how contemporary cultural trends and technologies jeopardize 'essentials of social life' and 'prioritize self-interest'. Communication, Harvie writes, 'may appear to be enhanced by contemporary technologies, for example, but in many ways they inhibit it, isolating individuals in silos of blinkered attention to personal mobile communication devices' (2013, 2).

This 'blinkered attention' is captured by Keren Zaiontz (2014) in similar terms. Zaiontz is mostly concerned with performances that are in their set-up already spectator-centric (in this context, Punchdrunk's Felix Barrett [2007] speaks of 'the audience as epicentre' on which the performance hinges). Zaiontz examines 'how the consumption of self through interactive and immersive performances produces a narcissistic spectatorship' (2014, 407), by which she does not mean the clinical definition but rather 'how self-absorption serves as a primary mode of experience for audiences within particular types of participatory art and performance' (407). The spectator is, therefore, positioned not as an author or agent but as an experiencer (Nelson 2010, 45).

These positions form the nodes of my analysis as well, but in contrast to Zaiontz, I am interested in highlighting how a specific practice of presenting (and, by extension, advertising) theatre and performance can foster a 'narcissistic' encounter quite similar to that she describes in the context of immersive performance. Crucially, however, spectator-centrism may have different effects and includes different factors. This is why seeing it only in a negative light should be avoided; instead, it is necessary to speak of the welcome manifestation of the 'feeling I'. The frame this is embedded in does not oppose depth of emotion to depth of thought: I am not suggesting that the responses, as 'off-the-cuff' as they are, do not represent a form of cognitive labour and post-show reflection. The boundaries between cognition and emotion are fluid, as Alf Gabrielsson has observed in his study *Strong Experiences with Music* (2011), assigning a multitude of experiential dimensions to the listening of music, from bodily, to mental, to religious and therapeutic sensations (see especially 120–44). The responses are not as complex as what Axelson calls 'vernacular meaning-making' in the context of film studies but related to that: the viewers who then tweet about their experiences do evaluate the aesthetics of the narrative, they engage with them emphatically, and they relate them to (their own) life (2015, 144, 151).

For this reason, a concept that is even more relevant for my earlier considerations is Andrew Eglinton's 'first-person experiences', which he has coined after examining the work of immersive theatre companies such as Punchdrunk, Blast Theory, Shunt and others. He argues that through its

> persistent blurring of boundaries between theatre and non-theatre, and its emphasis on first-person experiences, Punchdrunk has captured something of a 'coming of age' in general perceptions of British theatre in a twenty-first-century digital age: that is, the recognition that the

theatre contributes to a society driven by networked digital technology and real time media, marked by the myriad 'social gestures' and 'sites of gesture' that communication devices induce. (2010, 48–9)[11]

Eglinton here thinks of the specific context of immersive theatre and the intramedial employment of all sorts of new technological devices as 'new "frames" of performance' which focus and hinge on the first-person experiencer. My point is to extend this notion also (a) to the realm of livecasting and (b) that of post-livecast discourse. As much as they bear the potential for opening up a new and vast field for experience (both that of a given performance and that of reflecting on it afterwards), these new 'sites of gesture' can also create quite an opposite effect, namely a limited one that consists of a sharpening of the private, first-person singular position. Oddey and White's remark that the 'new mode of spectating is to focus only on what "I" want to see; on my perception of the world as "I" see it' (2009, 8) thus also applies to the playground available on social media for twenty-first-century spectators of livecasts.

It should not come as a surprise that such a kind of engagement 'works' so well, for it is precisely this *assumption* of engagement that Alan Read has identified as characteristic of 'performance in general, and theatre in particular' and that he calls 'the "immunisatory paradigm" to protect us, the spectator, the audience, from the implication of involvement' (2014, 13). This logic, or the 'pathogen of performance' as he calls it,

> is the contract *we make* as an audience member at each stage of the dissembling of the stage to reassert the very protocols of distance from involvement we thought we were paying to see dispelled. My proposal here is that this repertoire of *affects of adjustment* is what makes sitting in the dark watching illuminated stages so interesting. This is the 'immunisatory logic' of theatre, something that performance in all its guises has done little to destabilize, so powerful is its hold on us. And, in my view, this is the inherent *power of theatre* that uses all its theatricality to unpick its own communitarian stupidity. (13, emphasis in original)

In the livecasting context, too, the invitation to engage, to get closer (behind the scenes even, or to see a performance from 'the best seats in the house', see NT n.d.), suggests a dispelling of distance not dissimilar to that in immersive theatre performances, yet the immunizatory logic, that is, the notion that one is *actually* free from engagement is more pronounced here. One has the option of sharing one's feedback and telling others about the livecasts one has seen, but this does not have any direct or immediate influence on the outcome of a given show.

The responses on Facebook and Twitter are united in their cheerfulness, which casts a long shadow of doubt on Anne Ubersfeld's statement that 'one is less happy when alone'. (1982, 128) Similarly to McAuley's (and others') emphasis on the social dimension of theatre, Ubersfeld holds that 'theatrical pleasure [. . .] reverberates through others. [. . .] The spectator emits barely perceptible signs of pleasure as well as loud laughter and secret tears [. . .] One does not go alone to the theatre – one is less happy when alone' (1982, 128).

The 'OMFG Goosebumps' tweet you see pop up on your smartphone screen – while probably verbalizing a very similar emotion – certainly cannot have the same somatic effect on you as the hearty laugh or gasp of disbelief emitted by the stranger or friend sitting in the seat next to you. Yet when one looks at the responses, one clearly sees the joys of a first-person encounter with theatre and a solitary reflection, no matter how casual it may be. Even if one attended the broadcast with other people, the reflection itself takes place when the individual is on their own. For you, for me, it is exciting. While the experience of a 'we' manifests itself implicitly, it is not more valuable than the experience of an 'I', and certainly not a greater source of pleasure: on the contrary, the latter is a central characteristic of the experience as a whole. In the context of NT Live, where the programme attempts to 'impose a collective voice on its audience', as Kirwan has observed, it is quite pleasant to see how these attempts fail and are dispersed in the shape of individual, whimsical and nevertheless productively engaged responses (2014, 278).

In his discussion of livecasting and its effects on the experience of the viewers, Daniel Schulze briefly discusses whether Twitter and blogs manage to create a kind of (virtual) community and borrows the concept of 'hyperimmunity' from Read with regard to the experience of the audience watching a livecast on the laptop screen at home. By this Schulze means the wish to be 'safe' (and isolated) as a spectator who at the same time is part of a (virtual) community (2015, 321). 'Hyper-immunity' seems to be a rather pleasant manifestation in this presentation, but Schulze is not explicit enough about this matter. He argues that in the context of NT Live broadcasts, 'in terms of politics, audiences are condemned to absolute passivity, they are deprived of their voice in the form of booing, heckling or cheering' (315), which he contrasts with the 'participatory climate' surrounding Forced Entertainment's broadcasts. There, spectators 'become active, emancipated spectators in Rancière's sense' (316) whose social media responses are, for instance, included directly below a broadcast on the same webpage – a simplification that I disagree with. Thus, while Rancière has dismantled the dichotomy between spectator/passive and actor/active, Schulze introduces a new puzzling dichotomy, namely between NT Live spectators as passive, on the one hand, and Forced Entertainment spectators as active, on the other hand. While Schulze then relativizes the quality of this 'activity' by asking whether tweeting can indeed be considered a form of social exchange, a more nuanced assessment of what is manifesting here is necessary. Schulze's observation – made with regard to the tweets in response to Forced Entertainment's *Quizoola24* (#Quizoola24) and *Speak Bitterness* (#FESpeaklive) – that 'the vast majority of the Twitter users were not seeking any meaningful exchange but only had the aim to be recognised [. . .] an almost exhibitionist pleasure that seeks to display one's own partaking in a cultural exercise' (2015, 230–1) is certainly apt. Yet it should be acknowledged that there is another dimension belonging to the spectrum of 'theatrical pleasure' that gains greater importance in the context of livecasting: namely the pleasure the individual derives from the experience for him- or herself. Schulze's phrase 'schizophrenic state of mind' (321) is problematic in that it pathologizes the complexity of being an audience member. His argument seems to exclude the possibility of the need to engage in a self-sufficient way, to be primarily a feeling I, alongside being a member of an audience.

In my analysis I have agreed with Keren Zaiontz, who critically maintains that most discussions suggest that spectators want to be agents, emancipated, those 'reading' theatre, and argues that sometimes they want to (just) be an integral part of the performance. She therefore outlines how in the performances she has analysed, the spectator is positioned not as an author or agent but as an experiencer (Zaiontz 2014, 408); a position that I share, with the specification of identifying a feeling experiencer, and that embeds my reflections in spectator rather than performance studies, thus following Susan Melrose's suggestion (2006, 120–2). One can also draw a parallel to Nicholas Ridout's term of the 'mis-spectator' that forms the starting point of my discussion in the next chapter. The mis-spectator can (and wants to) rely on their opinion or impressions, however subjective they may be. One can see tendencies of more communitarian communities of inexpert (understood positively) critics emerging as well and livecasts as constitutively embedded in the digital space of social media do bring about a slight shift in this regard. Yet the solitary tweeter and the presence and the need to verbalize a 'feeling I' is an equally important part of this discourse in the context of twenty-first-century theatre production.

5

Quasi-experts in the context of livecasting

In Bernardine Evaristo's novel *Girl, Woman, Other*, the activist Morgan rises to some fame on Twitter, tweeting about 'trans issues, gender, feminism, politics' (333), and with over a million followers they are considered an 'influencer' and get invited to write reviews of, for instance, plays. The chapter on Morgan argues that '[s]oon there'll be no need for proper critics, the so-called "experts" who've been running the show since forever, most of them here in London, it's all about the democratization of critical opinion' (Evaristo 2020, 333). Evaristo's novel opens with one of the protagonists, the playwright Amma, going to the opening night of her play, *The Last Amazon of Dahomey*, about which Morgan (@transwarrior) later tweets:

> Just seen #TheLastAmazonofDahomey @NationalTheatre. OMG, warrior women kicking ass on stage! Pure African Amazon blackness. Feeeeerce! Heart-breaking & ball-breaking! All hail #AmmaBonsu #allblackhistorymatters Book now or cry later, peepalls!!! @RogueNation' (334)

This fictional tweet is representative of larger trends in recent years with regard to responses to theatrical performances and other cultural events on social media and Twitter in particular. First of all, it is written in colloquial language and employs acronyms such as 'OMG', second, it is characterized by extreme subjectivity and personal emotions (many exclamation points, unconventionally spelled words like 'Feeeeerce!' to underline the tweeter's enthusiasm) and third, it evokes the sense of immediacy and proximity to the event and suggests that it was written directly from the field ('*Just seen*'). Indeed, various theatres have started to use spectators' responses to plays captured in tweets to advertise their shows – I discussed this in Chapter 2 with regard to *A Midsummer Night's Dream* (Bridge Theatre/NT Live) but there are other examples, such as the Royal Opera House, which, after their livecast of *La Bohème* on 29 January 2020, asked audiences for 'Your Reaction: What did you think of The Royal Opera's *La bohème* live in cinemas?'[1] and presented a selection of audience members' tweets along with official production photos, thus creating the impression of a virtual collaboration between the reviewers and the ROH. Similarly, the Hampstead Theatre in its Reviews trailer for *Botticelli in the Fire* posted on 1 November 2019 on YouTube used the usual words of praise from publications such as the *Evening Standard* or *The Guardian* alongside selected tweets, creating an even landscape of reactions that did not seem to prioritize one over the other.[2]

This is a relatively recent development; it is only one of the shifts theatre criticism[3] has been undergoing in recent decades. The former lead theatre critic of *The Guardian*, Michael Billington, stated already in 1999 that theatre criticism had undergone a massive shift from the 1960s, when, for instance, critics were sent off to review even the plays staged by small companies and amateurs. From the 1990s on, the plays chosen to be featured in newspapers were narrowed down and the status of theatre itself became a threatened and marginal one (Billington 2002, 55). Billington linked both theatre's and theatre' reviewing's loss of status to the Thatcherite social revolution and how '[p]rofitability in the 1980s became a test of worth: popularity an index of quality. Inevitably, if you start to play the numbers game, theatre is vulnerable: it cannot easily compete with the mass-audiences commanded by film, television, popular music' (Billington 2002, 55). Another threatening factor to the status of theatre criticism is the role of the press and public relations 'language', which has, for instance, brought about the existence of 'star ratings' in reviews. Whatever the changes are, theatre reviews have the power to be like 'paper bullets', and especially commercial theatre plays depend on a 'favorable tide of critical opinion' (54). It is telling that Billington is evoking the image of a war: he creates a gulf between the theatre or theatre plays and those reviewing them with the latter either firing bullets or deciding not to use their guns in a manner that would be destructive for the theatre-makers involved.

To create such an antagonism is detrimental to a more accessible and democratic view of both theatre – to which livecasting contributes – and theatre reviewing practices. Billington's bullets have recently found their very own counterpart, when the set and costume designer Anna Fleischle spoke about *any* kind of review on a show as the 'finishing touch' to a production.[4] I would like to draw two conclusions from this statement: first of all, rather than conceiving of criticism as being necessarily antagonistic to what it criticizes, one should think of both the performance and the review of it as contributing to the theatre experience as a whole. To reiterate: theatregoers who tweet about the play afterwards also prolong the sense of liveness of that play, and this should also be considered as part of the theatre experience. The main difference between livecasts and theatre is that during the livecast event audiences are strongly encouraged to post contributions on social media, which is why in the case of livecasts these responses on the paradocumentational brim belong to the arrangement of the livecast. Second, when one enters the realm of an already more accessible and less rigidly (with regard to genre conventions) demarcated form of theatre, as is the case with livecasting, one should pay attention to and take into account how this also fosters different kinds of 'criticism' and 'expertise'. Notably, in the case of livecasting there are almost no long-form reviews of livecasts – as I mentioned in Chapter 1, this is because there is little awareness of the fact that these productions are the results of complex artistic process in their own right. Who steps in? The spectators, who tweet about the livecast and thus in fact valorize it.

With regard to livecasts, tweets resemble and substitute the coughs or the wiggling of fellow theatregoers; they are 'here I am' expressions from people who need a substitute for the post-show chatter in the theatre foyer. Through the tweets, a keying together of spectators can happen which can find their expression in an informal form of reflecting online. In the context of the contemporary theatrical experience, a loosening up of regulations as well as a merging of the etiquette(s) and/or repertoires of action associated with both theatre- and cinema-going occurs, which also has an impact on the situation of the spectator.

The aspect of immediacy characteristic for tweets is something that provides the greatest contrast to forms of criticism that are published in long-form in journals or newspapers: such reviews that have been pondered upon, imbibed with some contextual information and are thus, one might assume, more distant to the event that is reviewed. Such an opposition reiterates the dichotomy between non-experts (in the passage from *Girl, Woman, Other* quoted earlier: 'someone like Morgan') and experts ('the proper critics'). Being an expert is, qua distance and objectivity, associated with more thorough knowledge, work and rigour; or, as the media and theatre history scholar and RSC producer John Wyver has put it, for him

> the most valuable, or the richest responses to cultural texts almost exclusively come from professional voices whether in journalism or in academia. Although it is very important that those responses come from a much more diverse range of places and responses than they did 20 years ago. The [. . .] amateur – very problematic word – but the amateur critical response, while it can extend and come from an enthusiasm and excitement about a production – I'm not sure it, very often, deepens the critical discourse around the case. But that's not necessarily a very democratic position. [. . .] And there's no question that the range of voices that are recognized and the professional context is much wider

and broader than it has ever been. And that's a very good thing. [. . .]
Personally, [. . .] I don't find . . . individual enthusiasts writing about this
work or theatre in general being very fruitful for me. (Wyver 2020)

Several aspects are mentioned in the remarks of Wyver, who frames his position very thoughtfully and carefully: diversity, value, professionalism versus amateurism and the question what role (individual) enthusiasm and excitement about a production should play in an assessment of it. Professional voices deepen the critical discourse – such experts are trained in their profession, more rational and qualified. Historically, they have been 'defined according to narratives of power, excluding those with other forms of expertise such as practical know-how, indigenous knowledge, embodied skill passed down from one generation to another' (Gilbert et al. 2020, 6). Billington epitomizes this position and such rather old-fashioned notions of expertise when he says that it is a theatre critic's obligation to 'write better', in a 'voluptuous style' and with 'moral passion' (2002, 57). But even he concedes that 'theatre critics have a duty to question prevailing values' (2002, 57).

It is precisely the aspect of exclusion and the necessity to broaden the understanding of 'expertise' that is in the process of being tackled in the present moment, and at a time which has already been dubbed the 'anti-expert' age (Sedgman 2018b). This is a positive development, as I show in the following, as 'amateurism', 'anti-expertise' or 'quasi-expertise', as I prefer to call it, can destabilize prevalent power structures and challenge conventional ideas, not only, but especially about all kinds of cultural products.

Discussions of who is or is not an expert also pick up on Walter Benjamin's assessment of the relationship between a work of art and its recipient. Contrasting the 'extremely backward' attitude of the masses towards Picasso with the 'highly progressive' one towards Chaplin, Walter Benjamin in 'The Work of Art in the Age of Its Mechanical Reproducibility' (1935) characterizes the latter as 'an *immediate, intimate fusion of pleasure in seeing and experiencing* with an attitude of *expert appraisal*' (29). Benjamin links this new feeling of agency among people and audiences to two developments: first of all, the expansion of the press, that, through 'letters to the editor', has started to dismantle the divide between authors and readers. Readers can more easily become writers, too. Second, with the rise of film as a genre, basically anyone can lay claim to being filmed. And most importantly for the creation of the attitude of expert appraisal, 'nowhere more than in the cinema are the reactions of individuals, which together make up the massive reaction of the audience, determined by the imminent concentration of reactions into a mass' (29). This tension between the individual and the mass is thus central to the cinema experience; the cinema needs these reactions. The individuals having them are therefore at the core of the cinema event and can also lay claim to talking about it as something *they* have experienced. In other words: knowledge about a film, artwork, etc. is acquired via the experience of it, and it is this hierarchy of experience and knowledge that makes somebody an expert.

What Benjamin describes then is linked to the effect the reproduced work of art (the copy) can have on the viewer, namely an increased closeness. Thinking about film and cinemas where the masses seek and find entertainment, he characterizes the viewing situation as one of '[r]eception in distraction [. . .] which is increasingly noticeable in all areas of art and is a symptom of profound changes in perception' (34). That is, the copy of the work of art and film changes the ways in which perception is performed and makes its parameters shift. Benjamin holds that while concentrating before a work of art means being absorbed by it, being distracted by a work of art (which is something he links to the masses' relation with the cinema especially) means absorbing it into oneself. The former seems to be associated more with the individual's experience in Benjamin's thinking, whereas the latter is a description of the distracted masses, who encompass the work(s) of art, for instance, buildings or the cinema, 'with their tide' (33).

In the twenty-first century, however, to continue a thought from the previous chapter about contemporary modes of spectating, to concentrate on and be distracted by a work of art are not mutually exclusive anymore. Hybrids between performance and film such as livecasting provide a realm in which phases of distraction (in the form of responding to it, for instance) and concentration (silent watching) alternate in waves. Thus, while the historical context is a very different one, questions raised by Benjamin are relevant again in this context. Certainly, theatrical performances have been telecast to private homes before and British and American television were built upon foundations of live telecast theatrical drama.[5] Those latest livecasts are both a reproduction (a two-dimensional copy of the three-dimensional production) *and* an artistic product in their own right; they are also firmly enmeshed in social media as the space in which they are advertised and then commented on, thus presenting a fruitful ground to think about how experiencing, perceiving and critically assessing a work of art changes in the context of these new developments. As Michel Foucault has put forward, critique can be 'the art of not being governed quite so much' (2007, 45). In my argumentation, this resistance to 'government' is understood as a deviation from conventions and automated patterns of evaluation and appreciation, from a 'consensus around value' (Ridout 2012, 173).

When Benjamin, as quoted in the passage earlier, describes the relationship between consumers and art, he prioritizes the visual quality of this encounter. Such an encounter combined with an attitude (personal positioning) of expert appraisal creates an immediate and intimate feeling of pleasure. What is an *attitude* of expert appraisal? If you are not an expert, what are you – a quasi-expert? I propose to shift the (hegemonic) hierarchy that prioritizes experts over non-experts in the context of cultural criticism in general and livecasting in particular and explore the positive ramifications of this latter concept/persona. To this end, I investigate a form of expertise on social media uttered in response to livecasts that takes on the form of a disruption of this consensus.

Foucault defines critique as a mechanism that lays bare power structures that have been accepted for a long time, and have been dictated either by religion, jurisprudence, science or the sovereign (or all of those). Critique does not accept that such existing rules are subsumed under the categories 'natural law' and 'indefeasible right' (Foucault 2007, 46); critique is 'the movement by which the subject gives himself the right to question truth on its effects of power and question power on its discourses of truth' (47). This questioning also entails wanting to understand where established rules seem to come from (Foucault mentions, for instance, reading the Bible in order to question religious authorities).

What I suggest is the necessity for a further dissection of the power structures within the discourse of 'critique' itself. Taking up Nicholas Ridout's concept of the mis-spectator (2012), I think about quasi-expert appraisal and transfer and apply the thrust of Benjamin's argument to the context of twenty-first-century criticism and livecasting. The prefix 'quasi-' puts the focus on the temporariness and playfulness of the endeavour of being an expert; it aligns the form of criticism with the emphasis on the liveness of the livecasts as they are framed in their marketing.

This performative playfulness also contributes to an elimination of distance between artwork (here: broadcast performance) and spectator. As a consequence, this can create higher levels of engagement, as spectators control where and when they are watching what, and turn them more easily into valuable quasi-experts – their opinion matters, at least potentially. The key questions this chapter puts in parallel are, thus, what kind of spectator/critic emerges through social media and how this figure and process is shaped by live broadcasting as a new form of mediation and mediation of liveness especially. Livecasting, which in itself presents an example of a de-hierarchicalization of the theatrical experience in that it does away with some of the barriers or obstacles surrounding the 'typical' theatre visit (especially with regard to the location and the less formal setting of the cinema), also provides a fruitful ground to think about the role of spectators' responses to theatre more broadly but especially livecasting in particular.

Immediacy and afterlife

Before commencing a discussion of what kind of potential a less hierarchical form of criticism entails, a few words on the *act* or the *how* of commenting on a performance are warranted. In performance research, some theorists problematize the dangers of articulating a (performance) experience (at all), and others describe the process of post-performance contemplation as a different experience in its own right. The reasoning behind referring to articulations about performances as dangerous is that, as Patrice Pavis suggests, 'the act of converting phenomenological reactions into words results in "fixing" the memory of that experience forever' (2006, 117). Eugenio Barba argues along similar lines that 'the memory of experience lived as theatre, once translated into sentences that last, risks becoming petrified into pages that cannot be penetrated' (2005, 11). I agree with Rebecca Schneider's argument to think of performance as having the potential to be(come) alive (again) through the diverse 'remains' it leaves behind (see more on that in the concluding discussion in Chapter 7). It makes sense to link this position to that phrased by Matthew Reason, who, with regard to writing about performance, contends that the process of post-performance contemplation, be it in verbal or written form, should be understood not as a pale or distorted reflection and thus an increasing of the gap between the now and then of the performance but rather 'a *connected but different* experience in its own right' (2010, 26, emphasis in original). Much like live performance is encountered at its moment of disappearance, writing about the livecast event, too, begins with loss. As de Certeau has said about the act of writing, it is an attempt to capture what cannot fully be expressed in words (cf. 1988, 195). This is why it is so important to recur to acts of writing, remembering and recording in order to say the unsayable. Also, while personal and private contemplation of a performance is valuable and enriching for the individual, the act of *sharing* it with others is equally crucial: as Bucknall and Sedgman point out, 'unless [these] recollections are shared more widely this embodied knowledge becomes lost to cultural memory' (2017, 117). Writing about a performance keeps it alive and is not a static end product. On the contrary, any kind of review or reflection is 'an act of generosity' and invites critical questioning and such reflection on 'performative events keeps them alive by breaking down the polarity between process and product, between past and present, theory and practice' (Nicholson 2006, 1).

The livecasting context provides a particularly rich and fruitful ground to think about the concomitant shifts with regard to criticism and expertise. I share Reason's (and Shaughnessy's, 2012) positions and regard responses to performances as activities and responsive acts that entail the making of a choice (of what one wants to respond to, write about, remember, and of how much one wants to share), and I extend this idea to those responses in tweet form. The responses to a livecast on Twitter, no matter how short or 'off the cuff' they may be, are as much part of the livecasting event as the performance itself, hence the idea of a paradocumentational brim. Most importantly, I am interested in the concept of quasi-expertise in the livecasting context. The prefix 'quasi-' points to the temporariness of the act of responding – those who tweet are only experts for the time of the tweeting act. This claim hinges on the distinction between 'attitude of an expert' and 'becoming' such an expert; that is, once you tweet, your attitude of an expert is translated into action. It is no longer merely a potential but expresses itself in an active taking on of the role of the quasi-expert. Quasi-expertise is related to the discourses on amateurism,[6] fandom[7] and criticism.

Apart from their expertise as experiencers (see Nelson 2010) when taking part in pre- or post-livecast assessments online, quasi-experts also bring another dimension to the table: their membership to the *live* audience. This 'liveness' increases their quasi-expert status because livecasts are primarily marketed as 'a live event' so that liveness becomes an especially dominant perceptual frame for those attending the livecast and arguably also those wanting to learn more about it by, for instance, reading reviews or tweets. Yet each live transmission *is* being recorded and thus turned into a document, which is constantly re-shaped by those watching it, when they review it. Even those livecasts which are archived can never be static or finished. Livecasts are inherently dynamic: they are not only made up of the filmed content of the theatre performance but also the (informal) texts surrounding them and the feedback loop they create in the virtual space in which audiences can talk about them and especially their experiences of them. In this sense, it is through the participation of quasi-experts that the liveness of the performance can be prolonged and shaped even after its 'now' has passed.

In 'Mis-spectatorship, or, 'redistributing the sensible', Ridout argues for a re-distribution of the (non-)sensible by the mis-spectator, which I am reading partly as a revaluation of the seemingly banal or private experience. The term 'sensible' is taken from Jacques Rancière's phrase 'the distribution of the sensible', to which Ridout refers and which Rancière uses to describe the existing consensus around value,

> the entire system of social and cultural processes, codes, values and material realities through which we jointly understand the world, and according to which we make our judgements about what and who

belongs where, who has the right to speak and be heard [. . .] and who gets to be recognized as an expert. (Ridout 2012, 173)

The sensible and the system it refers to are therefore related to what Foucault (2007) has in mind when he writes about systems of rules. Ridout uses the compound figure of Marcel (from Proust's *A la recherche du temps perdu*) to develop the figure of a spectator who – self-reflectively, laboriously – shifts those (evaluative) terms dominating especially the critical consensus, a kind of consensus that bears worrying similarities to habit/habituation, conforming and 'imaginary yardsticks' (2012, 181). The mis-spectator ignores those yardsticks and therefore makes 'mis-takes' which enable him [*sic*] to disrupt 'the consensus which masquerades as collectivity in the folklore of the institution of the theatre' (182). According to Ridout, '[t]his inexpert figure closely resembles Rancière's "emancipated spectator" who [. . .] emerges as the producer of meaning upon whom the theatre does not exercise its powers of educational reform' (2012, 174). What Ridout and Rancière (2011) put to the fore is the appreciation of a kind of spectator who does not *need* or does not *want* (educational) support. As Sedgman has pointed out, the use of the word 'expert' is not unproblematic within an arts context as it seems to suggest that those writing about theatre from 'highly invested positions' are something other (better) than 'mere' audiences (2018b, 309). Referring to Paul J. Sylvia, Sedgman draws attention to the fact that recently in arts research the distinction between the 'emotional physical and cognitive responses of "experts"' – those whose knowledge has been gained variously 'through training, formal study, and experience' – and those of 'novices', who, 'in contrast, generally lack such knowledge and hence apply [. . .] personal experiences when judging art' (309) has opened up. To speak of 'novices' is to add another term to the list of describing a non-conforming way of assessing art. In order to provide some continuity, I find it more fruitful to talk about mis-critics and quasi-experts. Recent work acknowledging the development(s) towards spectator-centrism in contemporary British drama provides a context here and has been discussed in the previous chapter.

Coinciding with this spectator-centrist awareness, there is an acknowledgement of what Oona Hatton sums up fittingly with the term 'crowdsourced theatre criticism' (2014) and that Duška Radosavljević thinks about as the potential of 'the democratizing and creatively empowering technological developments of the twenty-first century' to free the idea of criticism from 'the constraints of pre-Enlightenment structures of authority and power hierarchies.' The possibility this opens up is that 'the idea of criticism [can] redeem itself of its association with power and authority' (2016, 29).

In an age of user-submitted web content, livecasts allow their audiences (the feeling of) a key role in determining the shape of the paradocumentational brim of the livecast, and theatres reach out to audiences to engage with their shows on social media. Yet a placing on the map of the value of such leisurely critics is not explicit enough, and attempts in this direction do not sufficiently link these roles with criticism. Exceptions in this regard are Megan Vaughan's *Theatre Blogging. The Emergence of a Critical Culture* (2020), Michelle MacArthur's article in Radosavljević's *Theatre Criticism. Changing Landscapes* and brief essays by Linda Hutcheon.[8] Hutcheon's claim that 'in the digital age experience has replaced expertise as the prime criterion for critical authority' (in MacArthur 258) is very much to the point, but she talks about this in a very short essay in the context of consumer culture.

Following Abercrombie's and Longhurst's terminology (1998), livecasting spectators belong to the categories of both 'diffused audience' and 'simple audience'. The essential feature of the audience-experience of diffused audiences is that 'everyone becomes an audience member all the time' (68) since in 'a media-drenched society' being an audience member and consumer of media is '*constitutive* of everyday life' (1998, 69). Livecast attendees are also part of a 'simple audience' since they are usually also first gathered bodily for the broadcast in a cinema. Whimsical tweets reflect that 'audiences are not [. . .] homogenous social and psychological groups, [. . .] their reactions are chiefly private and internal, and recording their encounters with events, [. . .] is usually belated and inevitably partial' (Kennedy 2009, 3). What it means to be a spectator differs from person to person (see Dolan 2005, 15). Crucially, when journalists review plays, they tend to make assumptions about 'the audience' in generalized conclusions about their reception.

This changed attitude towards the act of spectating as replacing expertise and, linked to this, that spectators are not a homogenous group, and the role of social media in facilitating reflection on and responses to theatrical performance brings about a new paradigm of criticism and can contribute to a shift in the understanding of 'expertise'. One of the most succinct definitions of the 'critic' and the two-facedness of this figure has been formulated by Matthew Arnold (2010) already in the nineteenth century in 'The Function of Criticism at the Present Time', first delivered as a lecture at Oxford on 29 October 1864, and then published in the *National Review* in November 1864. Arnold's definition of the critic is oxymoronic: one part would correspond with the playfulness that the prefix 'quasi' aims to attest to in my phrasing, whereas the other reaffirms hegemonic power structures. Arnold defines criticism as 'sincere, simple, flexible, ardent, ever widening its knowledge' (703). He points out that in contrast to other languages, the word 'curiosity' has a somewhat negative connotation in the English language. Criticism, however, should be guided precisely by this instinct of curiosity as an attempt 'to know the best that is known and thought in the world, irrespectively of practice, politics, and everything of the kind; and to value knowledge and thought as they approach this best, without the intrusion of any other considerations whatever' (691). It is an instinct that Arnold identifies as being opposite to the 'practical English nature' (see 691). He tethers criticism to a rigorous duty and detachment; criticism, he explains, 'tends to *establish* an order of ideas' and seeks to 'make the best ideas *prevail*' (686, emphases added). As his choice of verbs indicates, criticism is challenging work; the campaign must be waged with 'inflexible honesty' (692). Arnold firmly believes that some ideas are right and others wrong; he is well aware of the ways in which the impulse for change can become destructive. A good literary critic is, inevitably for Arnold, a good critic in general: a person of culture embarked on a steady, steadfast inquiry into self and society.

In the twenty-first century, some of these characteristics are still relevant, yet for about twenty-five years now, theatre scholars and practitioners have redefined criticism as 'a cooperative endeavor and collaborative engagement' (Román 1998, xxvi).[9] David Román inaugurated the column 'The *Theatre Journal* Auto/Archive' in 2003 (from 55.1) in which authors write reviews/ reflections that focus on the material details of theatre-going – 'with whom we went, how it made us feel, and what a performance made us think' – that can form a trail of notations 'of how performances felt in very local, historicized moments in time' (Dolan 2005, 10). To think about such subjective responses as leaving a trail echoes the messiness of such a kind of criticism; if criticism is 'about sorting out the morass of perception into something orderly and interesting [. . .] about discerning relationships and making meaning' (Daly 2002, xiv), then one might argue that tweets about how 'feeeeerce' somebody finds a performance, as seen in the beginning of this chapter, may increase rather than do away with a cohesive and comprehensive impression of it. Yet I argue that coherence is precisely not desirable; on the contrary, when one accepts that the carpet knotted by the quasi-experts is a flying one rather than one on which one can tread comfortably and perhaps more predictably, this can open up the doors to an embracing of a polyphonic discourse. Such an accommodation of plurality can ultimately 'better promote the ideal of participatory parity than does a single, comprehensive, overarching public' (Fraser 1992, 122).

Quasi-experts at work: Liveness and after-liveness enabled by social media

Theatre livecast attendees are not just spectators. They are performers, fans, participants and (mis-)spectators; they can be all this because their repertoires of action have been expanded. They can be all this because they are experiencing a loosening up of etiquette which also lowers the barrier of wanting to and actually contributing to a (critical, but also affective) discourse of theatre assessment.

The context that affords such a loosening up of parameters is that of millennial digital media practices and participatory culture; crucially, these practices are not just practices by millennials, but the term is used to describe a 'construct and [...] [a] evolving, self-defined culture' (Stein 2015, 7). Henry Jenkins (2006) argues that commercial media producers, for better or worse, have to deal with the expectations of participatory culture, much of which he sees as having roots in fandom (see Stein 2015, 9). More than that, they should (and increasingly are) consider(ing) fandom as offering 'a vital model for present and future media culture en large' (Stein 2015, 9–10).

Perhaps the most valuable contribution Stein's study makes is to identify the centrality and realizations of celebrating and sharing collective passion in millennial fan practices. She draws on a multitude of sources, such as posts on Tumblr and blogs, and argues that millennial fans often

> tout emotional response – or what is known in millennial culture as 'feels' – as a driving force behind their creative authorship communities. [...] We can think of emotionally driven collective authorship as a quality of the blog and of digital culture more broadly. (2015, 156–7)

Any blog post[10] – and I would like to extend this to tweets, too – is always already a collective text 'waiting to be elaborated upon' (157) and drawing on the repository provided by 'feels culture', which 'combines an aesthetics of intimate emotion – the sense that we are accessing an author's immediate and personal emotional response to media culture – with an aesthetics of high performativity, calling attention to mediation and to the labor of the author' (158). What is at stake here, thus, is the performance or the enactment of the personal from behind the front (that, which is visible) of the digital space as a whole but also the linguistic conventions dominant within it (when talking about Twitter: word limit, and therefore shorter sentences, layout of tweet, the use of emojis and hashtags, which both make the tweets searchable and thus more widely accessible and individual). When these tweets are about capturing the experience one had witnessing a cultural product, as the following examples demonstrate, this is not just 'blabber'. While based on the affective and therefore not a form of expertise acquired by education, it is still labour. From the perspective of the institutions producing that which is tweeted about, every tweet is an advertisement for a production, a currency, a commodity or social thing 'whose qualities are at the same time perceptible and imperceptible by the senses' (Marx 1988, 83). The tweeters also sign the unspoken 'theatre contract' that Darko Suvin defined in 1985 as a 'two-way relation between spectators and performers' (9) for the context of traditional, representational theatre. The actors' visible, physical and emotional labour onstage is assisted (and in fact made possible) by the 'invisible', mostly silent presence of spectators who agree to suspend their disbelief. In the contemporary world of theatre-making, going 'to "the theatre" does not always mean going to *a* theatre; being an audience member does not always mean watching, listening, being quiet, sitting down' (Sedgman 2018a, 13). And it certainly does not mean being passive.

Continuing Ridout's argumentation, he suggests that 'a measure of inexpertise may be crucial to an interruption of the consensus around value to experts, both performance makers and spectators, routinely contribute, a consensus in which we agree only to see and hear what we already know' (2012, 173). In this line of thought, to know (to be an 'expert') is to be 'lazy', to already have done the work – it is a comfortable position. To not know, however, is laborious, it is uncomfortable. As Ridout illustrates, for Proust's Marcel attending a play is clearly a highly (self-)reflexive act driven by the awareness of the fakeness of theatrical representation with regard to reality; at the same time he willingly submits himself to the illusion. Knowing is equated with 'mere' spectatorship, while disrupting the consensus through not knowing is linked to the figure of the mis-spectator who labours. The live broadcast attendee's position between comfort and discomfort is thus a particular case of twenty-first-century (mis)spectatorship and illustrates how spectators deal with the ways in which they are engaged.

Theatres often think they engage their spectators in only one way, but there are always unintended moments of failure. Attending theatre is a process of negotiation, on the side of the spectators but also on the side of theatre critics or theatres. For the context of livecasting, especially, these negotiations are extended into the online space, where 'the affordances of digital tools supposedly enable cultural participants to connect across national boundaries'; as is the case with online fan and millennial cultures (Stein 2015, 6). How do the spectators' reflect on their positionality and how do they verbalize their experience?

In addition to the tweets that verbalize a spectator's somatic experience, such as the ones referred to in the previous chapter ('OMFG Goosebumps

#macbeth @NTLive'), the following responses provide further examples: After the livecast of *Antony and Cleopatra* on 6 December 2018, @VibhutiJPatel tweeted, 'This was just all sorts of brilliant. Ralph Fiennes and Sophie Okonedo are dazzling. And the fact I was able to watch it from my local cinema @CamPicturehouse because of @NTLive still amazes me. #AntonyandCleopatra #Shakespeare'. @PhilofBeeston thought that '#AntonyandCleopatra from @NTLive was superb. Fast moving production inhabited Hildegard Bechtler's amazingly versatile set. Verse speaking was perfectly articulated by whole cast. Sophie Okonedo gave an outstanding Cleopatra – no wonder Ralph Fiennes' Antony was so love-struck.' And @BethanMedi summed it up as: 'I am absolutely blown away by the @NationalTheatre broadcast of #AntonyandCleopatra. It was exciting and full of passion from start to finish. There is nothing quite like theatre!!' These are instances of mis-spectating: the mini reviews deviate both from 'the sensible' and standard reviews, as they blend the personal with the experience of the livecast, use the tweeters' quasi-expertise as a valid point of reference and the tweeters use idiosyncratic language.

A special category are the responses to livecasts of performances featuring performers with a big fan base. For those instances, Martin Barker has suggested the categories of 'immersive' audiences who embrace 'all the bonus materials, because [they] allowed them to become audiences in a way that previously they had not been able to', whereas 'expert' audiences display 'a feeling that the event was almost being misappropriated', seeing themselves as 'holding expertise which the livecasts undercut' (2013, 66). Daisy Abbott (2015) and Rachael Nicholas (2018) have investigated these categories in relation to the reception of the *Coriolanus* livecast in 2014 featuring the actor Tom Hiddleston in the title role. Those audience members who posted about the livecast on social media would qualify their positions with statements such as 'I'm a big Hiddleston fan' or 'I'm a Shakespeare lover'; both groups tended to be offended by the ways in which Hiddleston was reduced to his physicality in the mid-show interview as they felt it 'undercut' their expertise (Abbott 2015, n.p.). This sense of having more entitlement than others to approach a Shakespeare play also extended to more general arguments about filming in theatre and demands for a DVD release. Whereas Hiddleston fans exerted their right to perform as fans, 'theatre aficionados demonstrated anger in reaction to what they saw as the undermining of their rights to access Shakespeare' (Abbott 2015, n.p.). Despite its mixed reception from Hiddleston fans, the mid-show interview reinforces 'Hiddleston fandom' as a legitimate viewing position, one that viewers focused on Shakespeare saw as demeaning of their own values and expertise (Nicholas 2018, 83). Applying the previous argument made by Ridout about the mis-spectator as rendering present some of the things that 'the machinery of the theatre normally works to obscure' (2012, 173), this would refer to the ways in which the machineries of theatre and theatre criticism create a distinction and even divide between legitimate and illegitimate (i.e. fan-ish) ways of engaging with a performance. Fandom, therefore, is a specific category of quasi-expertise that critiques prevalent discourses around a given play – especially with regard to canonical plays – and adds layers based on personally acquired knowledge, for instance about the lead performers, to an assessment of a performance.

Similar forms of engagement could be observed in the tweets about the NT Live screening of *Hamlet* featuring Benedict Cumberbatch on 15 October 2015. There were tweets such as 'I prepare to swoon' (@MDockrayMiller) (posted ten days before the livecast) or 'Benedict Cumberbatch you are amazing x I hope the skull in Sherlock is called Yoric' (@PentaholixUk), thus coming from Cumberbatch and/or *Sherlock* fans (Cumberbatch plays the title role in the BBC series *Sherlock*) or tweets that put this performance in context with others, thus positioning the tweeter as a knowing Shakespeare enthusiast: 'The last Hamlet I saw that comes close to Cumberbatch was Kenneth Branagh 23 years ago. Amazing performance' (@darkfienix) or 'I've never seen grief be dominant in the character of Hamlet before. Incredible performance from Cumberbatch' (@larkinaround).

When looking at all the tweets mentioned earlier, first of all, one notices different degrees of seriousness and that some users go into more detail than others. Second, the format of the tweet posted casually from one's smartphone brings about a – certainly also performative – colloquialization of responses, something that Ong, with regard to the digital age more generally, has fittingly described as 'secondary orality' (Ong [1982] 2002) and which we now, given how drastically the implications of 'the digital' have changed since the early 1980s, might refer to as tertiary orality. This casualness increases the immediacy of the experience because the responses reflect spontaneous responses to the performance right after leaving the cinema (they were all posted on the night of the show). It is crucial to note that the social dimension of theatre-going differs from the social dimension of the online space: both have their own (behavioural, linguistic) etiquettes. The online space allows for a more fragmented, catchy way of reacting to something, which both increases the ambivalence (and thus can relativize any 'absolute' statements) and the playfulness of the engagements, when, for instance, emojis or GIFs are used.

Complicating the issue of what exactly is limited or expanded, Cochrane and Bonner utter their scepticism towards live broadcasts and argue that they take away or deprive audiences of 'the ability, indeed the right, of each audience member to select and compile his or her own edit of the proceedings' (2014, 127). While this comes close to a sort of aesthetic censoring, one can ask if such editing does not inadvertently create a channelling of one's view. In my experience, the fact of being forced to look at particular spots on the stage creates high levels of impatience and annoyance, unnervingly so in livecasts of productions starring famous actors. For instance, in the NT's livecast of *Macbeth* on 10 May 2018, the focus was mostly on the protagonists' faces (played by Ann-Marie Duff and Rory Kinnear) instead of giving a permanent sense of the stage design. Many viewers, however, do not mind this tunnel vision at all: a NESTA study into the impact of NT live in its early stages reported that levels of absorption and emotional engagement in a given production were actually higher with regard to NT Livecasts (Bakhshi, Mateos-Garcia, and Throsby 2010, 5, 9). It seems that if a spectator accepts and perhaps even wishes for a mildly 'pre-shaped' show in the first place, then they can thoroughly plunge into it.

In order to grasp what else is entailed in this purported closeness of the performance to the recipient, it is necessary to think about the connection between response-ability, liveness and Twitter as a form of personalized live feed that all are part of the closeness or plunge experienced. The parameters according to which liveness is assessed shift. A brief reminder of Peggy Phelan's (among others) definition is due: Phelan focused on the temporal dimension of liveness, saying that '[p]erformance's only life is in the present' (1993, 146), meaning that 'performance is so radically "in time" (with time considered linear) that it cannot reside in its material traces and therefore "disappears"' (Schneider 2012, 66). Rick Altman (1986) usefully argues, however, that for an event to be perceived as live it does not necessarily have to happen at the same time as it is viewed. What matters is whether 'the television experience itself is [. . .] *sensed* as live by the home viewing audience' (45, emphasis added). As Hitchman paraphrases, in the livecasting context liveness is not seen in the nature of the original but 'as a condition of *viewing*' (2018, 176). This means that being part of an audience and being an audience member at the same time with others attending a film, a performance or a film of a performance, defines liveness and not the relation between oneself and the work of art. Social media such as Twitter contribute to this loosening up of parameters since they create an after-liveness that enables the user to operate much more independently. Twitter also emphasizes the individual viewing experiences in constituting, in many instances, the only documented form of one's memory of a performance. I would, thus, agree with the statement that 'social media enables the experience of liveness to travel outside the confines of physical co-presence' (Bucknall and Sedgman 2017, 124), but the *sense* of a co-presence of audience members is still crucial.

We are in it together: Critiquing the experience online

'In the case of crowdsourced theatre criticism', MacArthur points out, 'there is no need to hide one's inexperience' (MacArthur 261). The same holds true for livecasts. While MacArthur describes instances where social media users would assess a review somebody else had written while admitting they had not seen the show, this unabashedly personal, experiential dimension of the 'feeling I' dominates responses on social media to livecasts. In addition to the responses by spectators on Facebook and Twitter to the livecasts of *Yerma* and *Angels in America* that I discussed in the previous chapter, there were also tweets that were more specifically about the main actor's performance: for instance, after the livecast of *Angels in America* on 20 July 2017, @NicLeeBee wrote that 'Andrew Garfield has broken my heart tonight. Amazing stuff. Incredible performances all round but Andrew kills me. #NTlive #angelsinamerica' and @floridiangoblin felt that 'Andrew Garfield's portrayal of Prior Walter is honestly outstanding. I was deeply moved by his very raw performance #NTlive #AngelsinAmerica'. On the NT Live Twitter page, the livecast of *Present Laughter*, elicited comments such as the following in response to the post 'Congratulations to the absolutely marvelous cast of #PresentLaughter. We hope you enjoyed the show?': 'Fantastic, such virtuosity, Andrew Scott was primus inter pares, congratulations all!' (by @EevaTenkanen on 28 November 2019) and 'Loved it all over again. Happy memories of seeing this live a few weeks back. Wonderful night. Now looking for an encore showing. And the lovely @oldvictheatre looked great, too' (by @genesian61 on 29 November 2019). The comments are mini reviews, yet not only with a focus on the plays themselves, or the quality of the livecast (in typical responses to NT Live, there are occasional complaints about glitches in the transmission), but on the experience of attending them.

A survey of these responses presents one with a huge collection of private glimpses, of different emotional perspectives on a given livecast. One can connect this with the aforementioned remarks about what Benjamin referred to as 'reception in distraction' for his time and how these are no longer mutually exclusive in our context. Indeed, being attentive to one's smartphone distracts the user; it isolates them from the artwork/theatrical performance they are experiencing and creates a distance. At the same time, it can focus one's attention when one goes online to check what others are saying about a play, for instance, or to tweet about it. To be precise, this is a reception of the play, which then can feed into how one perceives the play, or, if read afterwards, how one has perceived the play. This form of reception that happens *via* distraction is situated on the paradocumentational brim and thus feeds back into the experience as a whole, bringing about new forms of attention as well.

Thinking back to the effect of the implied presence of other spectators, one must note that there is a friction between the 'we', or the communal viewing situation, and the 'I' that is created. Looking at cinema audiences, Julian Hanich argues that, first of all, being a spectator is being active and sharing an activity with others, which is based on a *we-intention* even if it is not spelled out (2014, 339). Thus, in addition to acting in the form of perceiving – Hanich aligns his argumentation with the enactivist approach of, for instance, Alva Noë (2004) – the spectators are also acting – and this is my take on Hanich's elaborations – in the form of forgetting the physical co-presence of other spectators but at the same time retaining a sense of their co-presence. Quite rightly, 'they have simply receded to the fringe of the field of consciousness. What is more, throughout the film this [. . .] prereflective *acting* jointly may be supplemented by *feeling* jointly' (Hanich 2014, 339–40). And thus, despite the mutual forgetting in exchange for a focus on the film/broadcast watched, and despite the fact that levels of attention vary, in its communality all these perceptions 'contribute their individual share to the joint action of the attentive audience' (Kennedy 2009, 14). This is why social media when used as channels for post-show reflections prolong the being part of an audience out of which a given individual experience has materialized.

Against a stagnation of theatre

It is necessary to acknowledge quasi-expertise and the role played by the experienced but inexpert commenter, whose response has its own validity. Here we are back at Benjamin's description of the masses' reaction to Chaplin as 'an immediate, intimate fusion of *pleasure* in seeing and experiencing with an attitude of expert appraisal' (Benjamin 1935, 29). The responses reflect the joys of a first-person encounter with theatre and a solitary and spontaneous reflection. One gets the impression that for viewers it is quite pleasant to verbalize their feelings because they know there is a forum for it. One can link this to a freeing from rules and hierarchies that Radosavljević observes when thinking about the secondary orality of the digital age:

> When it comes to writing, the hierarchies of the publishing world have demanded that we abide by certain orthographic standards. Even the pedagogies of literacy have been governed by the same rules. However, with the removal of those editorial hierarchies in the digital world we

have been freed to revert to more personal, more creative and more conversational means of expression. (2016, 18)

The responses that the paradocumentational brim surrounding NT Live elicits from spectators may not be according to the standards of the Critic's Circle or the American Theatre Critics Association, but they are still an equally valid part of the discussion. In the same way in which theatre changes and keeps on existing in new medial environments, the ways in which people talk about it are changing and need to change. It would be too myopic of a thesis, perhaps, to assume that soon 'there'll be no need for proper critics' because, as Arnold already knew, it is balance that is needed for a society striving towards the appreciation of culture and knowledge. But what livecasts especially make a contribution to is the diversification of *forms* of expertise. When livecasting loosens up the parameters of liveness, the tweets by quasi-experts who share their enthusiasm are part of the same discourse, namely one which makes use of the elasticity both of the current media environment and the online space. As was discussed in the panel discussion as part of the Young Vic's 'Pressing Concerns' series on 3 March 2021, (professional) reviewing is indeed a responsibility and reviewers are also responsible to care for and about new audiences. At the same time, *any* comment is the finishing touch to a production – if all reviews were perfect, where would the conversation be? Quasi-experts' tweets, thus, are of course very different from 600-word articles; some may regard them as 'individual enthusiasts' (which they certainly mostly are); yet they contribute to the diversification of performance response. Theatre needs recollections in order to live on – recollections that are disseminated by audiences and makers. These recollections are mediations because if we have not seen a show ourselves, we rely on these voices to tell us about it (and all aspects of it) for us. Precisely because these mediations influence *our* impression of a show, it is important to have a varied and diverse pool to draw from, both in terms of the background of the mediators and the form in which they are writing about a show. As Megan Vaughan puts it:

> When we only learn about theatremaking processes in the classroom, or from the memoirs of old white men on their retirement, a traditional way of doing things, and a traditional *route* into doing those things, is reinforced. When those with the power to communicate what theatre is, how it is made, what it means, how it makes us *feel*, all look and sound the same, and all share the same educational background and life experiences, then theatre stagnates. It is starved of new ideas, its audiences either get bored or get old and die, and it sacrifices its relevance

to the numerous other (cheaper) art forms and cultural activities that do actually reflect people's lives. (2020, 3–4)

Theatre, more than other art forms and cultural activities, only lives on if it is imbibed with new ideas and made relevant. It is for this reason that livecasting makes such a valuable contribution to the genre, even if some regard it as a commodification of theatre (Vaughan 2020, 3). It gives a new spin to theatre-making processes, thus preventing them from stagnating and from repeating themselves. The same holds true for theatre reviewing and criticism: the point is not that tweets should *replace* long-form reviews. But the voices of quasi-experts can liven theatre reviewing up and can, as a side-effect, also let theatre-makers and livecasting directors know what it is that spectators pay attention to in a show and what feeling or impression it is that they want to share usually immediately after they have been to a livecast. It can thus also contribute to a more audience-friendly experience – in other words: make theatre-makers understand audience engagement[11] – and shape the future of mediated performance.

6

Covidian theatre

The move to small screens and into homes

On or around 26 March 2020, the character of theatre changed. The change was not sudden and definite, but a change there was, nevertheless. What is a reference to Virginia Woolf's assessment of the arrival of Modernism on the world stage and its impact on human consciousness in her essay 'Mr. Bennett and Mrs. Brown' (Woolf 1924, 4) can be used analogously to describe the steps towards a new theatrical aesthetic that emerged out of the grip the Covid-19 pandemic has had on people all around the world since early 2020. When theatres closed in the UK, the search for alternatives to in-situ performances began. The closure of theatres is not unprecedented in British history, as throughout the late sixteenth and early seventeenth centuries theatres in London had to close several times when the plague was ravaging the city. As early as in 1569, the city was concerned about people attending 'certayne stage plays [. . .] and there being close pestered together in small romes [. . .] all not being and voyd of infeccions and diseases, whereby great infeccion with the plague, or some other infeccious diseases, may rise and growe' (in Chambers 1923, 267).[1] In 1577, during one of the first outbreaks of the plague in London, a preacher named T. White said in a speech from Paul's Cross that the theatre was to blame in the first place since 'the cause of plagues is sin' and 'the cause of sin are plays' and thus 'the cause of plagues are plays' (G. Evans et al., 1997, xliv). In the years that followed, playhouses could open depending on the death rate per week (varying between thirty and fifty) and while the restrictions were not always strictly followed, 'the visitations of plague nonetheless were by far the most severely limiting phenomenon the players encountered' (Gurr 2009, 98). While the plague was detrimental to acting companies, it also, conversely, contributed to the creation of plays, as Shakespeare scholar James Shapiro (2015) suggests. In 1606, during another month-long closure of playhouses, Shakespeare produced three of his most famous plays, *King Lear*, *Macbeth* and *Antony and Cleopatra*. In other words: as destructive and disruptive pandemics have been and are, one can also observe creative and productive responses to them coming from many societal fields, and the cultural sector in particular. The Covid-19 pandemic of 2020 is no exception to that.

The National Theatre posted first (public) considerations of making available its archived performances on 18 March 2020. It announced on its Facebook page that it was 'very actively looking' at how to make available shows from its archive – a move that seemed to follow requests from the public. This post was met with enthusiasm (as of 17 November 2020, 276 comments, 215 shares and 3.7K reactions, either 'likes', 'hearts' or 'laughs') that, already in these early days of lockdown, brought to the fore the yearning for theatre and the central role it plays in the lives of many people (Figure 17).

While some comments referred to specific plays, for most users who posted their comments the yearning seemed to be primarily for an affective, communal experience. The adjectives used were exclusively positive – for example, 'wonderful', 'fabulous', 'amazing', 'useful for schools' – and the phrase we/I would be 'happy to pay' came up fourteen times out of 276 (some of the comments only contained tagged names or emojis, however). People asked for streams of performances they had seen and of which they had 'wonderful memories' (Ashley Morgan-Davies), that they would be 'happy to pay for some nights at the theatre' (Catherine Saker).

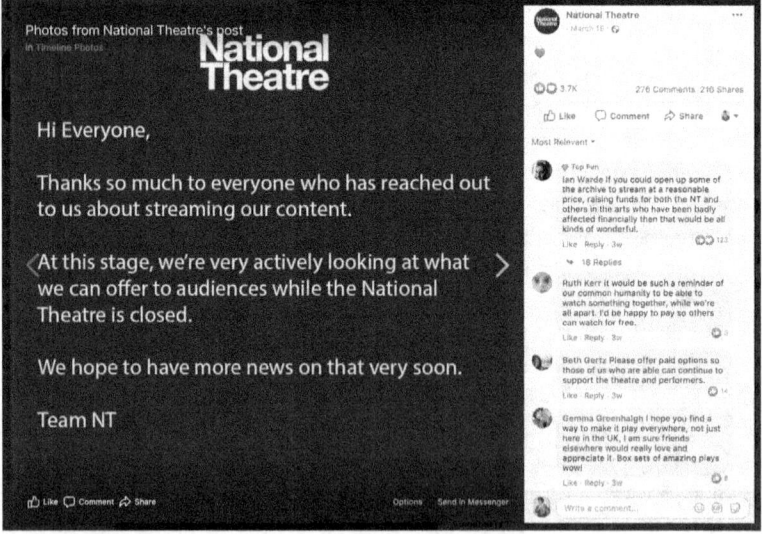

Figure 17 Screen capture of the National Theatre's Facebook Page on 18 March 2020.

On 26 March 2020, then, the initiative NT At Home was launched, showing sixteen of its archived – and previously partly livecast – productions on YouTube for free, for one week each, from 2 April until 23 July 2020. Its slogan was – just like that of NT Live – 'Get the best seats in the house', and the announcement post on Facebook received 1.2 K comments, 4.7K shares and 5.6K positive reactions ('likes', 'hearts' or 'wow') as of 17 November 2020, and 5740 retweets, 1774 quote tweets and 11.4 likes on Twitter.

In addition to making archived content available online, both the National Theatre and the Old Vic, among others, found ways to make new content accessible to audiences despite the lockdown and social distancing: theatres would film a performance of a show produced during the pandemic and share it on their websites or on YouTube, and the Old Vic launched a new series, called *In Camera*, which broadcast live shows via the communication programme Zoom from the theatre's empty auditorium. On a more experimental level, theatre companies, such as the Oxford-based Creation Theatre started to produce new shows online that were shown live to viewers all around the world via Zoom and where the performers were acting from their homes.

It is noteworthy that this is the penultimate chapter of a study on livecasting in/to cinemas which discusses more private forms of broadcast and mediated theatre in the context of a global pandemic. While the rise of online streaming in the performing arts has been taking place in parallel to the beginnings of livecasting but in a more quiet way, as Erin Sullivan points out (2020),[2] the forms it has taken when the Corona-induced lockdown began are unprecedented. Only a couple of years ago nobody could have predicted this new surge of online theatre and the topicality of theatre experienced on screens, albeit usually much smaller ones than those in cinemas. While it is thus a timely complement to the analysis conducted in the previous chapters, it continues and links up to the discussions of the tensions between non-mediated and mediated theatre, and more crucially, the tensions emerging out of the interaction between spectators and mediated performance.[3] The theatre on screens produced during the time of the Covid-19 pandemic reverberates with key issues identified for livecasting that function as the overarching anchor of this book: A changing understanding of *spectacle* (as it shifts from the public to the private sphere), *materiality* and made-ness of performance (in that performances are both made possible and limited by equipment, and, for instance, a specific socially distanced arrangement on stage) and *engagement* (when spectators are emphatically turned into bricoleurs or private experiencers that help co-create the theatrical experience). The discussions in the following connect ideas introduced in Chapter 1 about mediated theatre as compensation and the optionality of space with observations on the manifestations of mediated communitas in spectacles on screen as outlined in Chapter 2. These are intertwined with a revisiting of the play *Antony and Cleopatra* – included in the NT At Home programme – first watched as it was filmed for NT Live in 2018 and contextualized in its productive materiality in Chapter 3, with notions about spectator-centric theatre developed in Chapters 4 and 5.

This chapter offers a snapshot of the developments with regard to theatre produced in the year 2020 and considers the connection between different forms of performances that found their way to the online space. 'Covidian theatre' is not simply theatre produced and shown online during the time of the pandemic. Instead, I use this term to refer to plays which, in the wake of social distancing and lockdowns, explicitly address audiences *at home* and/or use various means to activate the pandemic frame. It is this specific positioning of the audience due to the pandemic that renders these plays 'Covidian'. The forms of addressivity unfolded in Covidian theatre are of particular concern for my analysis. I am interested in the different levels of engagement these plays foster, depending on the medium they use and to what end they choose to involve their spectators. By being exposed to a great and diverse variety of streamed performance, from no specific time and from no specific country, spectators in the year 2020 were made witnesses of how apparently disparate performances could bleed into and reverberate with one another in unexpected ways. Spectators' and theatre's understanding about their and its place in particular was again redefined. A new kind of theatre emerged, namely Covidian theatre, with 'viral theatre' as its most innovative category, as I have proposed together with Monika Pietrzak-Franger (2021).[4]

I suggest the term 'Covidian theatre' as an umbrella term for a broader thematic complex linking social practices with specific characteristics of theatrical performance and for different kinds of theatre shown and/or produced during the Covid-19 pandemic, that is, both pre-recorded or previously archived performance then made available online and those streamed and performed live. In a first step, the chapter comments on the role of masks – the symbol of the Covid-19 pandemic – in public life and in the context of socially distanced theatre and establishes a connection between vulnerability and the perception of community and citizenship or solidarity. In a second step, it looks at the characteristics of Covidian theatre and suggests that it emerges as a distinctly new quality of theatre and contributes to the creation of a new theatrical subgenre.

Masks and socially distanced theatre

As the sociologist David Inglis writes, '[m]asks both make some things present while occluding others. Their powers of affordance are great' (Inglis 2019). In the context of the Corona pandemic, putting on a mask has attained a new dimension – facemasks now evoke a different set of feelings. Social distancing has quickly become a whole code of conduct and politeness that is changing our affective responses to people we meet, the things we do and, a question relevant for this book, how or whether we experience theatre productions. In everyday life, the facemask or medical mask is an object with a set of specific, yet permanently shifting purposes: it protects people who fear infection, it is a symbol of solidarity for those who fear to infect others with their nasal secretion or spit, and it also symbolizes the adherence to and obeyance of new rules and restrictions imposed by the authorities (see Böhrer 2020). Following Foucault, the facemask manifests the relation and submission of humans to their corporeality and its frailties and deficiencies (Foucault 2013, 31–2). The mask is also a border between body and environment: it separates our body and bodily fluids from others, and it also marks what it excludes, that is, it excludes the danger emanating from the environment and potentially others from one's own body (Giesen 2011, 39).

In contrast, the origins of theatre point to a very different function of masks, depending on the context and operating both in religious and secular frames. They were and are used in rituals and in carnivals in particular. As Nourit Melcer-Padon points out, masks as 'agents of identity transformation assist in superficial transformations as well as in deep-rooted ones' and especially during a ritual, the person wearing a mask 'is identified with his mask, to the point of voiding himself of his own identity in order to become the mask-invoked deity' (2018, 9). The mask does something to the mask-bearer. When they become a vessel, they disappear and become an Other. The mask arms and obscures the bearer rather than exposing them as being vulnerable and in need of protection.

In his discussion of masks worn during carnival, Mikhail Bakhtin emphasizes that wearers of masks must obey the rules and temporal limitations of carnival while at the same time celebrating the 'temporary liberation from the prevailing truth and from the established order' (see Bakhtin 1968, 7–13). As Melcer-Padon comments, '[n]o society would survive a never-ending carnival, and by the same token, no society suffers impersonation masks to be used beyond their allotted limits and for other purposes than the ones they were made' (Melcer-Padon 2018, 97–8). Indeed, at first glance, the situation of the current pandemic and the ways in which theatre plays are made available are of a carnivalesque quality in Bakhtin's sense with regard to the conditions of exception, including the temporal dimension of an extraordinary time, and the subversion of at least some hierarchical structure. The pandemic, like the carnival, stands in contrast to normal life and creates spaces in which social hierarchies are reconfigured. They are not subverted, however, as would be the case with the carnival. On the contrary: as Cally Gatehouse (2020) has also pointed out, as the 'normal' rules are replaced with the new rules of the pandemic, they are 'in some senses an inversion of the carnivalesque' (34). The rules created by the pandemic are even 'a darker mirror image' (35) of the characteristics Bakhtin outlines when describing the carnivalesque: free and familiar contact among people is replaced by limited physical contact between people; eccentric behaviour, for instance, not wearing masks or other forms of non-conformance, and *carnivalistic mésalliance* are supplanted by the strict policing of deviance from those new rules of social distancing and the rigorous control of all things concerning the body. In addition, new societal divides are created, such as those between precarious and low-paid work, 'essential' and 'non-essential' work and the digital divide. With regard to theatre, lockdown regulations took away most sources of income for theatre institutions, thus taking away their agency. And despite all this, the creative energy and inventive drive to arrange with the current state and find new ways to live out social relationships endure. In parallel to the inversion of the carnivals, many life-affirming solutions – such as the examples of Covidian theatre that are the focus of this chapter – were produced amidst the pandemic. The pandemic opens up spaces of contingency when spectators are turned into their own 'performance editors' (when selecting from a multitude of offers from different theatres and points in time) – much more so than with regard to livecasts, where shows are limited and selected for the spectators by the NT or other theatres – and this is what makes me refer to the pandemic as bearing traces of a carnivalesque loosening of specific hierarchical structures in the cultural sector.

A protective mask in theatre is not about (carnivalesque) identity transformation, but about protecting the vulnerable body against a deadly disease. However, the very fact that people come to the theatre, even if this means wearing a protective mask and rendering themselves more vulnerable through exposure to others (vs. remaining at home), signals the enduring yearning for festivity, a theatrical event, that brings people together.[5] The quotes that I cited earlier in response to the NT At Home announcement are all about the appreciation of the magic of theatre, which echoes the Bakhtinian (utopian) understanding of carnival with its focus on the celebration of the communal and its life-affirming aspects.[6]

What is now new about masks in the context of theatre, then, is that our attention needs to be directed at those normally not wearing masks, namely the spectators, and in what ways masks have an impact on the experience of theatrical plays, and how the mask and social distancing have an impact on the set up of performances. In some German theatres, as the restrictions were lowered during the summer months of 2020, but also in the UK for several weeks in autumn 2020, it was possible to attend in-situ performances wearing a mask. At the local theatre in Freiburg, for instance, the Stadttheater, one had to book personalized tickets and was guided by ushers from the entrance of the building to the auditorium where a very limited number of chairs had been placed. When all audience members were in their seats and the lights went down, everybody could take off their masks. It was the spectators who literally made their masks fall and became both 'free' and more vulnerable during the duration of the performance that they watched without protection.

Both in public life and in theatrical performance, masks establish a connection between vulnerability and the perception of community and citizenship or solidarity. When attending an in-situ performance, one had the advantage of *being* there but the disadvantage of potentially putting oneself at risk and being vulnerable; when one watched such a performance streamed and saw the spectators in the auditorium, one might feel disadvantaged (one was *not* there), discomforted (those people were putting themselves at risk, even though they were keeping the social distancing rules) or comfortable (one was not at risk). As put by Alexis Soloski in his *NY Times* review of Sarah Kane's *Crave* that was performed at the Chichester Festival Theater and livestreamed from 29 October to 4 November 2020, the most shocking part of the play is its live audience:

> In the minutes before *Crave* began, remote spectators could watch as actual (masked) theatregoers took socially distanced seats. [...] I turned my computer volume up, the better to listen to the endangered language of hushed conversations and rustling programs [. . .] Those masked theatregoers are brave, for reasons beyond the pandemic. (Soloski 2020)

Masks as symbols of the pandemic and their call for social distancing, both directly and indirectly, had an impact on the aesthetics and theatricality of theatre produced and broadcast online, that is, its form, but also, if to a slightly lesser extent, its content. The plays shown in 2020 were produced in socially distanced circumstances: in most cases, such as the Zoom plays by the Oxford-based Creation Theatre, the performers were located in different cities in the UK and Ireland, thus adhering to the 2-metre social distancing rule with bravura. In other cases, such as the *In Camera* performances by the Old Vic, the actors either always kept a 2-metre distance from one another, thus never appearing in the same frame with one another (as was the case with *Lungs*, starring Claire Foy and Matt Smith), or there was a dominance of shows with one single performer, such as *Three Kings*, with Andrew Scott in the main role (see Liedke and Pietrzak-Franger 2021 for a discussion of these performances).

Viral affect on screens

As I have argued before in Chapter 2, theatre on screen can catch and carry affect successfully. For the spectators of the NT Livecast of *A Midsummer Night's Dream* at the Barbican on 17 October 2019, apart from the dynamic camera work and movement, it was seeing the in-situ spectators who functioned as carriers of affect. This observation can be complemented with insights offered by a Futurist play that at its core is about the effect of action seen on screen. There is a wealth of research literature on the affective impact of cinema and film that I have already referred to in Chapter 4,[7] but it is illuminating to also look at what theatre itself has to say on this subject. The following play is exemplary for how theatre displays a high self-awareness of its affective contagious nature and the rivalry between theatre and media. It positions itself to new media with regard to politics of affect. In the theatrical *sintesi* with the title *Madness* (1916–17) by the Italian Futurist Mario Dessy, the action takes place during a film screening. The film protagonists' madness breaches the movie screen and spreads through the cinema audience. As a consequence, 'everyone is disturbed, obsessed by the idea of madness that comes over them all. Suddenly the spectators get up screaming . . . gesturing . . . fleeing . . . confusion . . . MADNESS' (Dessy 2001 [1916–17], 282). This is an – admittedly very pithy – instance of filmic emotions having a contagious effect and a case where mediated emotions have a direct influence on those watching them. It can also be understood as serving to comment on the value of theatre in comparison to film. As John London argues, 'there is probably [. . .] something at the heart of the [Futurist] movement that argues against the exclusivity of the flat screen. [. . .] The message is clear: live action is more exciting than two-dimensional drama' (2017, 22). I suggest that there is also something quite different that can be gathered from this example: the play actually advocates a side-by-sideness of screen and live action. After all, if something can leave its medium and find ground in another frame, it must be powerful. The two-dimensional is so effective that it has a direct impact on live action – mediated emotions can be contagious, too.

In the context of media studies, the concept of 'virality' has been put to fruitful use by Tony Sampson (2012), who has suggested that a theory of contagion helps us understand how society comes together in assemblages, events and affects. More specifically, Sampson contends that 'virality' needs to be decoupled from representational approaches that tend to limit examples of social and cultural contagion to their resemblances to biological spreading phenomena. When such a limitation occurs, the emerging discourses centre on fears of contamination and neo-Darwinian biomechanisms forcefully transferred onto sociocultural processes. For Sampson, virality can describe new kinds of connectivity in the age of networks decoupled from such fears and limitations. While discredited by some (cf. Sugiera 2017), the concepts of 'contagion' and 'virality' have proved useful to the contemporary theorization of theatre and performance in times of heightened mediatization and digitalization. For Miriam Felton-Dansky, 'viruses, in their many forms – digital, biological, artistic – nearly always function as *disruptions in the fabric of daily life*' (2018, 4, emphases added). A virus can be contagious and so can emotions.

In this sense, then, Covidian theatre conceptually evokes and participates in the disruption of both extant generic expectations as well as the practice of spectating. What is more, it draws attention to the affordances of theatre as medium and as an event. In the context of theatre produced during the pandemic, its virality is of a threefold quality: it 'infects' or smudges generic expectations towards what a theatrical performance should look like *and* what the role of the spectator is, and it forces us to rethink what the framing of a theatrical event is and how stable its demarcations are. That this definition, taken by itself, would also work for livecasting, is a case in point: the developments towards a mediated experience of theatre are related. Yet the viral quality of Covidian theatre is distinct for this form, as it emerges out of a pandemic frame and enters people's homes when spectators experience plays on their own (small) screens.

Covidian theatre disrupts and redefines those constitutive elements of performance that make the theatrical experience contagious in the first place: the spatial and temporal co-presence of performers and the respective audience members and the notion of temporality and liveness more generally, when archived performances, for instance as part of NT At Home, are streamed as online events that have a 'premiere'.[8] Again, this definition would also work for livecasting; yet the plays that I term Covidian are all addressed explicitly to audiences *at home* or find various ways to activate the pandemic frame.

Looking at the statistics of NT At Home, one can see that on average, 25 per cent of viewers tuned in on the premiere date with 16 per cent across all titles watching in 'premiere mode'. The highest percentage of people watching on the premiere date was for *One Man, Two Guvnors* where it went up to 34 per cent (Buckeridge 2020).[9] However, since, as Auslander claims, theatrical 'liveness' emerges from a historical context whose characteristics have changed under the impact of new technologies, 'the concept of liveness has developed to only refer to temporality [. . .] at the expense of the once indispensable feature of corporeality' (Meyer-Dinkgräfe 2015, 71). More precisely, live media depend on configurations of real time and sociality to establish their value. Live media are characterized by an urgency, that is, the explicit disclaimer 'that something needs to be attended to *now* rather than later' (van Es 2017, 1249, emphasis added). This explains the nowness discourse set in motion by NT At Home that included countdowns to the respective opening nights of their selected shows. In addition, 'live media can make different selling points explicit by drawing on the particular relation they configure between real time and sociality' (1249). These selling points can be authenticity, unpredictability, presence and participation. Thus, both performance and live media are characterized by urgency, temporal limitations and participation – in as much as they create experiences, they cannot be contained in either a specific space or time.

One can identify various forms of theatre emerging out of the context of lockdown theatre, all of which supplement each other. In taking shape on a small(er) screen, this theatre is already intrusive and 'unruly' (defying the traditional form) in that it crosses the public-versus-private divide and enters people's homes. As a consequence, it has the potential to tackle, stir up and deconstruct attitudes towards theatre, the topics that are addressed within the theatrical frame and the spectators' subjectivities concerning them. The following section zooms in on the specifics of the different categories of Covidian theatre.

Covidian theatre

When remote audiences watch remotely collaborating performers or performers either on their own on stage or keeping a distance, this is not only socially distanced theatre but also a kind of theatre that is dominated by the notion of distance. One must note how this contrasts with definitions of theatrical spectacles in pre-pandemic times (see my discussion in Chapter 2), as Erika Fischer-Lichte has argued with reference to the early twentieth century. As an antidote to social isolation, ennui and what Simmel has termed the blasé attitude (Simmel 2002 [1903], 14) induced by the shifts in daily life in an industrialized society, theatre, as Fischer-Lichte proposes,

> appeared to be capable of transforming individuals into members of a community, albeit only temporarily, by focusing on the bodily

co-presence of actors and spectators, on the physical acts of the actors and their capacity to 'infect' the spectators as well as on the 'contagion' occurring among the spectators. (2005, 30)

It can be argued that temporal and spatial co-presence of performers and audiences, and the respective audience members among themselves, are constitutive elements of what makes the theatrical experience contagious in the first place. Fischer-Lichte states that for a performance to occur, it is necessary that actors and spectators *assemble* for a particular time span at a particular place and do something together' (Fischer-Lichte 2005, 23, emphasis added). According to this definition, the notion of proximity is required and cannot be widened to increase the distance between the participants, which creates impossible challenges in times of social distancing.

In the context of Covidian theatre, it is helpful to take a close look at the conditions that she sets for theatre. Co-presence, in Fischer-Lichte's sense, implies 'a relationship of co-subjects' and, crucially, not a replication or expression of a play text, but a bringing forth 'by the actions, perceptions, responses of both actors and spectators alike'. As the performance takes place '*between* actors and spectators', this calls for a 'social community' (2005, 23). Without this coming together of co-subjects (one group called 'spectators' and the other 'performers'), the performance would not exist and it then both needs a social community and creates one. Certain types of Covidian theatre do not fulfil the criterion of bodily co-presence, yet in most cases they manage to generate effects very similar to it. This is because the plays create this uniting relationship *across* distance. There are four criteria that all kinds of Covidian theatre fulfil and that are constitutive of the coming into being of this kind of theatre:

a) The paradocumentational brim and/or the interplay of form and content addresses the Covid-19 pandemic and the disruption it causes. The invoked 'pandemic frame' is not only established as an important context of the play but there is also, in varying degrees, a self-positioning of the plays in relation to the pandemic.
b) Space is multiplied, randomized and relegated to the realm of the coincidental and private.
c) There is a willingness on the part of spectators to engage with the new form and accept a novel role as spectators. As professional theatre depends on income through tickets, Covidian theatre ultimately rests on the willingness of spectators to buy tickets for theatre shown online.
d) Small(er) screens in general and communication technologies such as Zoom in particular are repurposed.

	Pandemic frame activated through...			Form requires direct forms of address of spectators at home		Liveness	
	paratext	Textual allusions in the play / stage design / depicted theatre venue	use of screens and medium	no	yes	no	yes
STREAMED THEATRE							
NT At Home via YouTube	✓	– / – / –	–	✓	–	✓	–
Live streams (e.g. *Crave*)	✓	– / ✓ / ✓	–	✓	–	–	✓
Theatre recorded during the pandemic and streamed online	✓	(✓) / ✓ / ✓	–	✓	–	✓	–
VIRAL THEATRE							
Readings of monologues or Zoom plays such as Creation Theatre's *Horatio! (And Hamlet)*	(✓)	✓ / – / –	✓	✓	–	–	✓
Performances presented via Zoom, e.g. Big Telly's and Creation Theatre's *Alice – A Virtual Theme Park*, *The Tempest* and *Macbeth* and Big Telly's *Dear World*	✓	✓ / – / –	✓	–	✓	–	✓
The Old Vic's *Lungs* and *Three Kings*	✓	(✓) / ✓ / ✓	✓	–	✓	–	✓
- performance pieces that can be downloaded, such as *Play at Home* and *1000 Scores* - 'Zoomies' such as Split Britches' *Last Gasp WFH*	✓	✓ / – / –	✓	–	✓	✓	–

← Greater traces of the pandemic

→ degree to which spectators become 'performers'

Figure 18 Typology of Covidian theatre.

The key question in my assessment of Covidian theatre is to find out who or what engages whom and how. As far as my understanding of 'engagement', a spacious term that can mean many things such as emotional involvement, connectedness, paying attention, taking part in an activity and so on, is concerned, I am building on definitions worked with in previous chapters of this book: first of all, I am picking up on the discussion in Chapter 2 on the conception of live theatre and livecasting as affective arrangements that can – to different degrees – exert a pull on their spectators. Second, continuing the discussion from Chapter 4, I conceive of engagement as specific effects of mediation. While in the previous chapters, the effects of the mediation and the affective arrangement of livecasting were focused, the ensuing discussion turns to smaller screens and the effects of the concomitant forms of mediation. In other words: to what extent is the form of the plays engaging spectators, that is, exerting a pull on them, or to what extent do the spectators have to do that themselves? What influence does the pandemic frame have on forms of engagement? To what extent are the spectators required or invited to become a performer themselves and be 'pulled' in the performance?

Given the manifold guises in which Covidian theatre appears, the overview in Figure 18 provides a typology of Covidian theatre to help map the field. This overview is by no means exhaustive, but it does illustrate the main tendencies that I have identified with regard to theatre emerging out of the lockdown context of 2020.

These three parameters (listed in the horizontal row) enable a mapping of the different forms of Covidian theatre in a grid table. The first parameter, the pandemic frame, allows a fine-tuning of the ways in which Covidian theatre positions itself to the ongoing pandemic. References to the pandemic may be restricted to the paratextual brim (e.g. the marketing of the play, the ways in which it is commented upon in social media and podcasts in which the artists involved are interviewed),[10] or they may be included in the play itself, either through textual allusions in the play, the stage design or the depiction of the theatre venue (e.g. showing mask-wearing theatregoers or protective screens between the actors). Furthermore, the way in which the affordances of communication technologies such as Zoom are used may be tailored towards evoking the pandemic as a frame of reference. As in the case of the Old Vic's *In Camera* series, the use of split screens and the 'spotlight feature' in Zoom, for example, can be seen as foregrounding impacts of the pandemic.

This parameter of the pandemic frame allows me to clearly distinguish two main tendencies that were discernible from instances of theatre that were shown online in the course of 2020: there was streamed theatre, and there was viral theatre. In contrast to streamed theatre, viral theatre employs the communication technology used to transmit the play in such a way as to evoke the pandemic frame.

The second parameter also hinges on the aspect of form. While all Covidian theatre addresses the audience at home, some forms of Covidian theatre *explicitly* address spectators as being at home and may even ask them to carry out specific tasks according to instructions. My second parameter captures these forms of explicit or direct address of the spectators at home as well as instances of participatory theatre or performance pieces. In the scenarios in which spectators are addressed explicitly, the form of engagement that is fostered is one of community with other spectators and performers across distance. This is not meant to imply that other streamed plays do not manage to engage their audiences (draw their attention, emotional responses, etc.), but instead this is about pulling the spectators into the live show to become part of it through creating entire sequences in the show which are filled out by the spectators (e.g. where they are encouraged to create the sound of rain by clapping, as in Creation Theatre's *The Tempest*, first shown in May 2020 via Zoom see Liedke 2020b).

The interplay between the different parameters becomes especially clear with regard to 'liveness', which is my third parameter. In those cases in which the plays were recorded in pre-Covid-19 times and were then simply streamed via YouTube, for example, the pandemic frame is not activated via textual allusions in the play, stage design or depicted theatre venue. The category of 'liveness' is important because my case studies actually complicate the seemingly easy opposition between 'liveness' and 'not live'. As will be shown, strategies are often employed to foster a sense of liveness even if that 'liveness' is not given in the temporal sense of the word.

Different forms of Covidian theatre are distinguished by their specific combination of these three parameters so that the table grid allows me to identify sub-categories of streamed theatre and viral theatre. Streamed theatre includes three categories: first, content that had already been available before the pandemic and was put online in the first weeks of lockdown; second, plays that were streamed live from a theatre during the pandemic (sometimes even with an actual audience in the auditorium); and third, plays that had been intended to run 'in situ' but had to be cancelled because of the second lockdown in the UK and the recordings of which were then made available online. Two prominent examples of the latter are the National Theatre's *Death of England – Delroy* that was streamed on YouTube for free on 27–28 November 2020 after it had been filmed on 4 November 2020, its opening and at the same time closing night. Similarly, the Almeida's *Nine Lessons and Carols* was originally scheduled to run from 3 December 2020 until 6 January 2021 and was then recorded live on 15 December 2020 and available to watch on the theatre's website (for the price of a ticket). Both shows activated the pandemic frame either indirectly or directly: in *Delroy*, there were see-through walls protecting the performer (Michael Balogun) from the audience and signs that were visible in the recording drew attention to social distancing measures. Both in *Delroy* and *Nine Lessons and Carols* one could see the on-site audience wearing masks and the main topic of the latter was loneliness and isolation. In general, when comparing the different categories of streamed theatre, there is a progression towards greater traces of the pandemic. Therefore, these categories have been grouped in such a way in the table grid that the traces of the pandemic become more prominent as one moves towards viral theatre.

Viral theatre encompasses several categories of theatre that differ from each other mainly because of the degree to which spectators are hailed as 'performers'. There are also three categories: first, shows that consist of monologues that are delivered but which do not pull audiences in by directly addressing them (through participation or through cues that one is told to follow, such as turning off the light, having a piece of paper handy etc.). This is different in the second category, such as the plays by Creation Theatre and Big Telly, and also the Old Vic, which not only activate the pandemic frame through their staging (in the case of the Old Vic: socially distanced shows with one or two performers performed in an empty auditorium) and textual allusions (Big Telly's *Macbeth*) but also pull spectators in by directly addressing them. The third category refers to performance pieces, for instance, *Play at Home* and *1000 Scores* (see 1000scores.com), that can be 'used' at the spectators' own discretion and turn their users into performers. These plays address the challenges of the pandemic and are geared towards encouraging their spectators to develop strategies of self-care as a vital and necessary response to the pandemic.

The crucial difference between streamed and viral theatre is, as mentioned earlier, that in the case of streamed theatre the pandemic frame is *not* activated through the use of screens and medium and the spectators are not pulled into a show directly; *they* do the 'pulling' themselves, and they choose to make connections (to other shows, to the pandemic frame, through willingly taking on the role of the bricoleur etc.). They are aided in this by the paratext that forges a connection to the pandemic frame and because streamed theatre is embedded in a media environment that invites surfing across the sprawling internet. In the case of viral theatre, the frame of the shows fosters spectatorial engagement and there are direct forms of address which hail the spectator to become part of the show, if only in an ornamental way. The ensuing sections will discuss NT At Home as a key category of streamed theatre in detail.

Retrospective synchronicity and NT At Home

Covidian theatre breaks up performance time and space: it cannot be contained within one structure or network in contrast to previous forms of mediated theatre such as livecasting. In both the case of Covidian theatre and in livecasts, the paradocumentational brim is a central part of the arrangement of the theatrical form: it does not play an equally important role in all instances of the former, however, while it is a constitutive part of the latter.

When investigating different broadcasts of Shakespeare plays in the early weeks of lockdown in the UK, Pascale Aebischer argued in an online talk on 20 May 2020 titled 'Viral Shakespeare – Binge-Watching *Hamlet* in Lockdown', that the broadcasts developed agency and, by inscribing themselves on the time and space in which they were being watched, became particularly alive. I argue that the agency of broadcasts is, however, a highly unstable one, one emerging out of an environment of contagion. The audience is the performer; being an audience member is to feel and enact one's vitality. When watching several broadcasts, a broadcast is only defined against other broadcasts: it is what it is not. For this reason, it is in fact the spectators – or 'spect-actors', to take up Augusto Boal's term (Boal [1979] 1985, 122) – who are the agencies forced to make the connections between the streams and creating equally unstable intra-textual (trans-textual) landscapes. Defying logical (or at least linear) orders of time and space, it is the agency of the spectator that creates an experience of retrospective synchronicity. In an environment characterized by attention, distraction and chopped-up performance, it is the spectators who become their own broadcast editors. In the context of the Covid-19 pandemic, one must ask if the form of streamed online theatre catapulted forward by it does contain an energy akin to radicalism that can truly shake up what we deem theatre to be capable of.

Several theatres in the UK, such as the National Theatre (with the initiative NT Home), the Royal Shakespeare Company (in partnering up with the BBC's 'Quarantine in Culture' programme and Marquee TV) and the Royal Opera House made former performances that had been archived available to the public online. Other London theatres, such as the Yard Theatre produced one-day online festivals.[11] The Berliner Ensemble encouraged their remote audiences to 'discover their digital offer in times of the Corona break' under the slogan 'BE at Home' and many other theatres around the world followed suit. In her talk Aebischer argued that – since it was possible to watch very different *Hamlet* productions from different countries and decades one after the other, they began to 'infect' one another in the mind of the viewer. The clarity of chronological order was 'smudged' by lockdown, and time was 'out of joint in a way that makes life slow down, pulls all together, while also accelerating' (2020). It was possible, therefore, to experience Thomas Ostermeier's *Hamlet* staged at the Schaubühne Berlin in 2008 alongside Federay Holmes's and Elle While's *Hamlet* at Shakespeare's Globe in 2018 interwoven with Dimiter Gotscheff's *Hamletmaschine* at Deutsches Theater Berlin in 2008.

With regard to the broadcasting of archived performances, there were different kinds of scenarios possible: either one could watch many streams within the course of a few days featuring the same actors or one could watch the stream of an archived performance that one had seen previously in situ. As a consequence, another type of performance that pushed itself onto the centre stage was the spectators' memory of 'original' performances they had seen or of those streamed performances they had watched in temporal proximity to one another. I want to suggest that what happened in these instances was the experience of retrospective synchronicity. What I mean by this is the notion that performances which had been staged at very different points in time, in some cases many years apart, could, by being watched within the course of only a few days or hours, be perceived side-by-side. Especially when seeing the same actors come up in different performances, unexpected connections could be made between plays or traits exhibited by a performer in one play were anticipated when they appeared in another play.

From 2 April to 23 July 2020, the National Theatre streamed sixteen of its archived – and previously partly livecast – productions on YouTube for free.[12] As mentioned at the beginning of this chapter, the NT announced its first considerations of offering such a service on 18 and 26 March (Figures 17 and 19).

The NT At Home initiative stood out because it went against the repeated assertions made by the National since the launch of NT Live in 2009 that it would not make the livecasts available in any other format, for instance on DVD, and that the only other way to watch them apart from the cinema would be to book an appointment in the theatre's archive – an offer hardly taken up by 'regular' audiences.[13] Once the decision was made to launch NT At Home, both the NT and the NT Live Twitter page advertised the initiative with posts such as the following:

> We're all about experiencing theatre together. At a time when many theatre fans around the world aren't able to visit National Theatre Live venues or local theatres, we're excited to introduce National Theatre At Home.
>
> You will be able to watch some of the best British theatre from the comfort of your living room, via YouTube for free for one week. (@NTLive)

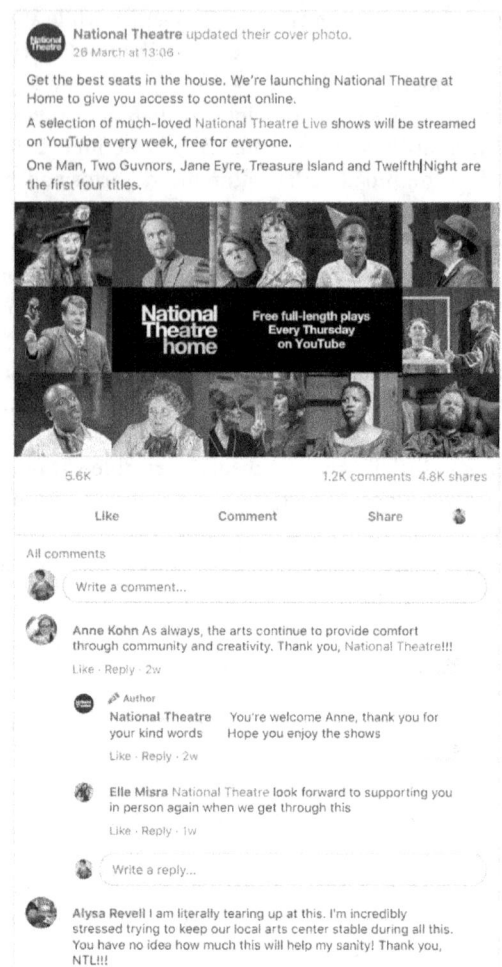

Figure 19 Screen capture of the National Theatre's Facebook Page announcing the launch of NT At Home on 26 March 2020.

Community and comfort are the keywords here: a virtual community of theatre lovers is evoked that will be given the opportunity to experience plays for free on their computer screens at home. Notably, in the post on 26 March (Figure 19) user Anne Kohn comments on how 'the arts continue to provide comfort *through* community and creativity'. The arts in general, and the NT in particular for the UK context, play the role of carers. They – or rather those at the NT responsible for their social media account – also took on the role

Covidian Theatre 163

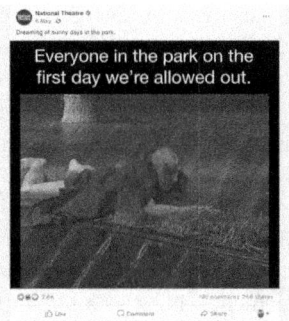

Figure 20 Screen capture of *Frankenstein* GIF posted on the National Theatre's Facebook Page on 6 May 2020.

of jesters, when GIFs were posted ahead of the streaming of *Frankenstein* on 30 April 2020, for instance, that functioned as meta-comments on the conditions of people's lives during the lockdown. The GIF in Figure 20 was edited as a ten-second contiguous clip of the video in which Frankenstein's monster, portrayed by Johnny Miller, crawls through grass and is visibly taken aback by touching something like that for the first time. The caption reads 'Dreaming of sunny days in the park'. GIF stands for 'Graphics Interchange Format' and can be either a short, looped animated sequence made from static images or a 5–10-second contiguous video clip. While GIF sequences can be accompanied by an audio feed, 'a large part of the humour of the format is derived from their absence of sound and the potential incongruity caused by the application of the original (silent) video to a new contexts' (Blackwell 2018, 112).

In the context of theatre, GIFs can thus subvert the associations spectators have with a text and make theatrical bodies speak (or move) in unexpected ways. This is also what happens with the *Frankenstein* GIF: it takes away the horror or disgust associated with the monster and ridicules it. One can draw a parallel to the observation made by Anna Blackwell with regard to GIFs made about Shakespeare plays (especially such performances featuring Tom Hiddleston, see Blackwell 2018, 113): The humour derived from a GIF like this lies in its refusal to treat both *Frankenstein* and Mary Shelley in the ways it has been as part of the Western canon: that is, mostly critical rigour and venerability. In analogy to Eckart Voigts' term 'para-cinematic' to refer to the modes in which animated GIFs operate, namely 'new modes of engagement (mobilised and manipulable, spreadable and sharable, accelerated, compact, and integrated in day-to-day activities' in 'a new cultural sphere of circulation' (2017, 23), and in line with my usage of the term 'paradocumentational brim' to refer to all texts and narratives produced outside of the core theatrical event, the *Frankenstein* GIF can be termed 'para-theatrical'. In this particular case, the GIF is not only integrated into day-to-day activities, it comments on them and creates a link between the everyday and the narrative of the play in question. The referring back to lockdown creates an unexpected sense of complicity between the monster and spectators but most importantly adds comic relief and silly play, something that the 1.3K likes, 1K 'laugh' reactions and 175 'hearts' (as of 3 December 2020) attest to. Crucially, such a use of paratext is both a way to activate the pandemic frame of the show *and* to foster spectatorial engagement with it as a connection between spectators and the show is established.

While it was indeed free to watch the plays that were part of NT At Home, there were reminders both before, during and after the streams to donate to the NT. This was complemented by video messages of the actors involved in the NT At Home repertoire, such as when Ralph Fiennes, who played Antony in *Antony and Cleopatra*, sitting in front of a nondescript white wall, wearing a casual sweater and with a dishevelled hairdo, thanked everybody who had watched the stream for supporting 'the fragile business of theatre' in a video message posted on the NT's Facebook page on 10 May 2020.

The agency OneFurther conducted research into what percentage of all the viewers who watched the first NT At Home performance, *One Man, Two Guvnors*, watched it on the night it was first broadcast, and whether there was a correlation between this premiere experience and the donations made. According to their research, the total number of views (i.e. the number of devices to which the play was streamed) was 2.6 million at the end of the week. Eight per cent of views came during the live premiere. By the end of the premiere, $41,600 were raised, and $82,500 shortly before the stream was taken offline a week later, which means that about 50 per cent of donations were raised on the first night (OneFurther.com). With regard to all the sixteen productions, as mentioned before, about 25 per cent of the total views a performance received did take place on the night of the premiere. That is, digital media indeed allow productions to keep '*living*' even if they are no longer '*live*' and 'remediated' theatre 'carr[ies] on performing in the present of the online environment even as the live event to which it is related has receded into the past' (Aebischer 2013, 146). There is, thus, another hierarchy discernible when it comes to theatre streamed for a limited time: it suggests that when a recording is shown for the first time, it lives more than when shown or watched later.

After the initiative was over, the 'Thank you' trailer put on YouTube showed moments from most of the sixteen productions and included phrases such as '16 world-class productions – brought to your homes for free . . . Over

4 months of entertainment – We've been overwhelmed by your support. But we still need you. Please keep donating' (National Theatre 2020). According to its own statistics, the initiative had nearly 15 million views, reaching 9 million households in 173 countries (most viewers in the United Kingdom, followed by the United States, Australia, Canada, Russia and Germany). As of 26 October 2020, there are 232 comments below this trailer and the vast majority of users asks for a streaming service or others ways to keep enabling access to the NT's plays. And indeed, on 1 December 2020, an announcement was made that few of those researching the NT would have expected: the NT launched a streaming subscription service, also called NT At Home, that offers currently over thirty productions for about 9 € per month and to which more productions are added. In their announcement tweet, they wrote: 'The National Theatre is coming home. This is unmissable theatre, whenever you want it.' The trailer encouraged audiences to 'take a front row seat in the comfort of your own home. . . . This is theatre for everyone – anytime, everywhere', thus effectively combining superlatives with affective language (spectators *want* theatre) and emphasizing the constant availability without spatial and temporal restrictions. Within eight hours, the post received 1.3K likes, 385 retweets and 318 quote tweets.

What did the offer made by NT At Home during lockdown add to an experience of theatre, apart from making it more accessible and reaching into people's living rooms? Linking this to my discussion of the livecast of *Antony and Cleopatra* in Chapter 4, watching the stream of the play on YouTube made it possible to add a third layer to my experience of the play which I had watched in situ and then on the night it was recorded in 2018. When I attended the filming of the broadcast of *Antony and Cleopatra* for NT Live in the National Theatre's Olivier Theatre on 6 December 2018, my attention was divided between the cameras on their tracks, Michael Bruce's sensual rhythmical music and my own role as a spectator who must not hide her emotions. Before the show the presenter, Samira Ahmed, had turned to us – the 'actual' audience in the auditorium – while the introductory film, in which Simon Godwin talked about staging the play, was being shown to cinema audiences around the world, and urged us not to be afraid to react 'because cinema audiences, wherever they are, really pick up on and respond to the atmosphere here in the auditorium'.

While a Foucauldian, New Materialist, or feminist reading of Godwin's production as watched on (a) screen might yield fruitful results, I am offering a Covidian reading.[14] As a spectator of the play when streamed as part of NT At Home on YouTube, I did not have to worry about contributing to a special atmosphere in my flat. My attention to the lavish setting was disrupted by my incredulity at seeing sun loungers beside a swimming pool at a time when travelling was restricted globally: the luxury of *Antony and Cleopatra* jarred with the relative quietude and isolation afforded by a global pandemic.

Godwin's production highlighted the lust and fury of love, war and megalomania. The main departure from the original Shakespeare lay in the choice to begin with the end. The first thing to be shown was a staircase in the centre of the stage going up – but who was climbing what ladder? – which was followed by a black screen (hovering my cursor over the screen confirmed that it was not a computer issue) for a few seconds. As the lights went on again, there was Caesar on top, addressing the audience in the Olivier and thus, both for NT Live and NT At Home audiences, seemingly looking into an undefined distance. He was at the height of his power, but also, since Cleopatra's body lay draped, snake-like, at the foot of the stairs, on top of the mischievous Egyptian monarch. Cleopatra had been conquered.

Philo's description of Cleopatra as a lustful 'gipsy', with which Shakespeare's text begins, was replaced by Agrippa asking: 'How came it then that we did see / The triple pillar of the world transformed / Into a strumpet's fool? Behold and see.'[15] I had not remembered the theatricality of the beginning of Godwin's production, and the grand arrangement seemed especially ill-placed watched on a small screen. In the next moment, Cleopatra was kissed awake by a prowling Antony, who lay down next to her. This choreography of two magnets clicking onto each other was repeated at the end of Act One when Antony left behind his wife Octavia and his wedding ring and fell into Cleopatra's arms in a seeming no-land between the two main settings: one half of the revolving stage represented Rome and the other Egypt and the passionate, impatient kiss took place in the section of the stage in between these two areas of the set. In the filmed version, the camera movement followed the revolving stage, thus increasing the dynamic and somehow natural sweep of this embrace.

In the same way in which Antony longed for Cleopatra – his reluctant grunts as she mocked him that he would have to go back to his duties were particularly amusing – the brown-orange colours of both the set and the protagonists' costumes made me long for a summer holiday resort. When Antony, wearing a less dishevelled outfit, confronted Cleopatra with the news that the other two-thirds of the triumvirate needed him, I could not help but read this as 'The holiday is over', and Cleopatra's reaction as that of a disappointed child and capricious diva.

As Antony 'went back to work', Rome was presented as a sterile command centre with a big six-part flat-screen on the wall. While the 2018 production also had Rome as a sterile command centre, in the context of the pandemic the presentation now gave rise to associations with daily Covid-19-necessitated routines consisting of tiled faces on screens. And when Caesar and Antony, their cognac glasses casually in hand, decided that the latter would marry the former's sister in a display of obnoxious patriarchy, they were at least keeping the proper 2-metre social distancing rule – only to get roaring drunk later, together with Lepidus and Pompey's men, and abandon all fears of contact in a mad and toxically masculine raging party in a submarine-turned-dive. When watched on my laptop screen, however, I could focus on details that had been inaccessible to me both on the bigger cinema screen and when attending the performance in situ: for instance, the plush seats Antony reclined on in the first half of the play shared the pattern of the fruit platter next to them and resembled exotic leaves. The lush colours of Cleopatra's dresses (a new one almost for every scene) had a hypnotic effect and made the surface of the water in the already very blue pool sparkle.

As much as it was impressive to watch, the stage design seemed to push the initially vibrant atmosphere off the stage. The clunky and luxurious marble of Rome again and again collided with the splendour of Egypt in scene changes that seemed heavy and bumpy. Combined with the lengthy dialogues and scenes, this got in the way of my longing for a summer breeze. A much-needed blob of that initial vibrancy came back when Cleopatra demanded 'some music' and danced to it with Iras and Charmian in her memorably yellow dress, which had been instantly recognizable to critics and audiences as an homage to Beyoncé's dress in the video to 'Hold Up'. Fittingly, it was Eros (and not the Messenger) that broke the news that Antony had gotten married in the meantime – Eros had to be dunked into the pool by way of punishment so that Cleopatra could maintain her dignity.

When watched at home, on a screen, during a time when many people were increasingly reliant on the internet for entertainment, such pop culture references created even stronger reverberations and echoes – images of Beyoncé, for instance, were just one click away, and one further click took me to Titus Andromedan's version of 'Lemonade-ing' in the Netflix show *The Unbreakable Kimmy Schmidt*, creating unexpected connections within the space of YouTube. Apart from these intertextualities that broke up time, space and genre, the performances shown as part of NT At Home created echoes between one another, hauntings even. Since I had watched *Twelfth Night* when it was available on YouTube between 23 and 30 April 2020, I had a fresh picture of Tim McMullan as the lasciviously tipsy Sir Toby Belch, so it made perfect sense to see him enter the stage – albeit as Enobarbus – with a beer bottle in his hand, swaying from one play into the next. Similarly, thinking of this character in *Twelfth Night* reminded me of Oliver Chris' performance in that production as Orsino, which linked up seamlessly with his performance as Oberon in the Bridge Theatre's *A Midsummer Night's Dream* that was shown on YouTube between 25 June and 2 July

2020, as I was writing down my notes on *Antony and Cleopatra*. Thus, the play was both on my screen and somewhere else, creating a dizzying array of retrospective synchronicities. In light of these new, vital connections made possible by online viewing, the much-vaunted appearance of the live snake that held such a thrill in the theatre felt less important: Covidian Shakespeare was most emphatically *not* about liveness, aliveness or the as-if-ness of a dangerous snake that might or might not be real. This Covidian *Antony and Cleopatra* was as much about itself and its traces of other Shakespeares and (inter)texts, as it was about being something it was not. When shown within the space of YouTube, it seemed to climb up the ladder from the opening scene itself, leaving the screen of my laptop, in order to rub shoulders with the other displaced performances, in defiance of any virus. While watching a stream of an archived performance online is not the same as watching it unfold before one's eyes when enacted by performers, digital media 'allow productions to keep "*living*"' and mediated theatre thus 'carr[ies] on performing in the present of the online environment' (Aebischer 2013, 146). The digital environment is both a protective enclave from the (dangerously) contagious world; yet it enlivens and positively connects and creates new content.

This perspective on the effects of virality is a positive one; while acknowledging how unsettling this experience is, it also points to the joy and enjoyment of play inherent in it. Even though we are disconnected, however, our subjectivities are not disembodied. Quite on the contrary: such a viewing situation characterized by a network structure rather than linearity reaffirms our presence in a very specific time and place and our agency as broadcasting editors, bringing together all the threads. While the situation of a lockdown, which many people all around the world experienced during 2020, encouraged and enforced high degrees of physical immobility (as in travel restrictions, curfews, etc.), in the context of consuming performance, it indeed recalibrates notions of agency and subjecthood. During lockdown, the division between inside (as 'safe' and advised by, for instance, health guidelines and governmental recommendations) and outside (the dangerous and 'unsafe') was pronounced. Being deprived of all these things characteristic of 'normal life' made one aware of how much one needed them in the first place.[16]

The creative agency of the spectators in the face of this craving for 'normality' comes very much to the fore when looking at the ways in which they respond to the spatial dimension of Covidian theatre. In all the different types of Covidian theatre, that is, the different forms of streamed and viral theatre, space – or more precisely: its exact set-up – is optional. Space is multiplied, randomized and relegated to the realm of the coincidental and private. The descriptions of where spectators watched plays during the pandemic are telling, as the following examples of tweets about the live stream of *Crave* as shown at the Chichester Festival Theatre demonstrate: @LauriettaEssien writes how she and her sister are dressing up in different cities to watch the play together as part of her sister's birthday ('My sis and I are dressed up and ready to watch from different cities tonight') and user Miss Hodgkin (@DramaHodgkin) wrote about standing ovations in their living room. Others, such as @AmeliaDonkor, watched the play from more unusual places like the bathroom, while @3nildown turned the lights off to simulate the darkness of an actual theatre and wanted to 'queue for [their] own toilet to complete the experience'. Another user, @e_schofield27, reflected on how the livestream came 'closest to live theatre since March' (when theatres had to close to adhere to social distancing rules) and added '+mega bonus, watched in my pjs'. Brief reports like these offer glimpses into how spectators 'make do' with the situation of having to compensate for what would normally be social nights *out*. When a night out becomes a night in, this can be negative or disappointing. The tweet reports speak of a playful arrangement and awareness that the situation is different, otherwise the rooms in which one watched the plays or the clothes one was wearing would not be mentioned. These creative adjustments of the Covidian theatregoers to experience a 'night at the theatre' point to how they act as bricoleurs, to use the concept coined by Claude Lévi-Strauss. The bricoleur 'is adept at performing a large number of diverse tasks [. . .] His universe of instruments is closed and the rules of his game are always to make do with "whatever is at hand" [. . .]' (1962, 17).

Spectators of Covidian theatre become bricoleurs as they tinker with the new and yet everyday situation and make it work for their own purposes. Bricolage also plays a prominent role with regard to the temporal and communal dimension of Covidian theatre, as, once again, the example of streamed theatre exemplifies. When the viewing situation has the structure of a network, the factor of time – a key factor during 'normal' times because the beginning of a show dictates audience's schedules – is upheld to some extent. On the one hand, there was the time-limitation of streams that was supported by their being framed as 'events' (taking place within a limited time frame, and Facebook events) and detailed temporal anchors, for instance in a Facebook post on 6 May 2020 about *Antony and Cleopatra* that there would be an 'online premiere, Thursday 7 May, 7pm UK time'. As Peter Kirwan discussed,

> the choice of many of these theatres to enhance the sense of live participation by imposing tight time limits on the availability of the

recording, or to hold a 'premiere' event hosted by the theatre that takes place at a particular time, seems to have had an enthusiastic take-up; and where theatres haven't done this themselves, audience communities have self-generated watch-parties to allow for collective viewing and live-tweeting. (Kirwan 2020)

That is, the notion of a communal assembly in Fischer-Lichte's sense still plays a role in the experience of spectators. But while normally, it is the plays and their being set in a particular place and at a particular point in time that invoke this assembling, in the setting of Covidian theatre it is the spectators who take up this part, quite willingly. Bricolage comes in again: it is playful and exciting to organize watch-parties, and there is something pleasingly subversive about it when Twitter is used as a schoolyard or speakerphone where one can shout out to one's friends and contacts to hurry up and get ready for a watch party. At the same time, though, these acts of organized conviviality should not be trivialized, or, even worse, overlooked. In the context of Covidian theatre, these acts of gathering are acts of spectatorial labour that in their entirety make the experience into what it is. While it is not always as structured and synchronized as a watch party, the self-generated moments of connectedness and spectatorial shared attention topple the autonomy of the theatrical space-time frame and create a kind of theatre that actually exists first and foremost because of the energy and goodwill of its spectators. To refer back to my typology: while neither live streamed theatre nor NT At Home as forms include calls of involvement or enact a sense of being part of a community of watcher-participants, it is the spectators themselves who willingly engage with these types of theatre and therefore 'pull' themselves into their affective arrangement.

NT At Home and other forms of Covidian and viral theatre have emerged out of a context of exception and are self-conscious about the framing and the limitations of the media they have to rely on. For many performance artists and theatre-makers this upsurge of what is called *Netztheater* in the German-speaking context is not a new phenomenon, however: the processes have been simmering for a few years now and the pandemic can also be understood as an acceleration of them. As the artistic director of the Young Vic, Kwame Kwei-Armah, has put it, the use of new digital technology as it has started during the Covid-19 pandemic 'will be in the DNA, and the subconscious of, an emerging generation of theatre-makers who will remember this time when they couldn't get into theatres and make their art' (Akbar 2020).

It is noteworthy that what *all* the forms of mediated theatre analysed in this book share is a concern with and movement towards a reclaiming of intimacy between spectators and performers, and spectators and performances, despite or through distance. It is therefore indeed timely to reshuffle the categories defining theatrical performance. Covidian theatre, as I have introduced it in this chapter, may recede into the background as theatres re-open, but it has left an impact on the possibilities of creating theatre that breaches the public and private divide. It fulfils several criteria at once that until now have been fulfilled by several heterogeneous forms of theatre: all forms of it are (by necessity) mediated, some are live, and they all foster spectatorial engagement in differing degrees – up until this point these are characteristics that could also be applied to livecasting. What is different is that most of the forms of Covidian theatre involve direct forms of address of audiences in their private homes and activate the pandemic frame, hence emphasizing even more the potential and responsibility of the performing arts to care for audiences and make them care for themselves through experiencing theatre.[17]

7

Concluding discussion and future directions

What remains of livecasting?

While the grounding of livecasting within a historical context in Chapter 1 has already indicated that early forms of broadcasting were tied to the optionality of theatre space, a different sense of liveness and new forms of conviviality, this study of present-day livecasting identifies it as a timely form of mediated theatrical experience. Several key claims have emerged out of *Livecasting in Twenty-First-Century British Theatre* that hark back to the hypotheses formulated in the Introduction: first, livecasts are part of the spectacle turn in the context of cultural production in general and theatrical performance specifically. They afford a multi-layered type of spectacle that creates a new manifestation of mediatized communitas. Through the use of cinematic techniques and as the spectators of the in-situ performance function as carriers of affect for those watching the livecast, the affective arrangement of the livecast can spill over into the cinema auditorium – the affective arrangement of the livecast exerts a pull on livecasting spectators to be engaged with what they are watching (hypothesis 1). Second, in livecasts the frictions between the aesthetics of film and theatre foreground the made-ness of materiality of theatrical performance and a spatially extended atmosphere is created in which spectators are invited to pay attention to all the spaces and elements a theatrical performance is made of (hypothesis 2). Third, as the livecast as such is a hybrid form, bringing together both different generic conventions and the connected practices of experiencing those genres, this, crucially, also reflects on the concomitant shifts in practices of spectatorship. Livecasts allow vastly different forms of engagement: this can be either an enacted sense of being part of a communitas of spectators or a hailing of spectators as 'feeling I's as orchestrated by the digital environment of the livecast. They also open the doors to a more flexible, less hierarchical form of expertise, namely quasi-expertise. The responses on the paradocumentational brim of livecasting are constitutive for this theatrical form (hypothesis 3). These new forms of addressivity and response have gained further ramifications recently in the context of the Covid-19 pandemic and Covidian theatre.

In this concluding discussion, I will revisit the notion of interdetermination with regard to livecasts outlined in the Introduction of this book and then place the livecasting discourse in the context of ongoing debates around liveness and the archive to emphasize, once again, how livecasts necessitate a thinking that resists a binary logic, such as the archive versus the live or ephemeral. When embedding these considerations in ongoing debates around liveness, the discussion shows that what 'being there' for a performance means and what of it is seen as 'remaining with us' is undergoing a marked shift due to the rise of livecasts. Livecasts, inadvertently, have put into motion ideas about performance and concerning the possibilities of mediated performance that are now developed further in the (post-)pandemic world.

Responsible responsiveness and liveness

The topics of spectacle and liveness, materiality and space, and engagement and the audiences' role are intertwined in the context of livecasting. They overlap with contingency, risk and spontaneity as defining theatricality. When we conceive of (regular) theatrical performance as place-bound, livecasts inhabit a realm on the threshold. This blending of spaces is related to a Bakhtinian understanding of adaptation and translation processes as fruitful acts of interdetermination.[1] Bakhtin was fascinated with translation processes because of the notion of simultaneity, that is, the awareness that something can be one thing and another at the same time (Cutchins 2017, 72). When thinking about literary language and translations of literary texts, Bakhtin argued that, once something was translated, the translation and that which had been translated were no longer a 'seamless whole (as they were for the creators of the epic), but were rather fragmented, separated from each other, had *to seek each other out*' (Bakhtin 1981, 377, emphasis added). If one seeks something, one either knows or suspects that the sought-after exists – when one knows that one watches, for instance, a movie adaptation of a novel, one becomes a 'knowing' participant (Hutcheon 2013, 120) or an 'elite' viewer (Venuti 2007, 37). While primarily focusing on literary texts, Bakhtin was interested in the interrelations between all kinds of texts as fabrics of utterances. According to him, '[t]he artistic act lives and moves not in a vacuum but in an intense axiological atmosphere of responsible interdetermination' (1990, 275).

Responsible interdetermination means that answerability within an axiological atmosphere requires effort. It also means that an act of response comes with responsibility for one's response. As my analysis in this book has shown, this logic can be applied in a fruitful way to livecasts because it categorizes them more specifically as interdetermined artistic or cultural acts being created out of complex artistic processes. The previous chapter on Covidian theatre has demonstrated that this responsible responsiveness can take on several shapes, especially when a type of theatre emerges which requires direct forms of address of spectators at home, such as viral theatre. These new forms of addressivity create a new awareness for subjecthood and the role of viewers in the reception process as both viewers and private individuals. This has also become obvious in the vastly different forms of participation in response on the paradocumentational brim that I have identified, that is, self-absorbed and subject-centred (with a focus on the 'feeling I') response(s) on the one hand and communal networking on the other.

Livecasts are characterized by a threefold hybridity with regard to genre, venue and reception. In terms of genre, they are determined *both* by the conventions of film and those of theatre in retaining the theatrical set-up on the screen. In terms of their status as spatially positioned art works, they are determined by the characteristics of both the theatres *from* which they are broadcast and the cinema venues *to* which they are broadcast. In terms of their reception by audiences, they are determined both by the cinema experience and the awareness or knowledge of their on-site quality. I am deliberately *not* speaking of their on-site or stage 'origin' because invoking such a hierarchy misses the point. It is reminiscent of the phrase with which Kelsey Jacobson recently found scorn when digital theatre produced during the Corona lockdown was described as 'merely a way of holding space before we can return to "real" theatre'. As Jacobson comments, and as my discussion of the status of space in livecasting also attests to, such a statement 'ignores the inventive responses of theatre artists who have shown that *theatre* is patently not tied to *theatres*' (Jacobson 2020, emphases in original). The reason for and the main motor behind the emergence and success of new forms of theatre and new spaces for them is the flexibility and openness of reception on the part of audiences. What the conceptual framework of livecasting as an example of 'the web-like quality of culture' (Allen 2011, 1) depends on is the labour done by audience members, who adapt to the new setting, of watching theatre in a cinema.

A final nod to the position of livecasting within the long and fraught discourse and debates surrounding the concept of 'liveness' is warranted. The question of liveness is linked to the question of the depiction of reality or realism in art, a question central to cultural and literary criticism. Past debates about reality and artificiality provide a fruitful backdrop when thinking about the current trends in performance aiming at manufacturing an experience that is going to be an excess of reality and liveness ('more real' and 'more live' than the original). The debates as such are not new; what *is* new is the existence of a frame that allows and fosters engagement from everyone, such as feeling spectators and quasi-experts (see Part II).

On a spectrum from Aristotelian mimesis (Aristotle 2013, 24) – which praises mimesis as distinctive of human nature and holds that a supposed non-reality perfects reality – to Wildean anti-mimesis[2] – which holds that life always already imitates art – livecasts fall squarely in the middle. On the one hand, they aim at a perfection of the reality (of the theatre) in capturing (thus imitating) it with the human-made means of technology that are available. On the other hand, since the reality they are capturing is already art(ificial), this reality and its liveness have already been informed by art and its dramaturgical set-up that make us see it as 'live'.

As Wyver observes, both 'the early television adaptations and recent live cinema broadcasts can be seen as exemplary of Philip Auslander's argument [...] about the general cultural tendency of mediatized forms to displace and replace live ones' (Wyver 2014b), which is connected to questions whether one form is somehow superior to the other – something that Wyver dismisses instantly saying that to watch a live (on-site) theatrical event and a mediated one are two very different experiences. I share this position. Accepting the experience of a livecast as a very different one still raises the question of how this difference also relates to a very different status of liveness (which, despite being troubled), is still a key element of livecast. In a final concluding step, I will identify the relevant conceptualizations of liveness for the purposes of a discussion of livecasting and responsible responsiveness, and then say how it can be helpful to connect livecasting to dynamic processes of archivization.

Referring to Gadamer's argument about how a work of art can be meaningful to an onlooker, Auslander discusses how in Gadamer's discussion 'contemporaneity' is picked out as a central factor to describe the type of engagement necessary for a meaningful effect. That is, even if a work of art is from a distant past, of which we only have abstract knowledge, once we *choose* to engage with it in our present – and presence[3] – it becomes fully present to us. This can be applied as well to the scenario in which, for instance, broadcasting technologies come into play, and 'an entity we know to be technological that makes a claim to being live becomes fully present to us when we *grasp* it as live' (Auslander 2012, 8, emphasis added). Whether something is perceived as live or whether the mediated event has a meaningful effect depends primarily on the perceiving subject, the consumer and the spectator: the willingness and the readiness to engage with especially less familiar forms of art and entertainment are the prerequisite for a successful exchange between spectators and mediated forms, such as livecasting. The readiness and willingness to engage were the focus of Chapters 4 and 5; the new urgency that these engagements have taken in Covidian theatre was discussed in Chapter 6.

What is noteworthy in Auslander's phrasing and also in the way in which I think about this exchange between artworks and spectators is that it is based on an embodied form of openness on the part of the spectators and described in terms of *grasping* (the quality of the mediated art form), accepting a claim and choosing to engage with it. These are all active verbs that imply a movement from the subject towards the object. Such descriptions privilege the role of the respective positions and with that the role of spatiality as more central to the experience of liveness than considerations of their temporality. The mechanisms of the performance of presence can be explained by recurring to phenomenology: There is an insistence on the audience's part consisting of an act of consciousness rather than visible action. Most importantly, to choose to be present is an active act – to be present is a process in the Heideggerian sense: '[t]he word "being" now no longer means what something is. We hear "being" as a verb, as in "being present" and "being absent." "To be" means to perdure and persist' (Heidegger 1973, 95). If being present is configured as a movement, it is also a process of definition; it is the subject who is present – the spectator who gives meaning to the performance/the livecast and not the time at which it is being shown.

Auslander criticizes several scholars for suggesting, that there is a certain technological determinism at play when it is specific technologies that influence the ways in which humans respond to them; yet they all centre on audience attention and spectatorship. What follows from this is that there is no technological determinism after all, which becomes obvious even in studies that overtly state otherwise. To sum up Auslander's 2012 take on liveness one can say that (a) the artefact makes the claim (on us) to be considered as live and (b) the audience chooses to accept this claim which is why, (c), 'liveness is an *interaction* produced through our engagement with the object and our willingness to accept its claim' (2012, 9, emphasis added). Such a phenomenological perspective illuminates that digital liveness emerges as a relation between self and other and the self's involvement or engagement with the other.

In light of the central role of social media and communication apps on the lived experiences of people, Nick Couldry has proposed two new forms of liveness, namely 'group liveness' as 'the "liveness" of a mobile group of friends who are in continuous contact via their mobile phones through calls and texting' and 'online' liveness as 'social co-presence on a variety of scales from very small groups in chat rooms to huge international audiences for breaking news on major websites, all made possible by the internet as an underlying infrastructure' (2004, 356-7). What such new terminology and the earlier considerations point to is that the experience of liveness does not lie in the 'properties of the thing experienced' but 'refers to a sense of always being connected to other people' (Auslander 2012, 6) and, in the context of livecasts, of the 'experience of belonging to a physical and networked community of fans that span [...] geographical locations and share [...] in the excitement of participating in a unique, ephemeral cultural event' (Aebischer, Greenhalgh and Osborne 2018, 7). As Sullivan (2020, 101–2) and Barker (2013, 30) have suggested, the *perception* of simultaneity (with in-situ audiences) is central to the success of a livecast for those watching it, especially when asked directly after the live transmission has taken place (Sullivan 2020, 101–2). As Victoria Lowe argues, 'liveness' in the livecasting context is reconfigured, 'marked more by the perception of it by audiences than a "being present" at the moment of creation' (Lowe 2020), a view I share. The tweets in which spectators post pictures of their tickets in the cinema or write from where in the world they are watching are comparable to the little waves audience members give one another when they spot a familiar face in the audience – only that in the livecasting context, strangers wave to each other.

What remains of livecasting?

Lastly, I want to revisit and connect the concept of the archive to my discussion of livecasting. In 1997, Margaret Benton, the director of the Theatre Museum and former television producer, who established the National Video Archive of Performance (NVAP), said that the purpose of archival recordings was 'to convey as faithful and as a [*sic*] detailed a record as possible of the original stage performance [. . .] It should aim to be an eyewitness to the event taking place in the presence of a live audience' (in Wyver 2019, 144–5). The term 'eyewitness' is noteworthy here as it attributes an active and even human role to the entity of the recording. Livecasts, too, are archival recordings. When we accept that livecasts evoke the experience of liveness, the liveness used to evoke this liveness is 'old' – there is never a livecast of an opening night, for instance. Yet it does not seem to play a significant role in which performance from a run is used to achieve these effects and to document a show and serve as proofs of its run. Crucially, the production and filming of a livecast understood as documentation does not relegate 'the activity of documenting performance as secondary to the artists' works' as has traditionally been the case by academics who privileged physical 'presence' for the cultural significance of a work (Sant 2017, 10). Livecasts indeed prolong and multiply the liveness of a performance and provide actors with an additional space to that of the audience's memory[4] – for Richard Schechner a crucial part of the performance ritual, whether social or artistic, that he calls 'aftermath' (2013, 246). For the multi-camera directors involved, to contribute to this aftermath is a crucial aspect. As Matthew Amos has put it:

> It's the work I feel the most proud of. To be part of something that will be there forever. If you think about some of the things they do at the National and NT Live has been going for just over ten years now – when my kids are my age, they'll still be able to look back on some of the performances and watch them. They will be available for people to look at and study them and learn from. That sort of legacy – It's our National Theatre and I always say to people, we own it, we *all* own it! [. . .] So the performances on that stage belong to everybody. I know there's some actors that aren't keen on it because they feel it should just be a one-off but, you know, if you live in Hull, or Belfast, to go and see something like that would cost you a fortune, there's lots of people who can't do it. So it's opening those things up and I think it's a very good tool in introducing more people to theatre. (2022)

While performance arts practitioners, scholars and critics agree that video recordings cannot replace the original live performance, they are the best way to capture a *sense* of live performance.[5] They can also contribute to conserving the creative work that is produced at a given time and thus conserve a nation's cultural history. Livecasts write history and make it available to the next generations.

In addition to Auslander, Rebecca Schneider has countered the claim that 'the live' has a privileged position over the mediatized by thinking about what remains after a performance and what performance remains are. Her considerations can be applied to the livecasting context as well. At the outset of her essay 'Performance Remains Again' (2012)[6] Schneider asks:

> If we consider performance as 'of' disappearance, if we think of the ephemeral as that which 'vanishes', and if we think of performance as the antithesis of preservation, do we limit ourselves to an understanding of performance predetermined by a cultural habituation to the patrilineal, West-identified (arguably white-cultural) logic of the archive? (2012, 65)

This passage needs a bit of unravelling. When we assume that what is archived constitutes history, and that which is archived follows 'the cultural habituation to the patrilineal', then what is archived has been recognized as constituting remains, and thus significant. Schneider also refers to Jacques Derrida, who in *Archive Fever* has argued in this context that 'archivization produces as much as it records the event' (1995, 17). The logic – that Schneider seeks to counter – goes that performance is so radically 'in time' (2012, 66) that it cannot produce remains or a document and therefore 'disappears'. What may have been postulated as a special characteristic of performance excludes it from a significant place in history when looked at from the perspective of the logic of the archive. Therefore, to think of performance as ephemeral is in fact not to elevate or praise it; it is to submit it to the logic of the archive and thus actively contribute to its erasure (from a society's cultural capital and collective memory). If we equate performance with impermanence and ephemerality, we affirm the binary between the archive and the live and fleeting, and we limit ourselves to an understanding of performance that regards it as non-archivable; if we say that performance disappears in the moment it appears, we exclude the possibility that it can constitute remains. It is necessary, therefore, to disrupt (and disturb) this binary and get away from the notion that something can only remain when it is isolated to an object or document. Rather, performance, as an embodied experience, remains and reappears in those who have experienced it. As Schneider puts it, 'performance becomes itself through messy and eruptive reappearance' and continuously challenges the binary between presence and absence (71). While for Phelan performance becomes itself through disappearance, for Schneider performance is a *medium* in which disappearance and materiality are passed through (75–6). Thus, in being recorded (also in spectators' memories) performance can both constitute remains and remain rather than disappear.

The experience of livecasting is an illustration of the validity of Schneider's arguments. What defines livecasting is a de-centred understanding of space and a hybrid set-up of cinematic and theatrical spaces in combination with the willingness to negotiate this hybridity on the part of the spectators. What gives a certain kind of stability to the form is its paradocumentational brim and the ways in which the NT's social media outlets enable an extended engagement with their livecasts that is not limited by the duration of the performance. The locus of liveness still lies to a great extent in the audience's experience, but it is also the setting of livecasting and its properties that offers the affordance of liveness. A livecast is 'something other' than a performance in that it makes one particular performance remain; but by doing so, it creates a performance of its own kind, one that prolongs the liveness of the livecast and, in overlapping with the former, creates another one in the cinema space. It is interdetermined at its core. If the debates around liveness seem to have reached something of a dead end, livecasts precisely move beyond the binary of the live and recorded (Bay-Cheng 2012, 40) and therefore beyond questions which of the two is more 'authentic'.

What Aebischer has argued with regard to recordings of performances watched online also holds true for livecasts and echoes Schneider's claims: rather than thinking about a performance or its recording as being live versus not-live, one can conceive of them as 'living' (Aebischer 2013, 146) in that they carry on performing in the moment of their reception. In connection with the negotiations in the cinemas and on social media, livecasts need to be understood as 'a network of interrelated components, both on- and offline, both overtly mediated and immediate to various and dispersed recipients' (Bay-Cheng 2012, 34, 35). They are hybrid events, happening on the threshold between theatrical and cinematic spaces and most importantly are put into play by those watching them.

A livecast is thus always made up of itself and either the *imagined* on-site performance that it implies and that spectators negotiate or the *remembered* on-site performance that it evokes for spectators who are familiar with it. As I attended all the performances on which the livecasts I analysed for this book were based, personal recollections and associations connected to the former overlapped and added to the experience in the cinema. During the scene changes in *Present Laughter*, which I started this book with, for instance, the camera captured close-ups of the ornament in the centre of the Old Vic stage, providing a curious sense of space that was immediately dispersed in the cinema frame. Any livecasting experience is at the same time characterized by a lack (of not being 'there', of not being acknowledged, of witnessing something else than the on-site event) and by the insight that rather than being subordinated to the theatrical 'thing' with its rituals and prescribed actions, as Schechner defines it so well, as a spectator one is choosing even more emphatically to be there.

What 'being there' means is currently undergoing a rapid shift within theatre and performance practices, as this book has shown. Livecasting has contributed to these shifts, and the Covid-19 pandemic has accelerated the processes involved and the needs and habits of spectators, as the previous chapter has discussed. In May 2021, the artistic director of the Young Vic, Kwame Kwei-Armah, announced that the theatre would livestream all of its future productions, as 'theatre can never go back to being something that can only be experienced by physically being there'. Kwei-Armah holds that the livestreaming of plays has become '"hard baked" into how the industry operates. As a consequence, the Young Vic will launch the project "Best

Seat in Your House", which will use multiple cameras between which online audiences can switch and thus change their view point' (Brown 2021). Two things are problematic about the argumentation in the article: first of all, the implication seems to be that theatre stagnated during the pandemic and now a long-wished-for solution to this stagnation has been proposed. This is a misrepresentation and a blatant blind spot, but may be partly motivated by the marketing rhetoric of the announcement. Second, the article implies that there is something like 'real' theatre and the one live experience that is better than anything that could be achieved by 'Zoom plays'. Such a misconception fails to recognize the mediating processes of cameras, mics, lenses and the work of those operating them. Sequences of images that are filmed create a narrative, too. In-situ theatre and mediated theatre are two different art forms in their own right, they come into being through the creative work of the people involved. And they do not have to be rivals. Yet it is crucial, especially in terms of access, that the Young Vic is taking that step so that, as Kwei-Armah puts it, 'each generation can think about how we define liveness versus access' (Brown 2021).

What will theatrical performance, and especially the experience of it, look like in the future? It will certainly be characterized by options and the side-by-sideness of experiences and ways of accessing them that are more personalized, more accessible and more varied than they used to be only twenty years ago. What *all* the forms of mediated theatre analysed in this book share is a movement towards a reclaiming of intimacy between spectators and performers and spectators and performances despite or through distance. Theatrical performance is bound to be more personalized, or rather more about creating the possibility for the personal and individual within an actual or virtual communitas of fellow watcher-participants.

It is likely that VR glasses will be more affordable and a whole new branch of performance-cum-video-game will emerge, such as the Royal Shakespeare Company has tried out in March 2021 with their *Dream*. One may also picture a scenario in which the audiences of NT Live shows and the filmed productions are intertwined more: there could be devices given to all ticket holders that report all tweets about the play live, or the NT could position a multi-media glass screen in front of the stage that would display the tweets from NT Live goers on its margin, creating a frame of livecasting reactions onto the on-site production.

While these are speculations for the years to come, already the past five years in which the research for this book has been conducted have witnessed a swift accommodation of livecasting practices into the broader discourse on theatre production. The developments brought about by the pandemic in early 2020, which are still ongoing, have further changed the way in which practitioners, performers and audiences think about performance, liveness and presence, but also precarity in the cultural sector more broadly. Theatre as a whole and the genre of theatre are still very much in a state on the threshold, with more revelations bound to follow.

Notes

Introduction

1. See also Nicholas (2018) who looks at the viewing experience of NT Live and RSC Live and analyses the 'audience performances'. In order to understand the power relationships at play when spectators have to engage in these processes, Michel de Certeau's distinction between 'strategies' and 'tactics' is helpful. 'Strategies' are set out by those whose power is derived from being located in a specific place, while 'tactics' are the actions taken by those who are dislocated in order to create space for themselves within a strategy (de Certeau 1988, 34–8).
2. See, for instance, the work of theatre company Dante or Die that in their production *User not Found* deals with the question of what happens to people's social identities after their death – audience members follow the performance via head- and smartphones; see also Klich/Scheer (2011); Bay-Cheng et al. (2010); Giannachi (2004); Parker-Starbuck (2012); Causey (2006); Kershaw (2007).
3. For Fiske, oral culture in particular is participatory, as in quiz or game shows 'distinctions among author, text, and reader, or between text and life, are blurred and minimized' (2001, 191).
4. For fan studies in general see especially Jenkins (1992 and 2006); Gray, Sandvoss and Harrington (2007); Gray (2003).
5. Other terms suggested – though not yet widely received – to describe the present age are Nicolas Bourriad's 'altermodern' (which was first mentioned at his Tate Modern exhibit in 2009) and Alan Kirby's (2009) digimodernism, both setting thematic foci as to how the present differs from what came before rather than coming 'after' it.
6. Cochrane and Bonner sum up the multitude of terms that has been tried out, some of which are simply inaccurate: streaming, broadcast (that the two authors counter with their neologism 'narrowcast' to acknowledge that the dissemination of the shows is not yet truly 'broad', and their reception not free) and event cinema. They suggest 'relay' as an alternative, as it also encompasses delayed reception, and call 'alternate content cinema' the most accurate (though the least informative) term (Cochrane and Bonner 2014, 122).
7. For the history of the National Theatre see Billington (2007); Sierz (2011); and Shellard (2007).

8 *Sea Wall* attended by the author on 21 June 2018, Old Vic; *My Name Is Lucy Barton* attended on 12 February 2019 at the Bridge Theatre. Both are monologues delivered by a single actor (in the productions mentioned Andrew Scott and Laura Linney, respectively) on stage, with no elaborate stage design (in *Lucy Barton* a hospital bed, an armchair and screens in the back that display pictures of a field or the Chrysler Building in New York; in *Sea Wall* a bare stage and a water bottle as the only prop) in which the characters tell their personal and emotional story. There is no interval in both cases, with *Sea Wall* lasting only thirty minutes and *Lucy Barton* about ninety minutes.

9 Key debates about liveness have been led by Phelan (1993), Auslander (1997) and Schneider (2011), with the discussion evolving around the concepts of presence, temporality, ephemerality of performance and the fraught connection between live performance and its status when it is mediated. In Giannachi et al. (2012) there is an excellent summary of these debates. Similarly, the 'value' and transformative effect of 'live' theatrical and performed presence has been restaged in Erika Fischer-Lichte's *The Transformational Power of Performance* (2008). Such perspectives are also elaborated in a range of other monographs exploring *Presence in Play* (Power 2008), which re-examines the theatrical literature on presence, *Stage Presence* (Goodall 2008), and Joseph Roach's examination of charisma in *It* (2007). It is this new engagement with presence in theatre theory and practice, too, that Giannachi et al.'s *Archaeologies of Presence* (2012) aims to reflect and capture, and to bring to this debate the processual character of presence, both in performance and its critical recovery.

10 While they do not mention Laurence Venuti, Cochrane's and Bonner's (2014) argument entails an echo of Venuti's discussion of translation and critique: Venuti outlines that the relation between second-order creations (such as films) and their source materials is hermeneutic, depending on the translator's or filmmaker's application of an interpretant (either formal or thematic). When it comes to livecasts, they are based on second-order creations (mostly plays based on dramatic texts) and thus are one step further removed, as they are third-order-creations. Although it is fruitful to think of them in terms of adaptations, analysis should be focused on their distinctiveness as a creation of their own. Venuti's logic has found its way implicitly into my discussion, yet I prefer not to use his terminology as such a way of numbering (first, second, third) implies, despite all, a certain hierarchy of 'authenticity' or 'value' that I precisely want to get away from, as do Cochrane and Bonner (2014) and later Cochrane (2018).

11 Performance philosophy is an emerging and interdisciplinary field of thought, which had its beginnings in 2012 and tries to grasp *how* performance thinks (not just performers or performance makers). See the work of the Performance Philosophy Research Network: https://www.performancephilosophy.org.

12 Some of these are the following: Bury (2017); Conner (2013); Evans (2019); Hill (2018); Pitts/Price (2021); Walmsley (2019).

Chapter 1

1 An earlier version of passages from this chapter has been published in (©2021) *Transmedia Practices in the Long Nineteenth-Century*, edited by Monika Pietrzak-Franger and Christina Meyer, as 'Transmedial Experience in Nineteenth-Century Live Theatre Broadcasting'. Passages are reproduced here by permission of Taylor and Francis Group, LLC, a division of Informa plc.
2 For a discussion of this with regard to contemporary livecasting see Liedke (2020). For an investigation of comfort in the context of contemporary culture more generally see Birke and Butter (2020).
3 See Denison (1901) and Talbot (1903). In the United States, the New Jersey Telephone Herald Company tried to follow the success of Telephon Hirmondó. It failed, however, because it could not keep up with the subscribers' interest and provide sufficient equipment – 1000 installations for 2500 subscriptions; the situation was complicated by the company's legal problems that made investments not profitable for third parties (Marvin 1988, 230; Sterne 2003, 194). Apart from that, from 1886, Milwaukee's Wisconsin Telephone Company provided orchestral concerts to its subscribers every evening and on Sunday afternoons; other telephone operators would even offer spontaneous jam sessions late at night, and operators in Cleveland provided baseball scores for their subscribers – all of which were precursors to radio broadcasting (Sterne 2003, 194).
4 I am grateful to John London for pointing out that this statement is not logical. For religious Jews it is not permitted to use any technology, including the phone, on the Shabbat. As the author here writes about ringing up the Great Synagogue on a Saturday, one can assume that they are not Jewish. Also, such a statement – and the sensational phrasing to 'take a dose of Judaism' – suggests that this may be an exaggeration as it is hard to imagine that a synagogue would be connected to the electrophone system for what seems like entertainment purposes.
5 W. J. Turner reached a similar conclusion in 1926 about broadcasting writing that it 'will initiate to the elements of musical enjoyment a vast new audience, and out of this audience the more sensitive, the more gifted, all the minds susceptible of development will emerge and, dissatisfied with what they are getting, will ask for more and will ultimately be driven into the concert hall to obtain it. To imagine that broadcasting will or can kill concerts is just the same as if we had imagined that the newspaper could kill the book' (1200).
6 See Owen (1861), Rupke (1994) and Keiling/Liedke (2021).

7 This echoes a sentiment uttered by Van Helsing in Bram Stoker's *Dracula*, as Sam Halliday discusses: when musing about how the use of electricity has changed the way people relate to the world, Van Helsing concludes that '[t]here are always mysteries in life'(see Halliday 2016, 598).
8 This form of experiencing plays, music or lectures in fragments rather than in their entirety is reminiscent of the ways in which many people described attending Zoom lectures or webinars during the Covid-19 pandemic. In the domestic setting, there seemed to exist less of a feeling of obligation to listen to, for instance, an online talk until the end, and people also had to attend to other duties at home. These issues will be taken up in detail in Chapter 6.
9 The perceiving and 'feeling I' has taken on a central role in the context of participatory culture and also in the set-up of twenty-first century livecasting practices and will be taken up in detail in Chapters 4 and 5 in Part II.
10 This document is held in the National Theatre Archive London in the Shakespeare Memorial National Theatre Collection (SMNT) as part of the correspondence about published articles and broadcasts between 1950 and 1959, reference number SMNT/7/4/5, which I consulted in March 2019. The material is quoted here by courtesy of the National Theatre Archive.
11 The correspondence referred to on this page is part of the documentation on cinema facilities and television in relation to the National Theatre between 1930 and 1955 and is held in the National Theatre Archive London in the Shakespeare Memorial National Theatre Collection (SMNT), reference number SMNT/6/1/4, which I consulted in March 2019. The material is quoted here by courtesy of the National Theatre Archive.
12 I am grateful to the reader of the final manuscript for their astute remarks concerning early television and theatre broadcasts and the dates of the first theatre broadcasts in the 1930s.

Chapter 2

1 An earlier version of passages of this chapter has been published previously as 'On being pulled: Spectator engagement and spectacle in the context of live theatre broadcasting and NT at Home' in *Participations* 18.2 (2021): 294–317.
2 See also Gregg and Seighworth (2010); Massumi (2002).
3 Ross MacGibbon in an interview with the author on 7 November 2019, at Gail's Café, Pimlico, London. All references to MacGibbon in this chapter are to this interview, the transcript of which can be requested from the author.
4 See John Harris's comment on how 'Guy Debord predicted our distracted society' in his *Guardian* article with that very title (2012).

5 The question what happens to theatre when it 'leaves the building' is even more pertinent in the context of theatre that is streamed online and will be taken up in Chapter 6, where I discuss Covidian theatre.
6 Experiences of events form a new economy of their own – at least this is the argument that has been made since the 1970s and that Joseph Pine and James H. Gilmore take up in their book *The Experience Economy* (1999) to argue how, increasingly, businesses rely on the production of memorable events for their customers so that not only a given product is bought but also the experience of it. One can see reverberations of these dynamics in many societal sectors and the cultural in particular.
7 It is a hope indeed that – perhaps under the auspices of the insights gained during the Covid-19 pandemic – smaller theatres, too, will take up the opportunity to provide livecasts of their shows and/or the NT will consider filming and broadcasting performances that have been produced on a smaller stage in the Dorfman Theatre, for instance.
8 See Barish's *The Antitheatrical Prejudice* (1981) for a historical overview of how theatre has been prejudiced against, rejected and condemned, for moral, political and aesthetic reasons.
9 The plays Brecht refers to are Henrik Ibsen's *Ghosts* and Hugo von Hofmannsthal's *Everyman* (21).
10 When Great Britain hosted the Olympic Games in 2012 an explicit parallel was drawn between sports spectacle and cultural spectacle as it was accompanied by a Cultural Olympiad. 'Culture' seemed to be synonymous with 'Shakespeare', however: the events presented were the 'World Shakespeare Festival' (RSC), 'Globe to Globe' (Shakespeare's Globe) and the 'Shakespeare Unlocked' season by the BBC. There were also livestreams of these performances of the Cultural Olympiad and *The Guardian* website streamed the Polish theatre company TR Warszawa's *Macbeth* (see Greenhalgh 2018, 31).
11 In total, people from 170 countries tuned into NT At Home with the most popular territories being the United Kingdom, United States, Australia, Canada and Russia (Buckeridge 2020).
12 See also Berkaak (1999) on the Olympic Games as 'mega drama.'
13 With regard to UK theatre, the word 'spectator' has been replaced in common English usage by 'audience' since the nineteenth century, which suggests a shift from the visual excess of a spectacle – which is spectated – to 'the serious art of theatre, where audiences listen to dialogue' (Finburgh 2017, 51–2). Yet in recent years, several scholars have encircled this development towards a positively understood spectator-centric theatre with new terminologies, such as Lavender (2016), Zaiontz (2014) and Alston (2016). Di Benedetto (2011) considers theatrical practice through the lens of contemporary neuroscientific discoveries and examines the ways in which the senses form the structure of a theatrical event and physiological aspects lay the foundation for theatre to affect human behaviour. In comparison

to previous centuries, in the twenty-first century, both a focus on spectacle *and* the spectator exist side-by-side, which is why I am speaking of a new spectatorial turn.

14 A similar claim has been made by Gareth White (2019), who argues that in overlapping with others, you become less of yourself.

15 The material referred to in this paragraph is part of the documentation of the press department of the National Theatre, and refers to the press releases concerning NT Live between 2010 and 2019. It is held in the National Theatre Archive London, with the reference numbers RNT/PR/2/5/526 and RNT/PR/2/5/459 (final quote), which I consulted in March 2019.

16 It is not possible to get an overview of how many times a given hashtag was used on Twitter, therefore it is not possible to say what kind of a percentage is reflected here. The aim of this comment is not to provide a quantitative analysis, but a qualitative one.

17 *Hamlet* (2015), *Who's Afraid of Virginia Woolf?* (2017), *The Lehman Trilogy* (2019), *Treasure Island* (2015), *Hansard* (2019), *A Midsummer Night's Dream* (2019), *A View from the Bridge* (2015), *All About Eve* (2019), *Everyman* (2015), *Small Island* (2019), *Follies* (2017), *Les Liaisons Dangereuses* (2016), *Coriolanus* (2014), *Fleabag* (2019), *Man and Superman* (2015), *No Man's Land* (2017), *Frankenstein* (2016), *Angels in America* (2017), *Macbeth* (2013 and 2018), *Twelfth Night* (2017), *Yerma* (2017), *Threepenny Opera* (2016), *Julie* (2018), *Peter Pan* (2017), *The Audience* (2016), *Amadeus* (2017), *Cat on a Hot Tin Roof* (2018), *King Lear* (2018), *Antony and Cleopatra* (2018), *Medea* (2014), *Young Marx* (2018).

18 It is noteworthy that it is especially women who are commenting here, in contrast to the still predominantly white male professional theatre criticism. Whether female online criticism can be regarded as forming a reclaiming of power, whether the women are there as women and/or as female critics, is a promising questions for a different research project. Chapter 5 will turn more specifically to diversity in online theatre criticism.

19 Event cinema 'is forecast to achieve annual revenues of £60 million–80 million in the UK and $1 billion worldwide by 2019' (Reidy et al. 2016, 9). According to its own statistics – the most up-to-date one that is available being from 2017 to 2018 – between 27 March 2017 and 1 April 2018, the NT had a gain in income from 'NT Live & Digital' of £6.4 million (6.0% of the total income). By comparison, the income generated by box-office sales (excluding West End and UK touring and international box-office sales) was £25 million (23.4 % of the total income) (National Theatre Annual Review 2017–18).

20 In his performance chart, Richard Schechner compares and contrasts the different characteristics of play, games, sports, theatre and ritual. In both

sports and theatre the social 'we' dominates; time is ordered in a special way, and a special value is given to objects. Rules are in place that (can) establish freedom and there is a balance between pleasure and reality principles (Schechner 1988, 12).

21 Reply on 31 December 2019 to a comment below NT Live tweet on 30 December 2019 (https://twitter.com/NTLive/status/1211699214792712192), which asked followers about their favourite line from *A Midsummer Night's Dream*.

22 The Bridge Theatre also used the promenade format of its auditorium in its production of *Julius Caesar* (20 January to 11 April 2018), where spectators – if they had a ticket in the pit – were involved in the action, either as the crowd greeting Caesar, the congress witnessing his murder or part of the civil war mob afterwards.

23 Audience members who attend a show on the night it is recorded agree to being filmed and appearing in the broadcast, which is why the spectators' faces in this shot have not been blanked out.

24 It was Denis Diderot (1771) who in meta-works such as *Discours de la poésie dramatique* and *Paradoxe sur le comédien* thought about questions relating to the philosophy of theatre and first used the term 'fourth wall of the theatre' to refer to the imaginary barrier separating an audience from the three dimensions of the stage it faces.

25 All references to MacGibbon in this chapter are to the interview I conducted with him on 7 November 2019.

26 See the preface by Henry Irving to Diderot's *The Paradox of Acting* [*Paradoxe sur le comédien*, 1830] (1883): 'If tears be produced at the actor's will and under his control, they are true art; and happy is the actor who numbers them amongst his gifts. The exaltation of sensibility in art may be difficult to define, but it is none the less real to all who have felt its power' (xx).

27 'Just watched @NTLive's broadcast of #MidsummerNightsDream and that might be my favourite theatre that I've watched this year. It was incredible. So clever and fun and captivating. I want to watch it again!' (@JadaAddo, 17 October 2019).

28 Examples include, notably, Lyndsey Turner's hugely successful *Hamlet* (5 August–31 October 2015) starring Benedict Cumberbatch in the title role, which opened with Nat King Cole's song 'Nature Boy' while the Young Vic used Alanis Morissette's 'You Oughta Know' to mirror Marina's fury in Joe Hill-Gibbins' *Measure for Measure* (the show ran from 1 October – 14 November 2015).

29 For a discussion of this see Liedke 2021b. Thanks to the NT At Home discussion group convened by Izzy Stuart and the discussion on 26 June 2020, 11.00–12.00 BST. Present: Amber Ash, Susanne Greenhalgh, Sophie Hamlet, Gill Lamden, Heidi Liedke, Izzy Stuart.

Chapter 3

1. See Bruno (2002), Chapman/Glancy/Harper (2007), Elsaesser (2016), Huhtamo and Parikka (2011) and Zielinski (2006).
2. See Bennett (2010), Barad (2007), Haraway (2016) and Latour (2017).
3. For a further discussion of the phenomenological qualities of objects and props used on stage, see Rayner (2006).
4. Bazin's work continues to be a (contested, but acknowledged) touchstone in film studies and adaptation studies and resonates with twenty-first-century concerns in media culture; in 2005, a new translation of his *What is Cinema?* by Hugh Gray was published and as recently as in 2014 a new translation of his work by Dudley Andrew was published as *André Bazin's New Media*. In her 2019 study, *Studying Film with André Bazin*, Blandine Joret adopts Bazin's methodology in a contemporary reading, linking his ideas to major philosophical and scientific frameworks such as CGI, 3D cinema and Virtual Reality. It is a mark of my study to transfer his theories to the study of livecasting.
5. In discussions of livecasts, such as Sullivan (2014) and (Wyver 2014b), the terms 'televisual' and 'cinematic' are used almost interchangeably, often also in the same breath, as in 'televisual and cinematic' versus 'theatrical'. The televisual and cinematic can indeed be grouped together in this particular context because they refer to related processes of mediation and production that are very much opposed to theatrical modes of production. Wyver (2014a) makes a further differentiation and uses 'the televisual' to describe the characteristics of the technology involved, that is image sequencing created when continuous feeds of multiple cameras are edited together in real time as in live television, and 'the cinematic' to refer more broadly to the spectacular and social contexts of the livecast's *reception*. Since the focus in my discussion is more on the reception, I am contrasting the term 'theatrical' with 'cinematic' throughout this chapter.
6. This version is available on YouTube as 'MOLIÈRE – Le médecin malgré lui (Pièce filmée, 1934)', directed by Pierre Weil. Available via: https://www.youtube.com/watch?v=J-KdRc8fqW0. Accessed on 17 February 2021.
7. For a detailed discussion of this aspect, see Liedke 2020a.

Chapter 4

1. An earlier version of this chapter was published in 2019 as 'Emancipating the Spectator? Livecasting, Liveness, and the Feeling I' in *Performance Matters* 5 (2): 6–23. I am grateful for the permission to reprint parts of this essay here.
2. For definitions of 'engagement' from a media psychology and media studies perspective, respectively, see Wirth (2006), Busselle/Bilandzic (2008) and Schlütz (2015).

3 See more on the role of GIFs in pulling spectators into the event in Chapter 6.
4 Jen Harvie (2013) has problematized the connection between immersive theatre practices and the unpaid labour contributed by spectators in this context. The connection and relevance of this discussion for livecasting is a vital one and will have to be taken up elsewhere.
5 By way of a general introduction to the question of adaptation in this context see Wyver (2014b, 104) and Krebs (2014).
6 This is also what Andreas Reckwitz (2017) describes when he writes that '*Wenn* es einem Gut gelingt, als singulär bewertet und erlebt zu werden, *dann* wirkt es authentisch' (139, emphases in original). 'Singular' in this case means 'special' or 'unique'. If one reads the 'wenn . . . dann' as 'when . . . then', this implies a temporal simultaneity of the realization of the given object's singularity and the experience of it as being authentic. This simultaneity is also crucial for the livecasting context.
7 Selected statements from the online survey posted on 18 July 2018, after the livecast of *Romeo and Juliet* on the RSC's Twitter Page.
8 The NT sometimes also livecasts plays produced by other companies, such as the Old Vic, the Young Vic and Donmar Warehouse. It also livecasts productions by companies that are not based in London: in 2018, for instance, the Chichester Festival Theatre's production of *King Lear* starring Ian McKellen in the title role, which was livecast on 27 September that year.
9 In the following, I am using the users' Facebook names as they appear on the page, even though they may not necessarily be their actual names, of course.
10 Selected responses on NT Live Facebook page December 25, 2017, accessed 12 July 2019, https://www.facebook.com/ntlive/posts/10155211513058857.
11 This 'first-person experience' appears in an extreme form in Punchdrunk's *The Masque of the Red Death* (2007) where some audience members (but not all) are led away by performers into separate rooms, something critic Lyn Gardner calls 'intimate theatre' (2009).

Chapter 5

1 https://www.roh.org.uk/news/your-reaction-what-did-you-think-of-the-royal-operas-la-boheme-live-in-cinemas, accessed on 4 March 2021.
2 https://youtu.be/GLqE6hAi2jM, accessed on 4 March 2021.
3 An earlier version of this chapter was published as 'In Appreciation of "Mis-" and "Quasi-": Quasi-Experts in the Context of Live Theatre Broadcasting' in *Platform: Journal of Theatre and Performing Arts* 13.1 (Autumn 2019): 86–102.
4 This was said in the panel discussion as part of the Young Vic's 'Pressing Concerns' series on 3 March 2021, 4–6 pm (GMT). The conversation

took place via Zoom, was convened by the Young Vic's Creative Associate Teunkie Van Der Sluijs and the panellists were Arifa Akbar (*The Guardian*), Dominic Cavendish (*The Telegraph*), Natasha Tripley (*The Stage*), Suba Das (director) and Anna Fleischle (set and costume designer).

5 For the American context, Playhouse 90 needs to be mentioned, a television anthology drama series that began as a live series and then used the recently developed videotape technology, and *Studio One*, a radio anthology drama series that was then adapted to television. For American, British, Canadian and Australian radio drama see Crook (1999).

6 The term 'amateur' is re-entering the twenty-first-century lexicon, redefining the ways in which cultural practices are performed and understood. There is also a revival of interest in folk art and craft, with some amateur bakers, knitters and gardeners becoming TV celebrities and others turning their skills to 'craftivism' (Greer 2008 and 2014) where guerrilla performance, slow art and other forms of amateur participation are applied to political activism. Amateur performance has only recently been the topic of a special issue ('On Amateurs', *Performance Research*), and Holdsworth, Milling and Nicholson even speak of an 'amateur turn' (Holdsworth, Milling and Nicholson 2017). The new patterns of labour and pleasure that are emerging in the digital age call for new definitions of the amateur. In the past, 'professional' and 'commercial' have been derogatory terms in some areas of cultural production, especially the so-called fringe; in others, such as music and dance, the boundaries have been less rigid and performers have moved between different modes at different times of their lives and even the day. Online performances produced in the context of the Covid-19 pandemic have further dismantled the 'professional' vs. 'amateur' binary as performers took to performing from their private homes, often with the 'props' that were at their disposal (see Chapter 6).

7 As Stein points out, both the 'fan' and the 'millennial' exist 'as constructs formed at the juncture of academic, popular, and commercial discourse. . . . Both are slippery concepts that shift depending on who is doing the defining' (2015, 4–5) and both groups 'spread and at times revise value systems created in commercial media' (23). For investigations of fandom and fan studies see Gray, Sandvoss and Harrington (2007); Jenkins (1992); the journal *Transformative Works and Cultures*.

8 The field of audience studies is on the rise, however, which should bring about a welcome new angle to think about criticism as well. See, for instance, the projects of the International Network for Audience Research in the Performing Arts and the work by Caroline Heim, Lisa Walsh and Kirsty Sedgman, and the Centre for Spectatorship and Audience Research at the University of Toronto.

9 Looking at the connection of activism, criticism and social media, Paulo Gerbaudo in his *Tweets and the Streets* (2012) suggests a new concept, namely 'choreographing', to explain how social media mediates between

online communication and actual physical gatherings thereby contributing to the emergence of new forms of protest. Building on this, Gerbaudo studies the role played by the politics of emotion and the risks of explosion which social media can add to contemporary protests.

10 An invaluable study on the young history of theatre blogging and its contribution to theatre is Megan Vaughan's *Theatre Blogging. The Emergence of a Critical Culture* (2020). Vaughan both contextualizes the key debates of fifteen years of theatre history and anthologizes the work of over forty theatre bloggers. The study highlights the innovative dramaturgical practices that have been developed and piloted by bloggers and offers insights into the precarious systems of labour and economics in which these writers exist. The five characteristics Vaughan identifies for a blog in her study are: (1) It isn't necessarily frequent, (2) it isn't necessarily chronological, (3) it doesn't rely on the acquiescence of gatekeepers, (4) it isn't formal in style, and (5) it isn't a marketing tool.

11 For a thorough study into the potential of live arts engagement more generally and an investigation of the debates about the place of arts and culture in contemporary society, see Stephanie E. Pitts and Sarah M. Price's *Understanding Audience Engagement in the Contemporary Arts* (2021).

Chapter 6

1 Chambers refers to a City precept from May 12, 1569, which he found in one of William Harrison's works, probably his *Description of Elizabethan England* (1577), which was first published in 1577 as part of *Holinshed's Chronicles*.

2 Sullivan argues in her article that connectedness replaces liveness in the experience of performances that are streamed online. What exact shape this meaningful connectedness can take, varies among spectators; a more stable factor is the connection between liking the broadcast production and feeling engaged by streaming as a medium (Sullivan 2020, 94).

3 One of the first monograph-length studies on the theatre of the pandemic is Barbara Fuchs's *Theater of Lockdown – Digital and Distanced Performance in a Time of Pandemic* (2021). The book offers several case studies from the Americas, Europe and Australia and complements them with interviews, while my chapter offers a more conceptual approach and embeds the recent developments in the discourse of mediated theatre more broadly.

4 See other publications that responded to the developments brought about by the pandemic, especially Aebischer (2022), Allred/Broadribb/Sullivan (2022), Fuchs (2021) and Mosse et al (2022).

5 See also Olive Senior's response to the implications of mask-wearing now in the poem 'M for mask' (2020).

6   See also, for example, Aurelie Godet's (2020) introductory comments on how the festive impulse endures in Covid-19 times.
7   See especially Hanich (2014), Kennedy (2009) and Noë (2004).
8   For historical context on liveness and TV history see, for instance, M. White (1999), Gadassik (2010), Zettl (1978) and Vianello (1985), and more generally Morley (1992).
9   In total people from 170 countries tuned into NT At Home with the most popular territories being the United Kingdom, United States, Australia, Canada and Russia (Buckeridge 2020).
10 Creation Theatre produced a few podcasts accompanying their productions or reflecting on theatre during lockdown, see https://www.creationtheatre.co.uk/category/podcast/.
11 'Yard Online' took place on 17 May 2020 (https://theyardtheatre.co.uk/theatre/events/yard-online/).
12 These productions – listed on the NT's page as 'National Theatre at Home streaming history' – were *One Man, Two Guvnors* (2–9 April), *Jane Eyre* (9–16 April), *Treasure Island* (16–23 April), *Twelfth Night* (23–30 April), *Frankenstein* (30 April–8 May), *Antony & Cleopatra* (7–14 May), *Barber Shop Chronicles* (14–21 May), *A Streetcar Named Desire* (21–28 May), *This House* (28 May–4 June), *Coriolanus* (4–11 June), *The Madness of King George III* (11–18 June), *Small Island* (18–25 June), *A Midsummer Night's Dream* (25 June–2 July), *Les Blancs* (2–9 July), *The Deep Blue Sea* (9–16 July), and *Amadeus* (16–23 July). See https://www.nationaltheatre.org.uk/nt-at-home.
13 Between 2015 and 2020, 18 per cent of those visiting the archive (based on about 6,500 enquiry forms relating to circa 18,000 people visiting the National Theatre Archive) identified as 'general interest', while the majority (54 per cent) identified as academics, students or teachers (Lee 2020).
14 An earlier version of this passage has appeared in *Shakespeare Bulletin* 39.1 (Spring 2021): 151–5.
15 In the original text, it is Philo who says: 'Take but good note, and you shall see in him / The triple pillar of the world transformed / Into a strumpet's fool. Behold and see' (Shakespeare 2015, I.1.11–13).
16 Indeed, when it is impossible to leave your home, or at least move about in the public space as one is used to it, questions around im/mobility and how it is embodied are of new importance. Crucially, as researchers at the School of Geography at QMUL postulate in their blog series 'Im/mobility in Coronatimes', '[t]he capacity to be immobile, by "staying at home", is both premised upon, and has radically different embodied consequences depending on, articulations of age, class, gender, racialization, migration/residency status and dis/ability. [. . .] Home cannot be considered simply a site of uncomplicated "safety"' (https://www.qmul.ac.uk/geog/research/

immobility-in-coronatimes-blog/). There are more studies on im/mobility and Covid-19 primarily from the angle of geography and politics.
17 See Liedke 2021a for a review of Split Britches' 'Zoomie' *Last Gasp WFH*, a play filmed entirely via the recording feature on Zoom and edited slightly afterwards, which I also subsume under the category of viral theatre as the whole piece is a highly personal reflection on humanity and subjecthood exacerbated by the pandemic and because it strongly hails its spectators to become observer-performers.

Chapter 7

1 While Bakhtin was not concerned with adaptations or adaptation theory, his ideas about translations and how texts relate to one another offer very useful answers to questions raised within adaptation studies about intertextuality (see Cutchins 2017 and Stam 1989).
2 In Oscar Wilde's essay 'The Decay of Lying' (1889), which consists of a dialogue between the writer Vivian and his friend Cyril, Vivian utters the maxime that 'Nature has good intentions [. . .] but, as Aristotle once said, she cannot carry them out. When I look at a landscape I cannot help seeing all its defects. It is fortunate for us, however, that Nature is so imperfect, as otherwise we should have had no art at all. Art is our spirited protest, our gallant attempt to teach Nature her proper place' (3). Art, therefore, can perfect nature and life and make it more comfortable – life must imitate art in order to be less defective.
3 A work of art or a performance needs to be seen in order to *be*. When thinking about the audience's role in meaning production, Herbert Blau takes up the first sentence of *Hamlet* uttered by Barnardo, which is 'Who's there?' Blau then problematizes the difference between 'audience' and 'spectator' to refer to those subjects who are present: 'We can speak as we wish of the audience's producing meaning, [. . .] but we are still left with the problem of evaluating the meaning which is produced and equilibrating it with the balance of power. While this is difficult enough with the individual spectator (or reader), what are we really to make of the continuing sentiments about collectivity that are, more than with other forms, still encouraged by the folk-lore and institutions of theatre?' (Blau 1990, 280). I am using the term 'spectator' throughout this study precisely in order not to make claims about collectivity of perception or meaning-making processes.
4 As Samuel Beckett has put it, 'of painters the paintings remain, of sculptors the sculptures, of writers the books, of actors remains only the memory of the audience which time quickly takes charge of erasing' (in Salazar 2017, 21).

5   See Salazar (2017, 24) and Taylor (2003, 19–20) for a more hesitant stance towards video recordings of performances.
6   The essay is an update to Schneider's previous essay entitled 'Performance Remains' (2011 in *Performance Research* 6.2, 100–8), which sets out to counter Phelan's claim that performance 'disappears' in the moment it is performed/staged and argues that (the) performance persists through its remains. In her 2012 essay, from which I am quoting here, Schneider expands on some of her claims.

References

1000 Scores. n.d. '1000 Scores – Pieces for Here, Now & Later – Homepage.' Accessed 19 June 2021. https://1000scores.com/.
Abbott, Daisy. 2015. '"Cut me to Pieces": Shakespeare, Fandom and the Fractured Narrative'. In *Proceedings of the Digital Research in the Humanities and Arts Conference DRHA 2014*, edited by Anastasios Maragiannis. Available online: http://radar.gsa.ac.uk/3827/1/drha2014_paper_a4_format-abbott.pdf.
Abbott, Daisy and Claire Read. 2017. 'Paradocumentation and NT Live's "*CumberHamlet*"'. In *Documenting Performance*, edited by Toni Sant, 165–87. London: Bloomsbury Methuen Drama.
Abercrombie, Nicholas and Brian Longhurst. 1998. *Audiences: A Sociological Theory of Performance and Imagination*. London: SAGE.
Aebischer, Pascale. 2013. *Screening Early Modern Drama: Beyond Shakespeare*. Cambridge: Cambridge University Press.
Aebischer, Pascale. 2018. 'South Bank Shakespeare Goes Global: Broadcasting from Shakespeare's Globe and the National Theatre'. In *Shakespeare and the 'Live' Theatre Broadcast Experience*, edited by Pascale Aebischer, Susanne Greenhalgh, and Laurie Osborne, 113–32. London: Bloomsbury.
Aebischer, Pascale. 2020. 'Viral Shakespeare – Binge-Watching *Hamlet* in Lockdown'. Online Talk hosted by the Royal Central School of Speech and Drama, University of London, 20 May 2020, 08.00-09.00 pm BST.
Aebischer, Pascale. 2022. *Viral Shakespeare. Performance in the Time of Pandemic*. Cambridge: Cambridge University Press.
Aebischer, Pascale, Susanne Greenhalgh and Laurie Osborne, eds. 2018. *Shakespeare and the 'Live' Theatre Broadcast Experience*. London: Bloomsbury.
Ahmed, Sara. 2006. *Queer Phenomenology: Orientations, Objects, Others*. Durham: Duke University Press.
Ahmed, Sara. 2008. *Happiness*. New Formations 63, Lawrence & Wishart.
Ahmed, Sara. 2010. *The Promise of Happiness*. Durham: Duke University Press.
Akbar, Arifa. 2020. 'The Next Act: How the Pandemic is Shaping Online Theatre's Future'. *The Guardian*, 21 September 2020. https://www.theguardian.com/stage/2020/sep/21/future-of-live-theatre-online-drama-coronavirus-lockdown.
Allen, Graham. 2011. *Intertextuality*. New York: Routledge.
Allen, Grant. (1877) 1977. *Physiological Aesthetics*. New York: Garland.
Allred, Gemma, Benjamin Broadribb and Erin Sullivan, eds. 2022. *Lockdown Shakespeare. New Evolutions in Performance and Adaptation*. London: Bloomsbury Publishing.

Alston, Adam. 2016. *Beyond Immersive Theatre*. London: Palgrave Macmillan.
Altman, Rick. 1986. 'Television/Sound'. In *Studies in Entertainment: Critical Approaches to Mass Culture*, edited by Tania Modleski, 39–54. Bloomington: Indiana University Press.
Amos, Matthew. 2022. Interview. 12 May 2022, 11.00–11.40 am (CET), Zoom.
Andrew, Dudley. 2014. *André Bazin's New Media*. Berkeley: University of California Press.
Aristotle. 2013. *Poetics*, translated by Anthony Kenny. Oxford: Oxford World's Classics.
Arnold, Matthew. (1867/1882) 2006. *Culture and Anarchy*. Edited with an Introduction and Notes by Jane Garnett. Oxford: Oxford World's Classics.
Arnold, Matthew. (1864/1875) 2010. 'The Function of Criticism at the Present Time'. In *The Norton Anthology of Theory and Criticism*, edited by Vincent B. Leitch and William E. Cain, 684–703. New York: Norton.
Assmann, Aleida. 2006. *Erinnerungsräume: Formen und Wandlungen des kulturellen Gedächtnisses*. Munich: Beck.
Assmann, Jan. 2013. *Das kulturelle Gedächtnis: Schrift, Erinnerung und politische Identität in frühen Hochkulturen*. Munich: Beck.
Atchison Globe. 1889. 'Foreign Gossip'. 23 July 1889 (4628): n.p.
Atkinson, Sarah. 2019. 'The Labor of Liveness: Behind the Curtain of Opera Cinema'. *The Opera Quarterly* 34 (4): 306–23.
Auslander, Philip. 1997. 'Against Ontology: Making Distinctions between the Live and the Mediatized'. *Performance Research: A Journal of Performing Arts* 2 (3): 50–5.
Auslander, Philip. (1999) 2008. *Liveness: Performance in a Mediatized Culture*. London: Routledge.
Auslander, Philip. 2012. 'Digital Liveness: An Historico-Philosophical Perspective'. *PAJ: A Journal of Performance and Art* 34 (3): 3–11.
Axelson, Tomas. 2015. 'Vernacular Meaning Making. Examples of Narrative Impact in Fiction Film. Questioning the "Banal" Notion in Mediatization of Religion Theory'. *Nordicom Review* 36 (2): 143–56.
Bakhshi, Hasan and David Throsby. 2009. *Innovation in Arts and Cultural Organisations*. Hamburg: Nesta Interim Research.
Bakhshi, Hasan, Juan Mateos-Garcia and David Throsby. 2010. 'Beyond Live: Digital Innovation in the Performing Arts'. *Nesta*. https://www.nesta.org.uk/report/beyond-live/.
Bakhtin, Mikhail. 1968. *Rabelais and His World*. Translated by Helene Iswolsky. Cambridge, MA: MIT Press.
Bakhtin, Mikhail. 1981. *The Dialogic Imagination*. Translated by Caryl Emerson and Michael Holquist. Edited by Michael Holquist. Austin: University of Texas Press.
Bakhtin, Mikhail. 1990. *Art and Answerability: Early Philosophical Essays*. Translated by Vadim Liapunow. Edited by Michael Holquist and Vadim Liapunov. Austin: University of Texas Press.

Baldwin, F. G. C. 1925. *History of the Telephone in the United Kingdom*. London: Chapman & Hall.
Balme, Christopher B. 2008. *The Cambridge Introduction to Theatre Studies*. Cambridge: Cambridge University Press.
Barad, Karen. 2007. *Meeting the Universe Halfway: Quantum Physics and the Entanglement of Matter*. Durham/London: Duke University Press.
Barba, Eugenio. 2005. *The Paper Canoe: A Guide to Theatre Anthropology*. Translated by Richard Fowler. London/New York: Routledge.
Barbican. 2018. 'Refunds for NT Live The Madness of King George'. Email received by Heidi Liedke, 23 November 2018.
Barish, Jonas. 1981. *The Antitheatrical Prejudice*. Berkeley: University of California Press.
Barker, Martin. 2013. *Live to Your Local Cinema: The Remarkable Rise of Livecasting*. Basingstoke: Palgrave Pivot.
Barrett, Felix. 2007. In Discussion with Josephine Machon. Battersea Arts Centre, London, 2 February 2007. http://people.brunel.ac.uk/bst/vol0701/felixbarrett/.
Baudry, Jean-Louis. 1986. 'Ideological Effects of the Basic Cinematographic Apparatus'. In *Narrative, Apparatus, Ideology. A Film Theory Reader*, edited by Philip Rosen, 286–98. New York: Columbia University Press.
Bay-Cheng, Sarah. 2007. 'Theatre Squared: Theatre History in the Age of Media'. *Theatre Topics* 17 (1): 37–50.
Bay-Cheng, Sarah. 2012. 'Theatre Is Media: Some Principles for a Digital Historiography of Performance'. *Theater* 42 (2): 27–41.
Bay-Cheng, Sarah, Chiel Kattenbelt, Andy Lavender and Robin Nelson, eds. 2010. *Mapping Intermediality in Performance*. Amsterdam: Amsterdam University Press.
Bay-Cheng, Sarah, Jennifer Parker-Starbuck and David Saltz, eds. 2015. 'Introduction'. In *Performance and Media: Taxonomies for a Changing Field*, 1–10. Ann Arbor: University of Michigan Press.
Bazin, André. 1951. 'Théâtre et cinema'. *Esprit* 180 (6): 891–905.
Bazin, André. 1967a. 'Theater and Cinema, Part One'. In *What is Cinema?* Essays selected and translated by Hugh Gray, 76–94. Berkeley: University of California Press.
Bazin, André. 1967b. 'Theater and Cinema, Part Two'. In *What is Cinema?* Essays selected and translated by Hugh Gray, 95–124. Berkeley: University of California Press.
Bellamy, Edward. 2007. *Looking Backward 2000–1887*. Oxford: Oxford University Press.
Benjamin, Walter. (1966) 1998. 'What is Epic Theatre? First Version'. In *Understanding Brecht*, translated by Anna Bostock, 1–14. London/New York: Verso.
Benjamin, Walter. (1935) 2010. 'The Work of Art in the Age of Its Technological Reproducibility [First Version]'. In *Grey Room. Walter Benjamin's Media*

Tactics: Optics, Perception, and the Work of Art 39, edited by Michael W. Jennings, 11–38.

Bennett, Jane. 2010. *Vibrant Matter: A Political Ecology of Things*. Durham/London: Duke University Press.

Bentley, Eric. 1965. *The Life of the Drama*. London: Methuen.

Berkaak, Odd Are. 1999. '"In the Heart of the Volcano": The Olympic Games as Mega Drama'. In *Olympic Games as Performance and Public Event*, edited by Arne Martin Klausen, 49–74. London: Berghahn.

Betancourt, Michael. 2017. *Glitch Art in Theory and Practice: Critical Failures and Post-Digital Aesthetics*. New York: Routledge.

Billington, Michael. 2002. 'The State of Reviewing Today'. In *Theatre in Crisis? Performance Manifestos for a New Century*, edited by Maria M. Delgado and Caridad Svich, 54–7. Manchester: Manchester University Press.

Billington, Michael. 2007. *State of the Nation: British Theatre since 1945*. London: Faber and Faber.

Billington, Michael. 2019a. 'All My Sons Review – Sally Field and Bill Pullman Deliver a Miller for Our Times'. *The Guardian*, 23 April 2019. https://www.theguardian.com/stage/2019/apr/23/all-my-sons-review-old-vic-london-sally-field-bill-pullman-jenna-coleman.

Billington, Michael. 2019b. 'Small Island Review – Levy's Windrush Epic Makes Momentous Theatre'. *The Guardian*, 2 May 2019. https://www.theguardian.com/stage/2019/may/02/small-island-review-andrea-levy-windrush-national-theatre-london.

Birke, Dorothee and Stella Butter, eds. 2020. *Comfort in Contemporary Culture. The Challenges of a Concept*. Bielefeld: Transcript.

Blackwell, Anna. 2018. *Shakespearean Celebrity in the Digital Age: Fan Cultures and Remediation*. Cham: Palgrave Macmillan.

Blau, Herbert. 1990. *The Audience*. Baltimore: Johns Hopkins University Press.

Boal, Augusto. (1979) 1985. *Theatre of the Oppressed*. Translated by A. Charles and Maria-Odilia Leal McBride. New York: TCG.

Böhrer, Annerose. 2020. 'Masking – "I Wear My Mask for You" – A Note on Face Masks'. *The European Sociologist* 45 (1): n.p.

Bolter, J. D. and R. A. Grusin. 1996. 'Remediation'. *Configurations* 4 (3): 311–58.

Bourdieu, Pierre. 1996. *On Television*. Translated by Priscilla Parkhurst Ferguson. New York: The New Press.

Bourriad, Nicolas, ed. 2009. *Altermodern: Tate Triennial 2009*. London: Tate Publishing.

Brecht, Bertolt. 1961. *Poems on the Theatre. (From a Work Called Messingkauf)*. Translated by John Berger and Anna Bostock. Northwood: Scorpion Press.

Brecht, Bertolt. (1930) 1964. 'The Modern Theatre is the Epic Theatre: Notes to the Opera Aufstieg und Fall der Stadt Mahagonny'. In *Brecht on Theatre: The Development of an Aesthetic*, edited by John Willett, 33–41. New York: Hill and Wang.

Brecht, Bertolt. (1920) 2015. 'Theater as Sport'. In *Brecht on Theatre*, edited by Marc Silberman, Steve Giles and Tom Kuhn, 20–1. London: Methuen.

Bridge Theatre Homepage. n.d. 'What's On'. Accessed 6 February 2019. https://bridgetheatre.co.uk/whats-on/a-midsummer-nights-dream/
Bridge Theatre. 2019a. 'A Midsummer Night's Dream Begins on 3 June'. Email received by Heidi Liedke on 25 May 2019.
Bridge Theatre. 2019b. 'Five Stars for A Midsummer Night's Dream'. Email received by Heidi Liedke on June 15 2019.
Bridge Theatre. 2019c. 'The End of The Dream Plus New Special Event Announced'. Email received by Heidi Liedke on 6 August 2019.
Broadhurst, Sue. 2012. 'Merleau-Ponty and Neuroaesthetics: Two Approaches to Performance and Technology'. *Digital Creativity* 23 (3–4): 225–38.
Brown, Mark. 2021. 'Young Vic to Livestream All Future Productions, Says Artistic Director'. *The Guardian*, 6 May 2021. https://www.theguardian.com/stage/2021/may/06/young-vic-to-livestream-all-future-productions-says-artistic-director.
Bruno, G. 2002. *Atlas of Emotion: Journeys in Art, Architecture, and Film*. London: Verso.
Buckeridge, Flo. 2019. 'Re: NT Live'. Email received by Heidi Liedke, 20 August 2019.
Buckeridge, Flo. 2020. 'Re: NT At Home Stats/Views'. Email received by Heidi Liedke, 21 October 2020.
Bucknall, Joanna and Kirsty Sedgman. 2017 'Documenting Audience Experience: Social Media as Lively Stratification'. In *Documenting Performance*, edited by Toni Sant, 113–30. London: Bloomsbury Methuen Drama.
Burwick, Frederick. 1996. *Poetic Madness and the Romantic Imagination*. University Park: The Pennsylvania State University Press.
Bury, Rhiannon. 2017. *Television 2.0. Viewer and Fan Engagement with Digital TV*. New York: Peter Lang.
Busselle, Rick and Helena Bilandzic. 2008. 'Fictionality and Perceived Realism in Experiencing Stories: A Model of Narrative Comprehension and Engagement'. *Communication Theory* 18 (2): 255–80.
Calvert, Louis. 1919. *Problems of the Actor*, with an introduction by H. B. Irving. London: Simpkin, Marshall Hamilton, Kent and Co.
Carlyle, Thomas. (1829) 2004. 'Signs of the Times'. *The Victorian* Web. https://victorianweb.org/authors/carlyle/signs1.html.
Causey, Matthew. 2006. *Theatre and Performance in Digital Culture: From Simulation to Embeddedness*. London: Routledge.
Cavell, Stanley. 1979. *The World Viewed: Reflections on the Ontology of Film*. Cambridge: Harvard University Press.
Chambers, E. K. 1923. *The Elizabethan Stage*. Vol. 4. Oxford: Clarendon Press.
Champagne, Christine. 2018. 'Now National Theatre Brings Its Live Plays to the Movies'. *Variety.com*, 21 September 2018. https://variety.com/2018/artisans/production/national-theatre-live-1202951785/.
Chapman, J., M. Glancy and S. Harper, eds. 2007. *The New Film History: Sources, Methods, Approaches*. New York: Palgrave Macmillan.

Cochrane, Bernadette. 2018. 'Blurring the Lines: Adaptation, Transmediality, Intermediality and Screened Performance'. In *The Routledge Companion to Adaptation*, edited by Dennis Cutchins, Katja Krebs and Eckart Voigts, 340–8. London: Routledge.

Cochrane, Bernadette and Frances Bonner. 2014. 'Screening from the Met, the NT, or the House: What Changes with the Live Relay'. *Adaptation* 7 (2): 121–33.

Conner, Lynne. 2013. *Audience Engagement and the Role of Arts Talk in the Digital Era*. Basingstoke: Palgrave Macmillan.

Copeau, Jacques. 1990. *Copeau: Texts on Theatre*. Translated by John Rudlin and Norman H. Paul. London: Routledge.

Corner, John. 2017. 'Afterword: Reflections on Media Engagement'. *Media Industries* 4 (1): 1–6.

Couldry, Nick. 2004. 'Liveness, "Reality," and the Mediated Habitus from Television to the Mobile Phone'. *The Communication Review* 7 (4): 353–61.

Crary, Jonathan. 1990. *Techniques of the Observer*. Cambridge: MIT Press.

Creation Theatre. 2020. 'The Tempest: LIVE, Interactive & in Your Living Room'. Creation Theatre Company, 23 July 2020. https://www.creationtheatre.co.uk/shows/the-tempest-live-interactive-in-your-living-room/.

Crook, Tim. 1999. 'The Electrophone or Théâtrophone. Broadcasting Audio Drama Before the Radio'. In *Radio Drama. Theory and Practice*, edited by Tim Crook, 15–20. London: Routledge.

Cutchins, Dennis. 2017. 'Bakhtin, Intertextuality, and Adaptation'. In *The Oxford Handbook of Adaptation Studies*, edited by Thomas Leitch, 71–86. Oxford: Oxford University Press.

Daily Evening Bulletin. 1889. 'Foreign News and Gossip'. 16 September 1889 68 (139): 4.

Daily Picayune. 1893. 'Operas by Telephone'. 9 August 1893 57 (197): 6.

Daily Picayune. 1899. 'Electrical Music'. 30 July 1899 63 (187): 6.

Daly, Ann. 2002. *Critical Gestures: Writing on Dance and Culture*. Middleton: Wesleyan University Press.

Daniel Judy, or: The London Serio-Comic Journal. 1902. 'Players and Playthings'. 13 August 1902 69: 392–3.

Daniel Judy, or: The London Serio-Comic Journal. 1905. 'Sauce Piquant'. 31 May 1905: 254.

Davis, Jim. 2016. *Theatre & Entertainment*. London: Palgrave Macmillan.

De Certeau, Michel. 1988. *The Practice of Everyday Life*. Berkeley/London: University of California Press.

Debord, Guy. (1967) 2005. *The Society of the Spectacle*. London: Rebel Books.

Denison, Thomas S. 1901. 'The Telephone Newspaper'. *World's Work*, April 1901: 641.

Derrida, Jacques. 1995. *Archive Fever: A Freudian Impression*. Chicago: University of Chicago Press.

Dessy, Mario. 2001. *Madness (La Pazzia)*. In *Futurist Performance*, edited by Michael Kirby, 282. New York: PAJ Publications.

Di Benedetto, Stephen. 2011. *The Provocation of the Sense in Contemporary Theatre*. London: Routledge.

Diderot, Denis. 1749. *Les Bijoux Indiscrets*, or, *The Indiscreet Toys*, translated from the Congese Language, Printed at Monomotapa, in two volumes. Adorned with Copper Plates. Vol. 2. Tobago: Re-printed for Pierrot Ragout. And sold by R. Freeman, near St. Paul's, 1749.

Diderot, Denis. 1771. *Œuvres de théatre . . . avec un discours sur la poésie dramatique*. Paris: Veuve Duchesne.

Dixon, Steve. 2007. *Digital Performance: A History of New Media in Theater, Dance, Performance Art, and Installation*. With contributed by Barry Smith. Cambridge: MIT Press.

Dolan, Jill. 2005. *Utopia in Performance: Finding Hope at the Theater*. Ann Arbor: University of Michigan Press.

Dream. 2021. 'Home'. 11 March 2021. https://dream.online.

Edmundson, Helen. 2019. *Small Island*. Adapted from the novel by Andrea Levy. London: Nick Hern Books.

Eglinton, Andrew. 2010. 'Reflections on a Decade of Punchdrunk Theatre'. *TheatreForum* 37: 46–55.

Elsaesser, Thomas. 2002. *Filmgeschichte und frühes Kino: Archäologie eines Medienwandels*. München: Edition text + kritik.

Elsaesser, Thomas. 2016. *Film History as Media Archaeology: Tracking Digital Cinema*. Amsterdam: Amsterdam University Press.

Elsom, John and Nicholas Tomalin. 1978. *The History of the National Theatre*. Jonathan Cape: London.

Etchells, Tim. 2015. 'Taking Time'. *Nachtkritik*, 22 June 2015. https://www.nachtkritik.de/index.php?option=com_content&view=article&id=11138:tim-etchells-on-live-streaming-forced-entertainment-s-durational-performances-and-complete-works&catid=53&Itemid=83.

Evans, Dean. 2017. 'The Tempest Is Live Theatre Reimagined, With Intel at Its Core'. 4 July 2017. https://iq.intel.co.uk/rsc-the-tempest-live-theatre-reimagined/.

Evans, Elizabeth. 2019. *Understanding Engagement in Transmedia Culture*. London: Routledge.

Evans, G. Blakemore et al., eds. 1997. *The Riverside Shakespeare*. Boston: Houghton Mifflin.

Evaristo, Bernardine. 2020. *Girl, Woman, Other*. London: Penguin.

Felski, Rita. 2020. *Hooked: Art and Attachment*. Chicago: University of Chicago Press.

Felton-Dansky, Miriam. 2018. *Viral Performance: Contagious Theatres from Modernism to the Digital Age*. Evanston: Northwestern University Press.

Finburgh, Clare. 2017. *Watching War on the Twenty-First Century Stage: Spectacles of Conflict*. London: Bloomsbury.

Fischer-Lichte, Erika. 2005. *Theatre, Sacrifice, Ritual: Exploring Forms of Political Theatre*. London: Routledge.

Fischer-Lichte, Erika. 2008. *The Transformative Power of Performance: A New Aesthetics*. London: Routledge.
Fischer-Lichte, Erika. (2004) 2014. *Ästhetik des Performativen*. Frankfurt: Suhrkamp.
Fiske, John. 2001. *Reading the Popular* London/New York: Routledge.
Foucault, Michel. 1986. 'Of Other Spaces'. *Diacritics* 16 (1): 22–7.
Foucault, Michel. 2013. 'Der utopische Körper' In *Die Heterotopien. Der utopische Körper. Zwei Radiovorträge*, 23–36. Berlin: Suhrkamp.
Foucault, Michel. 2007. 'What Is Critique?' In *The Politics of Truth*, edited by Sylvère Lotringer and translated by Lysa Hochroth, 41–81. Los Angeles: Semiotext(e).
Fraser, Nancy. 1992. 'Rethinking the Public Sphere: A Contribution to the Critique of Actually Existing Democracy'. In *Habermas and the Public Sphere*, edited by Craig Calhoun, 109–42. Cambridge: MIT Press.
The Friend of India. 1896. 'No Title'. 30 1896 LXXV (27): 13.
Frieze, James. 2016. *Reframing Immersive Theatre: The Politics and Pragmatics of Participatory Performance*. London: Palgrave Macmillan.
Fuchs, Barbara. 2021. *Theater of Lockdown: Digital and Distanced Performance in a Time of Pandemic*. London: Bloomsbury.
Fun. 1895. 'Fun by Week'. 9 July 1895: 62.
Gabrielsson, Alf. 2011. *Strong Experiences with Music. Music Is Much More Than Just Music*. Oxford: Oxford University Press.
Gadassik, Alla. 2010. 'At a Loss for Words: Televisual Liveness and Corporeal Interruption'. *Journal of Dramatic Theory and Criticism* 24 (2): 117–34.
Galveston Daily News. 1895. 'Multiple News Items'. 13 August 1895 142: 4.
Gardner, Lyn. 2015. 'Benedict Cumberbatch's Hamlet Comes into Its Own on the Screen'. *The Guardian*, 16 October 2015.
Gardner, Lyn. 2009. 'How Intimate Theatre Won Our Hearts'. *The Guardian*, 11 August 2009.
Gatehouse, Cally. 2020. 'Coronavirus and the Carnivalesque: What Speculative Methods Can Tell Us About Covid-19'. *Interactions* 27 (4): 34–6.
Georgi, Claudia. 2014. *Liveness on Stage: Intermedial Challenges in Contemporary British Theatre and Performance*. Vol. 25. Berlin: De Gruyter Mouton.
Gerbaudo, Paolo. 2012. *Tweets and the Streets*. London: Pluto Press.
Giannachi, Gabriela. 2004. *Virtual Theatres: An Introduction*. London: Routledge.
Giannachi, Gabriela, et al. 2012. 'Introduction. Archaeologies of Presence'. In *Archaeologies of Presence: Art, Performance and the Persistence of Being*, edited by Gabriela Giannachi, Nick Kaye and Michael Shanks, 1–25. London: Routledge.
Giesen, Bernd. 2011. *Zwischenlagen*. Velbrück: Göttingen.
Gilbert, David, Judith Hawley, Helen Nicholson and Libby Worth. 2020. 'On Amateurs: An Introduction and a Manifesto'. *Performance Research* 25 (1): 2–9.
Godet, Aurelie. 2020. 'Behind the Masks'. *Journal of Festive Studies* 2 (1): 1–31.
Goodall, Jane. 2008. *Stage Presence*. London: Routledge.

Gray, Jonathan. 2003. 'New Audiences, New Textualities: Anti-Fans and Non-Fans'. *International Journal of Cultural Studies* 6 (1): 64–81.
Gray, Jonathan. 2010. *Show Sold Separately: Promos, Spoilers and Other Media Paratexts*. New York: New York University Press.
Gray, Jonathan, Cornel Sandvoss and C. Lee Harrington. 2007. *Fandom: Identities and Communities in a Mediated World*. New York: New York University Press.
Greenhalgh, Susanne. 2014. 'Guest Editor's Introduction'. *Shakespeare Bulletin* 32 (2): 255–61.
Greenhalgh, Susanne. 2018. 'The Remains of the Stage: Revivifying Shakespearean Theatre on Screen, 1964–2016'. In *Shakespeare and the 'Live' Theatre Broadcast Experience*, edited by Pascale Aebischer, Susanne Greenhalgh and Laurie Osborne, 19–39. London: Bloomsbury.
Greer, Betsy. 2008. *Knitting for Good: A Guide to Creating Personal, Social & Political Change, Stitch by Stitch*. Boston: Trumpeter.
Greer, Betsy. 2014. *Craftivism: The Art and Craft of Activism*. Vancouver: Arsenal Pulp Press.
Gregg, Melissa and Gregory J. Seigworth, eds. 2010. *The Affect Theory Reader*. Durham: Duke University Press.
Grein, J. T. 1923. 'The World of the Theatre'. *The Illustrated London News*, 20 October 1923: 712.
Grotowski, Jerzy. (1968) 2002. 'The Theatre's New Testament. An Interview with Jerzy Grotowski by Eugenio Barba'. In *Towards a Poor Theatre*, edited by Eugenio Barba, 27–54. London: Routledge.
Groves, Nancy. 2012. 'Arts Head: David Sabel, Head of Digital, National Theatre'. *The Guardian*, 10 April 2012. https://www.theguardian.com/culture-professionals-network/culture-professionals-blog/2012/apr/10/david-sabel-digital-national-theatre.
Gurr, Andrew. 2009. *The Shakespearean Stage 1574–1642*. Cambridge: Cambridge University Press.
Halliday, Sam. 2020. 'Hearing and the Senses'. In *Sound and Literature*, edited by Anna Snaith, 37–55. Cambridge: Cambridge University Press.
Halliday, Sam. 2016. 'Electricity, Telephony, Communication'. In *Late Victorian into Modern*, edited by Laura Marcus, Michèle Mendelssohn and Kirsten Shepherd-Barr, 597–609. Oxford: Oxford University Press.
Halliday, Sam. 2013. *Sonic Modernity. Representing Sound in Literature, Culture and the Arts*. Edinburgh: Edinburgh University Press.
Hanich, Julian. 2014. 'Watching A Film With Others: Towards A Theory of Collective Spectatorship'. *Screen* 55 (3): 338–59.
Haraway, Donna. 2016. *Staying with the Trouble: Making Kin in the Curriculum*. Durham: Duke University Press.
Harris, John. 2012. 'Guy Debord Predicted Our Distracted Society'. *The Guardian*, 30 March 2012. https://www.theguardian.com/commentisfree/2012/mar/30/guy-debord-society-spectacle.
Harvey, David. 1989. *The Condition of Postmodernity: An Enquiry into the Origins of Cultural Change*. Oxford: Basil Blackwell.

Harvie, Jen. 2013. *Fair Play: Art, Performance, and Neoliberalism*. Basingstoke: Palgrave Macmillan.
Harvie, Jen and Paul Allain. 2006. *The Routledge Companion to Theatre and Performance*. Oxon Routledge.
Hatfull, Ronan. 2019. '"Finally You Put Me First": Love on Top in NT Live: A Midsummer Night's Dream @ The Bridge Theatre'. *Medium.com*, 28 October 2019. https://medium.com/action-is-eloquence-re-thinking-shakespeare/f...cé-to-nt-live-a-midsummer-night-s-dream-the-bridge-2e981a580118.
Hatton, Oona. 2014. '"Hey, Asshole: You Had Your Say." The Performance of Theatre Criticism'. *Theatre Topics* 24 (2): 103–24.
Hawes, Robert. 1991. *Radio Art*. London: Welds Green Wood Publishing.
Hawkes, Rebecca. 2015. 'Live Broadcast of Benedict Cumberbatch's Hamlet Watched by 225,000 People'. *The Telegraph*, 21 October 2015.
Heidegger, Martin. 1973. *Being and Time*. Translated by John Macquarrie and Edward Robinon. Oxford: Basil Blackwell.
Heim, Caroline. 2016. *Audience as Performer: The Changing Role of Theatre Audiences in the Twenty-First Century*. London: Routledge.
Henry V. Directed by Laurence Olivier, performances by Laurence Olivier and Renée Asherson. Two Cities Films, 1944.
Hill, Annette. 2017. 'Reality TV Engagement: Producer and Audience Relations for Reality Talent Shows'. *Media Industries* 4 (1): 1–17.
Hill, Annette. 2018. *Media Experiences: Engaging with Drama and Reality Television*. London: Routledge.
Hitchman, Lauren. 2018 'From Page to Stage to Screen: The Live Theatre Broadcast as a New Medium'. *Adaptation* 11 (2): 171–85.
Holdsworth, Nadine, Jane Milling and Helen Nicholson. 2017. 'Theatre, Performance, and the Amateur Turn'. *Contemporary Theatre Review* 27 (1): 4–17.
Huhtamo, E. and J. Parikka, eds. 2011. *Media Archaeology: Approaches, Applications and Implications*. Berkeley: University of California Press.
Hunter, Lindsay Brandon. 2019. '"We Are Not Making a Movie": Constituting Theatre in Live Broadcast'. *Theatre Topics* 29 (1): 15–27.
Hunter, Lindsay Brandon. 2021. *Playing Real. Mimesis, Media, and Mischief*. Evanston: Northwestern University Press.
Hurley, Erin. 2010. *Theatre & Feeling*. Basingstoke: Palgrave Macmillan.
Hutcheon, Linda, with Siobhan O'Flynn. 2013. *A Theory of Adaptation*. New York: Routledge.
Hutchinson, David. 2015. 'Benedict Cumberbatch Hamlet Takes £3m at NT Live Box Office'. *The Stage*, 9 December 2015.
Hytner, Nicholas. 2018. *Balancing Acts: Behind the Scenes at the National Theatre*. London: Vintage.
Inglis, David. 2019. 'Cover Their Face: Masks, Masking and Masquerades in Historical-Anthropological Context'. In *The Routledge International Handbook to Veils and Veiling*, edited by Anna-Mari Almila and David Inglis, n.p. London/New York: Routledge.

Irving, Henry. 1883. 'Preface'. In *The Paradox of Acting*, edited by Denis Diderot translated by Walter Herries Pollock, ix–xx. London: Chatto & Windus.

Jacobson, Kelsey. 2020. 'Theatre Companies Are Pushing Storytelling Boundaries with Online Audiences amid Covid-19'. *The Conversation*, 21 July 2020. https://theconversation.com/theatre-companies-are-pushing-storytelling-boundaries-with-online-audiences-amid-covid-19-141583.

Jenkins, Henry. 1992. *Textual Poachers: Television Fans and Participatory Culture*. London: Routledge.

Jenkins, Henry. 2006. *Convergence Culture: Where Old and New Media Collide*. New York: New York University Press.

Jenkins, Henry, Sam Ford and Joshua Green. 2013. *Spreadable Media: Creating Value and Meaning in a Networked Culture*. New York: New York University Press.

Johnson, Dominic. 2012. *Theatre & the Visual*. Basingstoke: Palgrave Macmillan.

Joret, Blandine. 2019. *Studying Film with André Bazin*. Amsterdam: Amsterdam University Press.

Keiling, Tobias and Heidi Liedke. 2021. *Faultiere: Ein Portrait*. Berlin: Matthes & Seitz.

Kennedy, Dennis. 2001. 'Sports and Shows: Spectators in Contemporary Culture'. *Theatre Research International* 26 (3): 277–84.

Kennedy, Dennis. 2009. *The Spectator and the Spectacle: Audiences in Modernity and Postmodernity*. Cambridge: Cambridge University Press.

Kershaw, Baz. 1999. *The Radical in Performance: Between Brecht and Baudrillard*. London: Routledge.

Kershaw, Baz. 2001. 'Oh for Unruly Audiences! Or, Patterns of Participation in Twentieth-Century Theatre'. *Modern Drama* 44 (2): 133–54.

Kershaw, Baz. 2007. 'Spectacles of Performance: Excesses of Power'. In *Theatre Ecology: Environments and Performance Events*, edited by Baz Kershaw, 206–38. Cambridge: Cambridge University Press.

Kirby, Alan. 2009. *Digimodernism. How New Technologies Dismantle the Postmodern and Reconfigure Our Culture*. New York/London: Continuum.

Kirwan, Peter. 2014. 'Coriolanus (Review)'. *Shakespeare Bulletin* 32 (2): 275–8.

Kirwan, Peter. 2020. 'The Tempest (Creation/Big Telly Theatre) @ Zoom'. *The Bardathon*, 19 April 2020. https://blogs.nottingham.ac.uk/bardathon/2020/04/19/the-tempest-creation-big-telly-theatre-zoom/.

Klich, Rosemary and Edward Scheer. 2011. *Multimedia Performance*. Basingstoke: Palgrave Macmillan.

Krausse, Alexis. 1897. 'The Telephone – Behind the Scenes'. *The Ludgate* 4: 535–6.

Krebs, Katja. 2014. 'Ghosts We Have Seen Before: Trends in Adaptation in Contemporary Performance'. *Theatre Journal* 66 (4): 581–90.

Kress, Gunther. 2010. *Multimodality. A Social Semiotic Approach to Contemporary Communication*. London/New York: Routledge.

Kushner, Tony. 1995. 'Playwright's Notes'. In *Angels in America. A Gay Fantasia on National Themes*, edited by Tony Kushner, 11. New York: TCG.

Latour, Bruno. 2017. *Facing Gaia: Eight Lecture on the New Climatic Regime*. Cambridge: Polity Press.

Lavender, Andy. 2016. *Performance in the Twenty-First Century: Theatres of Engagement*. London: Routledge.

Lawrence, Arthur H. 1897. 'Christmas – Then, and Now! Mr. George Jr. Sims at Home'. *The Idler: An Illustrated Magazine* 12 (5): 683–96.

Lee, Erin. 2020. 'Re: NT Archive Statistics'. Email received by Heidi Liedke, 2 June 2020.

Lehmann, Hans-Thies. (1999) 2006. *Postdramatic Theatre*. Translated and with an introduction by Karen Jürs-Munby. London: Routledge.

Lehmann, Hans-Thies. 1999. *Postdramatisches Theater*. Frankfurt: Verlag der Autoren.

Lévi-Strauss, Claude. 1962. 'The Science of the Concrete'. In *The Savage Mind*, edited by Claude Lévi-Strauss, 1–34. London: Weidenfeld and Nicolson.

Liedke, Heidi. 2018. *The Experience of Idling in Victorian Travel Texts, 1850–1901*. Cham: Palgrave Macmillan.

Liedke, Heidi. 2019. 'Emancipating the Spectator? Livecasting, Liveness, and the Feeling I'. *Performance Matters* 5 (2): 6–23.

Liedke, Heidi. 2020a. '"These Seats Are So Comfy": Livecasting and the Notion of Comfortable Theatre'. In *Comfort in Contemporary Culture: The Challenges of a Concept*, edited by Dorothee Birke and Stella Butter, 209–30. Bielefeld: transcript.

Liedke, Heidi. 2020b. 'The Tempest (2020) by Creation Theatre: Live in your Living Room.' *Miranda* (online) 21 (2020).

Liedke, Heidi. 2021a. 'Review: *Last Gasp (WFH)*'. *Theatre Journal* 73 (2): 225–7.

Liedke, Heidi. 2021b. 'On Being Pulled: Spectator Engagement and Spectacle in the Context of Live Theatre Broadcasting and NT at Home'. *Participations* 18 (2): 294–317.

Liedke, Heidi and Monika Pietrzak-Franger. 2021. 'Viral Theatre: Preliminary Thoughts on the Impact of the COVID-19 Pandemic on Online Theatre'. *JCDE* 9 (1): 128–44.

London, John. 2017. 'Introduction: Futurism, Anti-Futurism, and the Forgotten Century'. In *One Hundred Years of Futurism. Aesthetics, Politics, and Performance*, edited by John London, 1–45. Bristol: Intellect.

Lowe, Victoria. 2020. *Adapting Performance Between Stage and Screen*. Bristol: Intellect Books.

MacAloon, John. J. 2006. 'The Theory of Spectacle. Reviewing Olympic Ethnography'. In *National Identity and Sports Events*, edited by Alan Tomlinson and Christopher Young, 15–39. Albany: State University of New York Press.

MacArthur, Michelle. 2016. 'Crowdsourcing the Review and the Record: A Collaborative Approach to Theatre Criticism and Archiving in the Digital Age'. In *Theatre Criticism: Changing Landscapes*, edited by Duška Radosavljević, 255–72. London: Bloomsbury Methuen Drama.

MacGibbon, Ross. 2019. Interview. 7 November 2019, 10.00–11.30 am (GMT), Gail's Café, Pimlico, London.
The Magazine of Music. 1896. 'Accidentals'. September 1896 13 (9): 606–7.
Marinetti, Filippo Tommaso. 1914. *I Manifesti del futurism, lanciata da Marinetti et al*. Firenze: Lacerba.
Markwell, Celeste. 2020. 'Re: NT At Home – YouTube Statistics'. Email received by Heidi Liedke on 16 June 2020.
Marvin, Carolyn. 1988. *When Old Technologies Were New: Thinking About Electric Communication in the Late Nineteenth Century*. New York: Oxford University Press.
Marx, Karl. 1988. *The Communist Manifesto*. Edited by Frederick L. Bender. New York: W. W. Norton and Company.
Massumi, Brian. 2002. *Parables for the Virtual: Movement, Affect, Sensation*. Durham: Duke University Press.
McAuley, Gay. 1999. *Space in Performance: Making Meaning in the Theatre*. Ann Arbor: University of Michigan Press.
McLuhan, Marshall. 1964. *Understanding Media: The Extensions of Man*. London: Routledge & Paul.
McLuskie, Kate and Kate Rumbold. 2014. *Cultural Value in Twenty-First Century England: The Case of Shakespeare*. Manchester: Manchester University Press.
Melcer-Padon, Nourit. 2018. 'Chapter Three: From Theater to Novel: Luigi Pirandello'. In *Creating Communities: Towards a Description of the Mask-Function in Literature*, edited by Nourit Melcer-Padon, 59–100. Bielefeld: Transcript.
Melrose, Susan. 2006. 'Constitutive Ambiguities: Writing Professional or Expert Performance Practices and the Théâtre du Soleil, Paris'. In *Contemporary Theatres in Europe: A Critical Companion*, edited by Joe Kelleher and Nicholas Ridout, 120–35. London: Routledge.
Meyer-Dinkgräfe, Daniel. 2015. 'Liveness: Phelan, Auslander, and After'. *Journal of Dramatic Theory and Criticism* 29 (2): 69–79.
Milwaukee Daily Sentinel. 1891. 'Theaters This Week'. 27 December 1891 14 (11): 14.
Milwaukee Daily Sentinel. 1892. 'Foreign Odds and Ends'. 4 September 1892 14 (47): 4.
Milwaukee Journal. 1890. 'Recent ideas'. 20 August 1890: 3.
Monks, Aoife. 2013. 'Objects'. *Contemporary Theatre Review* 23 (1): 53–4.
Monks, Aoife. 2014. 'In Defense of Craft: A Manifesto'. *Scene* 2 (1–2): 175–8.
Morley, David. 1992. *Television, Audiences and Cultural Studies*. New York: Routledge.
Mosse, Ramona, Janina Janke, Judith König, Christian Stein and Nina Tecklenburg. 2022. 'Viral Theatres' Pandemic Playbook – Documenting German Theatre During COVID-19'. *International Journal of Performance Arts and Digital Media* 18 (1): 105–27.

National Theatre Annual Review 2017–2018.
https://review.nationaltheatre.org.uk/#2018/welcome/81.
National Theatre Annual Review 2018–2019.
https://review.nationaltheatre.org.uk/#2019/welcome/126.
National Theatre. 2019. 'Ten Years on Screen'. *YouTube*. Accessed 23 June 2021.
https://www.youtube.com/watch?v=T94kV4W24RE.
National Theatre. 2020. 'Relive the Memories'. *YouTube*. Accessed 23 June 2021.
https://www.youtube.com/watch?v=k_HhFCFMNr4.
National Theatre. 'Announcement for Final Titles Streaming as Part of National Theatre At Home'. *Facebook*, 11 June 2020, 12:00 BST, https://www.facebook.com/nationaltheatre/posts/10158729460534973.
Nelson, Robin. 2010. 'Experiencer'. In *Mapping Intermediality in Performance*, edited by Sarah Bay-Cheng, Chiel Kattenbelt, Andy Lavender and Robin Nelson, 45. Amsterdam: Amsterdam University Press.
The New Zealand Graphic and Ladies Journal. 'We Shall Be as Princes'. 6 August 1898 XXI (6): 162.
Nicholas, Rachael. 2018. 'Understanding "New" Encounters with Shakespeare: Hybrid Media and Emerging Audience Behaviours'. In *Shakespeare and the 'Live' Theatre Broadcast Experience*, edited by Pascale Aebischer, Susanne Greenhalgh and Laurie Osborne, 77–92. London: The Arden Shakespeare.
Nicholson, Helen. 2006. 'Collecting Memories'. *Research in Drama Education* 11 (1): 1–5.
Nield, Sophie. 2012. 'Are Curtain Calls a Clapped-out Convention?' *The Guardian*, 3 April 2012. https://www.theguardian.com/stage/theatreblog/2012/apr/03/curtain-calls-clapped-out-convention.
Nield, Sophie. 2019. 'Technologies of Performance'. In *A Cultural History of Theatre in the Age of Empire*, edited by P. W. Marx, 03–226. London: Methuen Drama.
NT Future. n.d. 'In-House Digital Facilities'. Accessed 23 June 2021. http://ntfuture.nationaltheatre.org.uk/explore/house-digital-facilities.
NT Live FAQs. 2017. 'NT Live FAQs'. Accessed 23 June 2021. https://www.nationaltheatre.org.uk/about-the-national-theatre/press/nt-live-press/nt-live-faqs.
NT Live FAQs. 2018. 'NT Live FAQs'. Email sent to author by Broadcast and Distribution Assistant Amaka Ejizu on 22 February 2018.
Noë, Alva. 2004. *Action in Perception*. Cambridge: MIT Press.
OED Online. 2020. 'spectacle'. February 2020. Oxford: Oxford University Press.
O'Neill, Stephen, ed. 2017. *Broadcast Your Shakespeare: Continuity and Change Across Media*. London: Bloomsbury.
Oddey, Alison and Christine White, eds. 2009. *Modes of Spectating*. Bristol: Intellect.
OneFurther.com. 2020. 'Visualized #3: National Theatre at Home'. *One Further*, 17 April 2020. https://onefurther.com/blog/visualised-3-national-theatre-at-home.

Ong, Walter. (1982) 2002. *Orality and Literacy: The Technologizing of the Word*. London: Routledge.
Ostmeier, Dorothee. 2001. 'Bertolt Brecht and the Internet'. In *New Essays on Brecht, The Brecht Yearbook* 26, edited by Maarten van Dijk, 35–255. The International Brecht Society, Madison: University of Wisconsin Press.
The Outlook. 1898. 'Notes'. 23 July 1898: 775.
Owen, Richard. 1861. *Memoir on the Megatherium*. London: Williams and Norgate.
Parker-Starbuck, Jennifer. 2012. *Cyborg Theatre: Corporeal/Technological Intersections in Multimedia Performance*. London: Palgrave Macmillan.
Parker-Starbuck, Jennifer. 2015. 'Cyborg Returns: Always-Already Subject Technologies'. In *Performance and Media: Taxonomies for a Changing Field*, edited by Sarah Bay-Cheng, Jennifer Parker-Starbuck, and David Z. Saltz, 65–92. Ann Arbor: University of Michigan Press.
Parsons, Elinor. 2014. 'Embracing Diversity: An Introduction to Contributions that Were Offered at the *From Theatre to Screen* Conference'. *Adaptation* 7 (2): 99–103.
Patteson, Thomas. 2015. *Instruments for New Music. Sound, Technology, and Modernism*. Oakland: University of California Press.
Paul, Christiane and Malcolm Levy. 2015. 'Genealogies of the New Aesthetics'. In *Postdigital Aesthetics*, edited by David M. Berry and Michael Dieter, 27–43. London: Palgrave Macmillan.
Pavis, Patrice. 2006. *Analyzing Performance: Theatre, Dance, and Film*. Translated by David Williams. Ann Arbor: The University of Michigan Press.
Petralia, Peter. 2012. 'Reach Out and Touch Someone: Technology and the Promise of Intimacy'. TAPRA, Kent University, 5–7 September 2012. Conference edit. http://www.drpetralia.com/wp-content/uploads/2012/09/Reach-Out-and-Touch-Someone_PAPER_EDITED.pdf.
Phelan, Peggy. 1993. *Unmarked: The Politics of Performance*. London: Routledge.
Pine, Joseph and James H. Gilmore. 1999. *The Experience Economy*. Boston: Harvard Business Review Press.
Pitts, Stephanie E. and Sarah M. Price. 2021. *Understanding Audience Engagement in the Contemporary Arts*. London: Routledge.
Play at Home. n.d. 'About Us'. Accessed 18 June 2021. http://www.playathome.org/who-are-we.
Power, Cormac. 2008. *Presence in Play: A Critique of Theories of Presence in the Theatre*. Amsterdam/New York: Rodopi.
Postlewait, Thomas and Tracy C. Davis. 2003. 'Theatricality: An Introduction'. In *Theatricality*, edited by Tracy C. Davis and Thomas Postlewait, 1–39. Cambridge: Cambridge University Press.
Proto-type Theatre. n.d. 'Fortnight'. Accessed 19 June 2021. http://proto-type.org/projects/past/fortnight/
Punch. 1881. 'The Way We Talk Now'. 14 May 1881 LXXX: 228.
Purcell, Stephen. 2014. 'The Impact of New Forms of Public Performance'. In *Shakespeare and the Digital World. Redefining Scholarship and Practice*,

edited by Christie Carson and Peter Kirwan, 212–25. Cambridge: Cambridge University Press.
Radosavljević, Duška. 2016. 'Introduction'. In *Theatre Criticism: Changing Landscapes*, edited by Duška Radosavljević, 1–36. London: Bloomsbury Methuen Drama.
Rancière, Jacques. (2007) 2011. 'The Emancipated Spectator'. In *The Emancipated Spectator*, translated by Gregory Elliott, 1–23. London: Verso.
Rascal, Dizzee. 2009. 'Bonkers'. *Tongue N' Cheek*. Dirtee Stank Recordings.
Rayner, Alice. 2006. *Ghosts: Death's Double and the Phenomenon of Theatre*. Minneapolis: University of Minnesota Press.
Read, Alan. 2014. 'From *Theatre & Everyday Life* to *Theatre in the Expanded Field*: Performance Between Community and Immunity'. *JCDE* 2 (1): 8–25.
Reason, Matthew. 2010. 'Asking the Audience: Audience Research and the Experience of the Theatre'. *About Performance* 10: 15–34.
Reckwitz, Andreas. 2017. *Die Gesellschaft der Singularitäten*. Berlin: Suhrkamp.
Reidy, B. K., B. Schutt, D. Abramson and A. Durski. 2016. 'From Live-to-Digital: Understanding the Impact of Digital Developments in Theatre on Audiences, Production and Distribution'. *Arts Council England*, October 2016. Available online: https://artswork.org.uk/resources/from-live-to-digital-understanding-the-impact-of-digital-developments-in-theatre-on-audiences-production-and-distribution/.
Ridout, Nicholas. 2012. 'Mis-Spectatorship, or, "Redistributing the Sensible."' In *Archaeologies of Presence*, edited by Gabriela Giannachi, Nick Kaye and Michael Shanks, 172–82. London: Routledge.
Roach, Joseph. 2007. *It*. Ann Arbor: University of Michigan Press.
Román, David. 1998. *Acts of Intervention: Performance, Gay Culture and AIDS*. Bloomington: Indiana University Press.
Rosenthal, Daniel. 2013. 'Coming to a Cinema Near You'. In *The National Theatre Story*, edited by Daniel Rosenthal, 793–802. London: Oberon.
Rowell, George. 1978. *The Victorian Theatre 1792–1914: A Survey*. Cambridge: Cambridge University Press.
Rufford, Juliet. 2015. *Theatre&Architecture*. London: Red Globe Press.
Rupke, Nicolaas. 1994. *Richard Owen: Victorian Naturalist*. New Haven: Yale University Press.
Sabel, David. 2020. '#DigitalWorks10: David Sabel – Livestreaming and Distribution'. *YouTube*, 21 April. https://www.youtube.com/watch?v=w5yJt64rJpk.
Salazar, Daniela. 2017. 'Performance Arts and Their Memories'. In *Documenting Performance: The Context and Processes of Digital Curation and Archiving*, edited by Toni Sant, 19–28. London: Bloomsbury Methuen Drama.
Sampson, Tony. 2012. *Virality: Contagion Theory in the Age of Networks*. Minneapolis: University of Minnesota Press.
Sant, Toni, ed. 2017. *Documenting Performance: The Context and Processes of Digital Curation and Archiving*. London: Bloomsbury Methuen Drama.

Schechner, Richard. (1988) 2003. *Performance Theory*, rev. and ex. ed. London: Routledge.
Schechner, Richard. 2013. *Performance Studies: An Introduction*. London: Routledge.
Schlütz, Daniela. 2015. 'Contemporary Quality TV: The Entertainment Experience of Complex Serial Narratives'. *Annals of the International Communication Association* 40 (1): 95–124.
Schneider, Rebecca. 2011. 'Performance Remains'. *Performance Research* 6 (2): 100–8.
Schneider, Rebecca. 2012. 'Performance Remains Again'. In *Archaeologies of Presence*, edited by Gabriela Giannachi et al., 64–81. London: Routledge.
Schulze, Daniel. 2015. 'The Passive Gaze and Hyper-Immunised Spectators: The Politics of Theatrical Live Broadcasting'. *JCDE* 3 (2): 315–26.
Scott, Derek B. 2019. *German Operetta on Broadway and in the West End, 1900–1940*. Cambridge: Cambridge University Press.
Sedgman, Kirsty. 2018a. *The Reasonable Audience: Theatre Etiquette, Behaviour Policing and the Live Performance Experience*. Basingstoke: Palgrave Pivot.
Sedgman, Kirsty. 2018b. 'Audience Experience in an Anti-expert Age: A Survey of Theatre Audience Research'. *Theatre Research International* 42 (3): 307–22.
Senior, Olive. 2020. 'M for Mask'. *The Gleaner*, 17 May 2020. https://jamaica-gleaner.com/article/art-leisure/20200517/meeting-ground-poems-time-covid-19.
Shakespeare, William. *Antony and Cleopatra*. London: Bloomsbury Arden, 2015.
Shapiro, James. 2015. *1606: William Shakespeare and the Year of Lear*. London: Faber and Faber.
Shaughnessy, Nicola. 2012. 'Preface: Defining the Terms'. In *Live Art, Socially Engaged Theatre and Affective Practice*, edited by Nicola Shaughnessy, xiv–xxi. London: Palgrave Macmillan.
Shellard, Dominic, ed. 2007. *Kenneth Tynan: Theatre Writings*. London: Nick Hern Books.
Sierz, Aleks. 2011. *Rewriting the Nation*. London: Methuen Drama.
Simmel, Georg. 2002. 'The Metropolis and Mental Life'. In *The Blackwell City Reader*, edited by Gary Bridge and Sophie Watson, 11–19. Malden: Blackwell.
Slaby, Jan, Rainer Mühlhoff and Philipp Wüschner. 2019. 'Affective Arrangements'. *Emotion Review* 11 (1): 3–12.
Smith, Alistair. 2013. 'Nicholas Hytner: The Final Lap'. *The Stage*, 20 October 2013, https://www.thestage.co.uk/features/nicholas-hytner-final-lap/.
Sofer, Andrew. 2003. *The Stage Life of Props*. Ann Arbor: University of Michigan Press.
Soloski, Alexis. 2020. 'Review: 'Crave' Is a Timely Ticket for a World on Fire'. *New York Times*, 4 November 2020. https://www.nytimes.com/2020/11/04/theater/review-crave.html.
Sontag, Susan. 1966. 'Film and Theatre'. *Tulane Drama Review* 11 (1): 24–37.

Spence, Jocelyn and Steve Brenford. 2018. 'Sensibility, Narcissism and Affect: Using Immersive Practices in Design for Embodied Experience'. *Multimodal Technologies and Interaction* 2 (15): 1–22.

The Sporting Times. 1899. 'Multiple News Items'. 4 November: 2. Nineteenth Century UK Periodicals.

Stam, Robert. 1989. *Subversive Pleasures: Bakhtin, Cultural Criticism, and Film*. Baltimore: Johns Hopkins University Press.

States, Bert O. 1981. 'Phenomenology of the Curtain Call'. *Hudson Review* 34 (3): 371–80.

States, Bert O. 1985. *Great Reckonings in Little Rooms: On the Phenomenology of Theatre*. Los Angeles: University of California Press.

Stein, Louisa Ellen. 2015. *Millenial Fandom: Television Audiences in the Transmedia Age*. Iowa City: Iowa University Press.

Sterne, Jonathan. 2003. *The Audible Past: Cultural Origins of Sound Reproduction*. Durham: Duke University Press.

Stone, Alison. 2016. 'Not Making a Movie: The Livecasting of Shakespeare Stage Productions by The Royal National Theatre and The Royal Shakespeare Company'. *Shakespeare Bulletin* 34 (4): 627–43.

Sugiera, Malgorzata. 2017. 'Theatre as Contagion: Making Sense of Communication in Performative Arts'. *Text Matters* 7 (7): 291–304.

Sullivan, Erin. 2014. Review of *Richard II*, directed by Gregory Doran. *Shakespeare Bulletin* 32 (2): 272–5.

Sullivan, Erin. 2017. '"The Forms of Things Unknown": Shakespeare and the Rise of the Live Broadcast'. *Shakespeare Bulletin* 35 (4): 627–62.

Sullivan, Erin. 2018. 'The Audience is Present: Aliveness, Social Media, and the Theatre Broadcast Experience'. In *Shakespeare and the 'Live' Theatre Broadcast Experience*, edited by Pascle Aebischer, Susanne Greenhalgh and Laurie Osborne, 59–76. London: Bloomsbury.

Sullivan, Erin. 2020. 'Live to Your Living Room: Streamed Theatre, Audience Experience, and the Globe's *A Midsummer Night's Dream*'. *Participations* 17 (1): 92–119.

Suvin, Darko. 1985. 'The Performance Text as Audience-Stage Dialog Inducing a Possible World'. *Versus* 42 (3): 1–16.

Tabbi, Joseph and Michael Wutz, eds. 1997. *Reading Matters: Narrativity in the New Media Ecology*. Ithaca: Cornell University Press.

Talbot, Frederick A. 1903. 'A Telephone Newspaper'. *Littell's Living Age* (Boston), 8 August 1903: 374–5.

Tally, Robert T., Jr. 2013. *Spatiality*. The New Critical Idiom. London: Routledge.

Tate. N.d.a. 'BMW Tate Live: Screening of Performance Room Series'. Accessed 19 June 2021. https://www.tate.org.uk/whats-on/tate-modern/film/bmw-tate-live-screening-performance-room-series.

Tate. N.d.b. 'BMW Tate Live'. Accessed 19 June 2021. https://www.tate.org.uk/whats-on/tate-modern/performance/bmw-tate-live.

Taylor, Diana. 2003. *The Archive and the Repertoire: Performing Cultural Memory in the Americas*. Durham: Duke University Press.

Terriss, Ellaline. 1955. *Just a Little Bit of String*. London: Hutchinson.
Toffler, Alvin. 1980. *The Third Wave*. New York: William Morrow.
Tomlinson, Alan and Christopher Young. 2006. 'Introduction'. In *National Identity and Sports Events*, edited by Alan Tomlinson and Christopher Young, 1–14. Albany: State University of New York Press.
Tonini, Paolo. 2011. *I Manifesti del Futurismo Italiano 1909–1945*. Gussago: Edizioni dell'Arengario.
Trueman, Matt. 2014. 'Hytner to Set up New Theatre Company When He Leaves National Theatre'. *The Guardian*, 9 January 2014. https://www.theguardian.com/media/2014/jan/09/nicholas-hytner-plans-new-theatre-company-national-nt.
Turner, Victor. 1982. *From Ritual to Theatre: The Human Seriousness of Play*. New York: Performing Arts Journal.
Turner, W. J. 1926. 'The World of Music'. *Illustrated London News*, 11 December: 1200.
Ubersfeld, Anne. 1982. 'The Pleasure of the Spectator'. Translated by Pierre Bouillaguet and Charles Jose. *Modern Drama* 25 (1): 127–39.
Valentini, Valentina I. 2019. 'National Theatre Live Marks Decade of Stage-to-Screen With Immersive "Midsummer"'. *Variety*, 17 October 2019. https://variety.com/2019/artisans/news/national-theatre-live-shakespeare-cinema-1203373312/.
van Es, Karin. 2017. 'Liveness Redux: On Media and Their Claim to Be Live'. *Media, Culture & Society* 39 (8): 1245–56.
Vaughan, Megan. 2020. *Theatre Blogging: The Emergence of a Critical Culture*. London: Bloomsbury Methuen Drama.
Venuti, Lawrence. 2007. 'Adaptation, Translation, Critique'. *Journal of Visual Culture* 6 (1): 25–43.
Vianello, Robert. 1985. 'The Power Politics of "Live" Television'. *Journal of Film and Video* 37 (3): 26–40.
Voigts, Eckart. 2013. 'The Performative Self: Reception and Appropriation under the Conditions of "Spreadable Media" in "Bastard Culture."' *Anglistik: International Journal of English Studies* 24 (2): 151–68.
Voigts, Eckart. 2017. 'Some Random Thoughts about Animated GIFs: Compact Meme Micronarratives in Everyday Remix Culture'. In *Anglistentag 2016 Hamburg Proceedings*, edited by Ute Berns and Jolene Mathieson, 19–31. Trier: WVT.
Voigts-Virchow, Eckart. 2000. 'Introduction: Post-Theatrical Drama/Post-Dramatic Theatre'. In *Contemporary Drama in English: Mediated Drama/Dramatized Media*, edited by Eckart Voigts-Virchow. Vol. 7, 7–11. Trier: WVT.
Wallace, Clare. 2010. 'Sarah Kane, Experiential Theatre and the Revenant Avant-Garde'. In *Sarah Kane in Context*, edited by Laurens de Vos and Graham Saunders, 88–99. Manchester: Manchester University Press.
Walmsley, Ben. 2019. *Audience Engagement in the Performing Arts: A Critical Analysis*. Basingstoke: Palgrave Macmillan.

Wardle, Janice. 2014. '"Outside Broadcast": Looking Backwards and Forwards, Live Theatre in the Cinema – NT Live and RSC Live'. *Adaptation* 7 (2): 134–53.
Way, Geoffrey. 2017. '"Together, Apart": Liveness, Eventness and Streaming Shakespearean Performance'. *Shakespeare Bulletin* 35 (3): 389–406.
Weil, Pierre, director. 1934. *Le médecin malgré lui*. Pelleyris. Available at https://www.youtube.com/watch?v=J-KdRc8fqW0.
Wells, H. G. n.d. *When the Sleeper Wakes*. Project Gutenberg. *EBSCOhost*, search. ebscohost.com/login.aspx?direct=true&db=nlebk&AN=1036700&site=ehost-live. Accessed 27 June 2020.
White, Gareth. 2013. *Audience Participation in Theatre: Aesthetics of the Invitation*. Basingstoke: Palgrave Macmillan.
White, Gareth. 2019. 'Playing with Intimacy and Intensity'. Introduction to the Symposium on 'Playing with Intimacy and Intensity' at the Royal Central School of Speech and Drama London, 16 November 2019.
White, Mimi. 1999. 'Television Liveness: History, Banality, Attractions'. *Spectator* 20: 38–56.
W. H. S. 1923. 'Radio Notes'. *Illustrated London News*, 27 January: 146. The Illustrated London News Historical Archive, 1842–2003.
Wilde, Oscar. (1889) 2010. 'The Decay of Lying'. In *The Decay of Lying and Other Essays*, edited by Ian Small, 3–38. London: Penguin Books.
Willems, Herbert. 1998. 'Inszenierungsgesellschaft? Zum Theater als Modell, zur Theatralität von Praxis'. In *Inszenierungsgesellschaft*, edited by Herbert Willems and Martin Jurga, 23–80. Wiesbaden: Westdeutscher Verlag.
Wingenroth, Lauren. 2018. 'We Need to Talk About Non-Consensual Audience Participation'. *Dance Magazine*, 12 October 2018. https://www.dancemagazine.com/we-need-to-talk-about-non-consensual-audience-participation-2611218336.html.
Wirth, Werner. 2006. 'Involvement'. In *Psychology of Entertainment*, edited by Jennings Bryant and Peter Vorderer, 199–213. New York: Routledge.
Woolf, Virginia. 1924. 'Mr. Bennett and Mrs. Brown'. In *Mr. Bennett and Mrs. Brown*, edited by Virginia Woolf, 3–24. London: Hogarth Press.
Wyndham Goldie, Grace. 1939. 'Television: From the Stalls'. *The Listener*, 19 January 1939: 171.
Wyver, John. 2014a. Review of *Hamlet*, directed by Nicholas Hytner. *Shakespeare Bulletin* 32 (2): 261–3.
Wyver, John. 2014b. '"All the Trimmings?": The Transfer of Theatre to Television in Adaptations of Shakespeare Stagings'. *Adaptation* 7 (2): 104–20.
Wyver, John. 2015. 'Screening the RSC stage: The 2014 *Live from Stratford-upon-Avon* Cinema Broadcasts'. *Shakespeare* 11 (3): 286–302.
Wyver, John. 2019. *Screening the Royal Shakespeare Company. A Critical History*. London: The Arden Shakespeare.
Wyver, John. 2020. Interview. 10 January 2020, 3.00–4.00 pm GMT, Illuminations Office, Studio 309, Screenworks, 22 Highbury Grove, London.

Yard Theatre. 2020. 'Yard Online'. 17 May 2020. https://theyardtheatre.co.uk/theatre/events/yard-online/.
Zahavi, Dan. 2014. 'You, Me, and We'. In *Self and Other: Exploring Subjectivity, Empathy, and Shame*, edited by Dan Zahavi, 241–50. Oxford: Oxford University Press.
Zaiontz, Keren. 2014. 'Narcissistic Spectatorship in Immersive and One-on-One Performance'. *Theatre Journal* 66 (3): 405–25.
Zettl, Herbert. 1978. 'The Rare Case of Television Aesthetics'. *Journal of the University Film Association* 30 (2): 3–8.
Zielinski, S. 2006. *Deep Time of the Media. Toward an Archaeology of Hearing and Seeing by Technical Means*. Cambridge: MIT Press.

Tweets Cited

@3nildown. *Twitter*, 6 November 2020, 10:15 p.m., https://twitter.com/3nildown/status/1324822674858823689.
@AmeliaDonkor. *Twitter*, 6 November 2020, 9:30 p.m., https://twitter.com/AmeliaDonkor/status/1324811531335454724.
@Becci_Nembs27. *Twitter*, 17 October 2019, 11:21 p.m., https://twitter.com/Becci_Nembs27/status/1184942473510113282.
@BethanMedi. *Twitter*, 7 December 2018, 12:05 a.m., https://twitter.com/BethanMedi/status/1070816533348343809.
@cathusmax. *Twitter*, 18 October 2019, 9:02 a.m., https://twitter.com/cathusmax/status/1185088763527139328.
@darkfienix. *Twitter*, 15 October 2015, 11:30 p.m., https://twitter.com/darkfienix/status/654771352671424513.
@DramaHodgkin. *Twitter*, 7 November 2020, 7:17 p.m., https://twitter.com/DramaHodgkin/status/1325140274683604994.
@EevaTenkanen. *Twitter*, 28 November 2019, 11:26 p.m., https://twitter.com/EevaTenkanen/status/1200179137480138759.
@e_schofield27. *Twitter*, 2 November 2020, 9:34 p.m., https://twitter.com/e_schofield27/status/1323362747271286790.
@floridiangoblin. *Twitter*, 21 July 2017, 3:16 a.m., https://twitter.com/floridiangoblin/status/888205990134509569.
@genesian61. *Twitter*, 29 November 2019, 12:22 a.m., https://twitter.com/genesian61/status/1200193266932703235.
@hvamitchell. *Twitter*, 18 October 2019, 12:06 a.m., https://twitter.com/hvamitchell/status/1184953746150903808.
@ironwrites. *Twitter*, 18 October 2019, 9:51 a.m., https://twitter.com/Ironwrites/status/1185100989382168577.
@JadaAddo. *Twitter*, 17 October 2019, 11:40 p.m., https://twitter.com/JadaAddo/status/1184947265225535489.

@Jenstra1. *Twitter*, 10 May 2018, 10:50 p.m., https://twitter.com/Jenstra1/status/994681076063891456.

@larkinaround. *Twitter*, 15 October 2015, 11:58 p.m., https://twitter.com/larkinaround/ status/654778499954151425.

@LauriettaEssien. *Twitter*, 6 November 2020, 7:43 p.m., https://twitter.com/LauriettaEssien/status/1324784600141488129.

@MDockrayMiller. *Twitter*, 5 October 2015, 8:50 p.m., https://twitter.com/MDockrayMiller/status/651107173628571649.

@NTLive. *Twitter*, 26 March 2020, 1:05 p.m., https://twitter.com/NTLive/status/1243146934182952963.

@NicLeeBee. *Twitter*, 27 July 2017, 11:22 p.m., https://twitter.com/NicLeeBee/status/890683921180090369.

@PentaholixUk. Twitter, 16 October 2015, 8:31 a.m., https://twitter.com/PentaholixUk/ status/654907412164562944.

@PhilofBeeston. *Twitter*, 7 December 2018, 12:15 a.m., https://twitter.com/PhilofBeeston/status/1070818974991048705.

@scraphamster. *Twitter*, 17 October 2019, 11:15 p.m., https://twitter.com/scraphamster/status/1184940963434848256.

@scrufflove. *Twitter*, 10 May 2018, 9:42 p.m., https://twitter.com/scrufflove/status/994663902570074113.

@VibhutiJPatel. *Twitter*, 7 December 2018, 12:45 a.m., https://twitter.com/VibhutiJPatel/status/1070826585627000834.

Index

1000Scores   156, 159

Ader, Clément   29
Aebischer, Pascale   81, 93, 160, 168, 181
Ahmed, Sara   2, 14
Allen, Grant
  Physiological Aesthetics   27
Alston, Adam   108
archive   13–15, 19, 26, 75, 132, 146, 148, 160–1, 174, 178–80
  and documentation   8, 13–16, 178
  and memory   10, 15, 70, 91, 131, 140, 161, 179–80
Arnold, Matthew, 'The Function of Criticism at the Present Time'   48, 134–5, 143
Assmann, Aleida and Jan   15
atmosphere   2, 51, 58, 61, 63–4, 67, 74, 81, 86, 93, 96–7, 101, 117, 119, 165, 167, 173–5
audience(s)
  in cinema   51, 52, 57, 60, 63, 66–7, 70–1, 76, 80–1, 86, 88, 90, 93, 94, 96, 99, 109, 112, 116, 126, 134, 142, 152
  remote   28, 41, 70, 105, 110–11, 132, 147–8, 153–4, 158, 160, 165, 171, 182
  in theatre   54, 60–5, 68, 77, 95, 97, 100, 107, 116, 151, 159
auditorium   1–2, 29, 42, 44, 63, 71, 76–7, 80, 94–5, 105, 147, 151, 158–9, 165, 173
Auslander, Philip   83, 111, 153, 176–7, 179

Bakhtin, Mikhail   18, 106–7, 117, 149, 174
  and carnival   150
Barker, Martin   10, 20, 138, 178
  Live to Your Local Cinema (2013)   16
Baudry, Jean-Louis   97, 99
  film apparatus theory   97
Bay-Cheng, Sarah   81, 90, 94
Bazin, André   82–6, 88, 97
BBC   38–9, 41, 43, 160
Bellamy, Edward, *Looking Backward: 2000–1887* (1888)   28
Benjamin, Walter
  aura   15, 115
  epic theatre   80
  'The Work of Art in the Age of Its Technological Reproducibility'   128–30, 141–2
Bentley, Eric   13
Berliner Ensemble   160
Big Telly   156, 159
Billington, Michael   86, 126, 128
Bonner, Frances   16–17, 105, 139
Bourdieu, Pierre   82, 84
Brecht, Bertolt   5, 54, 77
  'The Curtains'   77–8
  'The Lighting'   77–8
  neue Apparate   79–80
  'Theatre as Sport'   51
  'Weigel's Props'   96
Brexit   11, 44, 48, 112
bricolage, bricoleur   147, 159, 169–70
Bridge Theatre   60, 64, 66, 69
  My Name is Lucy Barton   14

broadcasting 25–45, 49, 53, 111, 161, 173, 176
  theatre companies working with
    Cheek by Jowl 11
    English National Opera 11
    Forced Entertainment 11, 110, 123–4
    Kenneth Branagh Theatre Company 11
    Royal Opera House 11, 30, 40, 125, 160
    RSC 11, 15, 17, 21, 42, 93–4, 107, 117
    Table Top Shakespeare 11, 110

cameras 12, 39–44, 51–2, 63–6, 68, 70, 77, 79, 84–9, 91, 95–6, 98, 115, 181–2
  'dirty' shots 68
  reaction shots 87
carnival. *See* Bakhtin, Mikhail
Cavell, Stanley 76
Chaplin, Charlie 83, 128, 142
Chichester Festival Theatre, Sarah Kane's *Crave* (2020) 151, 169
Cochrane, Bernadette 16–18, 52–3, 105, 139
Coleridge, Samuel Taylor 73
comfort 8, 14, 28, 31, 33, 35, 39, 75–6, 81, 86, 98–9, 137, 151, 161–2, 165
communitas 20–1, 47, 57–8, 60, 66, 72–3, 101, 106, 109, 116, 148, 173, 182
convergence (culture) 7, 80
Copeau, Jacques 28–9
Covid-19 pandemic 3, 21, 40–1, 45, 53–4, 74, 101, 145, 170, 174, 181
  lockdown 21, 146–8, 150, 154, 157, 158, 160, 163–5, 168, 175

social distancing 21, 147–51, 155, 159, 167, 169
viral theatre 3, 148, 156–9, 168, 170, 175
virus, virality 152–3, 168
Covidian theatre 21, 145–71
Cracknell, Carrie 88–9
Creation Theatre 147, 151, 156, 159
  The Tempest 156, 158
curtain call 2, 70

De Certeau, Michel 4, 113, 131
defamiliarization, disorientation 1–3
Diderot, Denis
  Les Bijoux Indiscrets 49
  The Paradox of Acting 65
digital performance 5–6
documentation. *See* archive

Electrical Exhibition at Crystal Palace 29
Electronovision 41
electrophone 25–38, 43–5
  acousmatic experience 20, 25–6, 31, 33, 35, 37
  théâtrephone 29, 33
Elsaesser, Thomas 76
embodiment 37–8, 93
engagement 18–21, 70, 94, 100–1, 106, 108–10, 113–16, 118, 122, 130, 135, 139, 144, 147–8, 157–8, 163–4, 173, 176, 180
ephemerality 12–13, 180
Etchells, Tim 110, 118
Evaristo, Bernardine, *Girl, Woman, Other* 125
Exposition International d'Électricité 25

feels culture 136
Felski, Rita 118
Felton-Dansky, Miriam 153

film   17, 19–20, 41, 56, 64, 76, 79–80, 82–95, 98–9, 107, 121, 128–9, 140, 142, 152, 175
film apparatus theory. *See* Baudry, Jean-Louis
Fischer-Lichte, Erika   13, 154–5, 170
Foucault, Michel   76, 129–30, 133, 149
  heterotopia   76
futurism
  Filippo Tommaso Marinetti, *Manifesto del Futurismo*   27
  Mario Dessy, *Madness*   152

GIFs   55, 139, 163
glitch, glitch aesthetic   45, 75–6, 81, 86, 98–100, 141
gramophone   25
Greenhalgh, Susanne   12, 17, 94
Grotowski, Jerzy, *Towards a Poor Theatre* (1968)   13–14

happiness   14
Harvie, Jen   7–8, 120–1
Heim, Caroline   99–100
heterotopia. *See* Foucault, Michel
Hurley, Erin   106
Hutcheon, Linda   134
Hytner, Nicholas   10–12, 34, 40, 44, 47, 60, 70, 75, 85

immersion   47, 62–3, 71, 90
immersive theatre   106–7, 121–2
In the work of Proto-type Theatre   7, 10
immunisatory paradigm   122
in situ   45, 49, 55, 60, 71, 73, 76, 86, 89, 112, 115, 145, 151–2, 161, 165, 167, 173, 178, 182
interactivity   113
interdetermination   18, 174–5
intermedial, intermediality   5, 7

Jenkins, Henry   7, 9, 55, 136

Kirwan, Peter   112, 123, 169–70

Lasdun, Denys   44
Lavender, Andy   107–8
Lehmann, Hans-Thies   50, 82
livecast
  as adaptive instantiation   17, 83
  affective arrangement *of*   46–8, 56, 58, 71–2, 74, 157, 170, 173
  affective dynamics *of*   58, 72
  as cross-over   17–19
  as distinct art form   17
  vs. encore   8, 53–4, 57–8, 76, 99, 141
  vs. filmed live screening   1, 63
  generic indeterminacy *of*   6
  as hybrid form   17, 76, 105, 107, 173
  multimodality *of*   114
  and pre-show features   4, 111
  as substitute   3, 27, 38, 48
  as threshold   174, 181
liveness   9, 12–19, 21–2, 31, 56, 96, 99, 101, 106, 111–13, 130, 132, 140, 143, 153–4, 156–8, 168, 173–83
  prolonged   19, 107, 126, 132, 140
London cinema venues
  Barbican   42, 63, 70, 98–9, 111–12, 152
  Curzon Bloomsbury   90, 92
  Hackney Picturehouse   86
  Rich Mix Cinema   1
London theatre venues
  Almeida   14, 158
  Hampstead Theatre   126
  Kiln Theatre   14
  Young Vic   14, 143, 170, 181–2

Index

MacAloon, John J. 53
McAuley, Gay 28–9, 123
McLuhan, Marshall 5
masks 148–51, 159
materiality 6, 18–19, 33, 63, 75–101, 147, 173–4, 180
media ecology 28, 31, 44–5, 73
memory. *See* archive
mimesis 176
mise-en-scène. *See* theatrical labour
mise-en-sensibilité 107–8
Monks, Aoife, 'In Defense of Craft' 20, 79
multi-camera directors
    Amos, Matthew 88–9, 98, 179
    Lough, Robin 42, 94
    MacGibbon, Ross 47, 51, 64–6, 68, 70

national (*meaning of*) 11, 38–40, 89–90
National Theatre
    Olivier auditorium 56, 77, 95–6, 165–6
    Shakespeare Memorial National Theatre Committee 39
    Southbank 56
Nield, Sophie 2, 27, 37
NT At Home, *plays shown as part of*
    Antony and Cleopatra 148, 164–9
    Death of England-Delroy 158
    Frankenstein 163–4
    A Midsummer Night's Dream 167–8
    One Man, Two Guvnors 53, 153, 164
    Twelfth Night 167
NT Live, *plays shown as part of*
    All About Eve 58
    All My Sons 85–7
    Angels in America 119–20, 141
    Antony and Cleopatra 47–8, 77, 94–5, 138, 164
    Coriolanus 138
    Frankenstein 54
    Hamlet 11, 139
    Julie 88–9, 114
    Macbeth 117, 137–8, 140
    The Madness of King George III 87, 98
    A Midsummer Night's Dream (2019) 55, 60–74, 118, 152
    Phèdre 10, 75, 85
    Present Laughter 13, 141, 181
    Small Island 89–92
    tenth anniversary *of* 56
    Yerma 119, 141

Old Vic, *plays shown at*
    All My Sons 85–7
    A Monster Calls 14
    Sea Wall 14
Old Vic: In Camera, *plays shown as part of*
    Lungs 152, 156
    Three Kings 152, 156
Olivier, Laurence, *Henry V (1944)* 88–9, 97
orality 139, 142

paradocumentation 8–9
    feedback loop 15, 132
    paradocumentational brim 8, 15, 18–19, 47, 55, 58, 72, 107, 109–10, 113–14, 127, 132, 134, 141, 143, 155, 160, 163, 173, 175, 180
participatory culture 9, 16, 19, 26, 136
perception 13, 17–18, 25–6, 35, 37–8, 46, 107, 122, 129, 135, 148, 151, 178
performers 2, 6, 29, 41, 68–70, 82, 96, 111–12, 136–9, 147, 151, 153–6, 159, 168, 170, 182–3
Phelan, Peggy 140, 180
plague (16th century) 145

Index

planned improvisation 64–5, 71
popular music 70, 126
(co-)presence 2, 13, 22, 42, 51, 54, 65, 73–4, 93, 99–100, 108–9, 117, 137, 140, 142, 153–5, 176–80, 183
proscenium 29, 112
proxemics 29, 58, 96, 105
Puskas, Tivadar 29

radio 25, 29, 38, 42–3, 80
Rancière, Jacques 106, 123, 132–3
Read, Alan 105, 122
response-ability 108, 140
retrospective synchronicity 160–1
Ridout, Nicholas 124, 130, 132–3, 137–8
Royal Shakespeare Company (RSC), *plays shown at/produced by*
   Dream (2021) 181
   The Merry Wives of Windsor (2018) 114
   Miss Julie (1971) 42
   Romeo and Juliet (2018) 111, 116–17
   The Tempest 5
   The Winter's Tale (1999) 42
Rude Mechanicals 62, 64, 67, 69

Sabel, David 3, 40–1, 44, 60
Sant, Toni 15–16, 179
Schaeffer, Pierre 25
Schechner, Richard 4, 70, 179, 181
Schneider, Rebecca 131, 140, 179–81
screen(s) 5–6, 11, 41–2, 46–9, 56, 63–4, 67–9, 71, 74, 76, 78, 83–5, 87, 93, 97–8, 101, 113, 119, 123, 147–8, 152–6, 159, 162, 166–8, 175
Shakespeare's Globe 161
Shakespeare studies 17
simultaneity 12, 63, 105, 174, 178
Sofer, Andrew 79

space
   cinema 13, 49, 181
   liminal 62
   optionality of 32, 37, 148, 173
   performance, audience and practitioner 28
   private *vs.* public 7
   social media 2
   theatrical 20, 81, 94–5, 97–8, 101, 170, 180
spatiality 13, 177
spectacle 46–74
   and Olympics 51
sports, sporting events 12, 28, 39, 50–4
soccer 54
States, Bert O. 70, 79
Sullivan, Erin 110, 147, 178

Tate Modern 9–10
telephone 25, 29–30
television drama 43
televisual 42, 71, 76, 81, 85, 88
temporality 13, 153–4, 177
theatre and emotions
   care 33, 35, 143, 159, 162, 171
   feeling I 106–7, 119, 121, 124, 141
   first-person experience 106, 117, 121–3
   intimacy 83, 114, 119, 170, 182
   pleasure 35, 50, 73, 123–4, 128, 130, 142
theatre criticism 126, 133–4, 139, 141
   (problematization of)
      expertise 105, 127–8, 130–2, 134, 137, 143, 173
   fandom 132, 136, 138–9
   mis-spectator 124, 130, 132–3, 137–8
   quasi-experts 128, 130, 132–3, 135, 138, 142–4
   writing about performance 131

theatre goers, theatregoing 4, 13, 41, 54, 71–2, 98, 105, 135, 139
  etiquettes 4, 71–2, 110, 127, 136, 139
  strategies and tactics (de Certeau) 4, 113–14
theatricality 17–20, 73, 75, 77, 80–2, 89, 91, 93, 101, 111, 122, 151, 166, 174
  contingency 18, 75, 150, 174
  risk 18, 65, 75, 81, 98, 131, 151, 174
  spontaneity 18, 75, 174
time-space compression (David Harvey) 30
theatrical labour 93
  crew 63, 69, 90
  equipment 4, 11–12, 77, 85, 93–6, 98–9, 147
  mise-en-scène 77, 81, 89, 93, 107
  objects 19–20, 26, 77–9, 96, 98, 101, 108
  props 20, 78–9, 81, 89, 91, 96, 101
  stage hands 62
Toffler, Alvin
  prosumer 9
trailer 4, 14, 55–7, 61, 126, 164–5
Turner, Victor. *See also* communitas
Twelfth Night (directed by Nicholas Hytner, 1998) 12

Twitter 4, 50, 58, 71, 99, 110, 113–14, 123–5, 140, 170

Ubersfeld, Anne 123

Vaughan, Meghan 134, 143–4
Victorian 26, 29–30, 32, 34–5
visuality, vision 13, 25–7, 43, 73, 75, 83
Voigts, Eckart 9, 82, 163
VR 5, 182

Weil, Pierre, *Le Médecin Malgré Lui* (1934) 84
Wells, H.G., *When the Sleeper Wakes* (1899) 28
White, Gareth 62
Windrush, the 91
Woolf, Virginia, 'Mr. Bennett and Mrs. Brown' 145
Wyndham Goldie, Grace 43–4
Wyver, John 10, 35, 42, 78, 127–8, 176

YouTube 11, 53, 56, 126, 147, 156, 158, 161, 164–5, 167–8

Zahavi, Dan 112
Zaiontz, Keren 108, 121, 124
Zoom (video conferencing programme) 147, 151, 155–8, 182

www.ingramcontent.com/pod-product-compliance
Lightning Source LLC
Chambersburg PA
CBHW071831300426
44116CB00009B/1509